Learning English as a Foreign Language

FOR

DUMMIES®

Learning English as a Foreign Language

FOR DUMMIES®

By Gavin Dudeney and Nicky Hockly

A John Wiley and Sons, Ltd, Publication

Learning English as a Foreign Language For Dummies®

Published by

John Wiley & Sons, Ltd
The Atrium
Southern Gate
Chichester
West Sussex
PO19 8SQ
England

Email (for orders and customer service enquires): cs-books@wiley.co.uk

Visit our Home Page on www.wiley.com

For general information on our other products and services, please contact our Customer Care Department within the US at 877-762-2974, outside the US at 317-572-3993, or fax 317-572-4002.

For technical support, please visit www.wiley.com/techsupport.

Wiley also publishes its books in a variety of electronic formats. Some content that appears in print may not be available in electronic books.

British Library Cataloguing in Publication Data: A catalogue record for this book is available from the British Library

ISBN: 978-0-470-74747-6

Printed and bound in Great Britain by Bell & Bain Ltd, Glasgow

10 9 8 7 6 5

WILEY

About the Authors

Gavin Dudeney is author of *The Internet & The Language Classroom* and co-author of *How To Teach English with Technology*. The latter won the 2007 International House Ben Warren Trust Prize for the most outstanding work in the field of language teacher education. Gavin is Project Director for The Consultants-E, a British Council award winning educational consultancy.

Nicky Hockly is a language teacher, teacher trainer and consultant, and Director of Pedagogy of The Consultants-E. She gives seminars, in-service workshops and teacher training courses all over the world, and writes regular articles and columns in teachers magazines and journals. Nicky is co-author with Gavin of the book *How to Teach English with Technology*.

Dedication

From Gavin: As always, this book is dedicated to my parents, without whom (quite literally) I wouldn't be writing it.

From Nicky: Heartfelt thanks to my students, who first made me aware of just how idiosyncratic the English language can be!

Acknowledgments

This book is inspired by all the people like us who've struggled – sometimes successfully, other times less so – to learn a foreign language. Between us we've tried French, Spanish, Catalan, German, Italian, Polish, Portuguese, Latin and Indonesian! Friends from those countries who know us will be better judges than we are of our expertise in each of those. As teachers of English, this book is particularly indebted to all the learners we've had the privilege of teaching over the past twenty years and from whom we have learnt more than they could possibly have learnt from us.

Publisher's Acknowledgments

We're proud of this book; please send us your comments through our Dummies online registration form located at www.dummies.com/register/.

Some of the people who helped bring this book to market include the following:

Acquisitions, Editorial, and Media Development

Project Editor: Rachael Chilvers

Development Editor: Colette Holder

Copyeditor: Charlie Wilson

Content Editor: Jo Theedom

Commissioning Editor: Wejdan Ismail

Assistant Editor: Jennifer Prytherch

Production Manager: Daniel Mersey

Cover Photos: © OJO Images Ltd / Alamy

Cartoons: Rich Tennant

CD Recording and Production:
Heavy Entertainment, with special thanks to Davy Nougarède and David Roper

Composition Services

Project Coordinator: Lynsey Stanford

Layout and Graphics: Samantha Allen, Claudia Bell, Carl Byers, Carrie Cesavice, Melissa K. Jester, Christin Swinford, Julia Trippetti

Proofreader: Melissa Cossell

Indexer: Ty Koontz

Contents at a Glance

Table of Contents

Introduction

O ver the past few decades, English has become *the* global language. Approximately 470 million people around the world currently speak English, and that number is growing. More people speak English as a second or foreign language than monolingual English 'native speakers'. Many countries include the compulsory study of English as a foreign language from primary school, and many parents are aware that some knowledge of English will help their children get better jobs in the future. Countries are keen to improve their citizens' English skills so as to ensure entry into the global market. In short, these days English is a language of worldwide importance.

What's Special about English?

When you talk about English-speaking countries, you may think of countries such as Britain, the United States, Australia, Canada or New Zealand. But in many other countries English is an official language and the citizens have high levels of English skills – think of India, Singapore, Malaysia, Nigeria, Kenya and Mauritius, to name a few.

One of the interesting things about English as a global language is that it is increasingly being used as a 'lingua franca' (or common language) so that people from *non*-English-speaking countries can communicate with those who do speak English. For example, at a business meeting in Bangkok, Thailand, with participants from China, Japan, Korea, Thailand and Indonesia, the common language is usually English. Likewise, a business meeting in Munich, Germany, with participants from Sweden, Greece, Italy, Germany and France, usually takes place in English.

Knowing some English is becoming increasingly important in today's global world. This is where *Learning English as a Foreign Language For Dummies* can help you. In this book we offer materials for communicating in social situations and in more formal situations such as at work, telephoning people and writing emails. We also show you how to deal with day-to-day situations such as ordering a meal, buying a train or bus ticket and renting a flat.

In *Learning English as a Foreign Language For Dummies*, we show you how to pronounce some of the more difficult words. Pronunciation and accents also come alive on the audio CD that supplements the book. You are just as likely to use English to communicate with non-English speakers in other countries as to communicate with English speakers in the UK, and so we use a range of accents on the audio CD.

About This Book

Learning English as a Foreign Language For Dummies provides you with useful words and phrases for short visits to the UK and longer work or study stays. The book contains phrases that you can use in a range of day-to-day situations, from a simple task such as buying something in the market to telling anecdotes in a pub. We help you communicate enough to complete basic tasks on a short visit to the UK, but also to interact with neighbours, new friends and colleagues if you plan to stay in the UK for a longer period of time. You can go through the book at your own speed and read the chapters in any order. Depending on your previous knowledge of English, you may want to skip some chapters and move directly on to other chapters where you feel you need extra support.

Conventions Used in This Book

Here are the *For Dummies* conventions we use in this book to make it easier to read:

- ✔ You'll be speaking as well as reading and writing English, so we include dialogues throughout the book. The dialogues are called 'Straight Talking' and they show you how to use certain words and phrases in conversation. Most of these dialogues are also on the audio CD that comes with the book. Appendix C has a full list of the dialogues.

- ✔ Memorising words and phrases is important in language learning, so we collect all the new words in the dialogues on a blackboard, under the heading 'Words to Know'.

- ✔ Fun & Games sections appear at the end of each chapter so you can put your skills to the test (relax – we also provide the answers!).

- ✔ Web addresses appear in the book in `monofont` type.

- ✔ English terms are set in **boldface**.

- ✔ Pronunciations are set in *italics*, following the English terms. Stressed syllables are <u>underlined</u>.

Foolish Assumptions

To write this book, we had to make some assumptions about who you are and what you want from a book called *Learning English as a Foreign Language For Dummies*. Here are some assumptions that we made about you:

✔ You already know a little English. Perhaps you studied English at school for a few years, or you've picked up a little English from pop songs, TV or films.

✔ You need a book to help you organise and review the English you already know. You want a book that shows you how to *use* English in real conversations.

✔ You want to learn real-life English that British people speak today. You plan to spend either a short time in Britain, for example on holiday or for a business meeting, or you want to spend a longer time in Britain working or studying.

✔ You like to study at your own pace, in your own time. You know where your strengths in English already lie, and which areas you need to review, or need some extra help with. You want to choose which chapters of this book to read and when.

✔ You want to have fun and review some useful English words and phrases at the same time.

If these statements apply to you, you've found the right book.

How This Book Is Organised

This book is divided by topics into five parts. Each part is divided into chapters. The following sections show you what types of information you can find in each part.

Part 1: Getting Started

In this part of the book we review some of the basics of English. If you already know quite a lot of English, you may want to skip this part and move directly on to the sections of the book dealing with communication. In Part I you find international words that you probably already know, the basics of English pronunciation and some survival phrases. You also find an overview of the main tenses in English (present, past, future and conditional), and see how to form questions and negatives.

Part II: English in Action

In this part we look at how to *use* English. Instead of focusing on grammar points, we look at everyday situations, such as talking to people, enjoying a meal, shopping, leisure and work skills such as talking on the phone and writing email.

Part III: English on the Go

In this part we give you the language you need to communicate in English in a bank, in a hotel, on the road, on a plane, on a train or in a taxi. We cover all aspects of getting around in the UK, including handling emergencies.

Part IV: The Part of Tens

If you want some small, easily digestible pieces of information about English, this part is for you. Here, we offer you ten ways to learn English quickly, ten favourite UK English expressions, ten public holidays that British people celebrate and ten phrases that make you sound fluent in English.

Part V: Appendices

This part includes important information that you can use for reference. We cover phrasal verbs, which English speakers use a lot in normal conversation but are difficult for non-English speakers to learn and to use correctly. We include some of the most commonly used English verbs and review some of the English irregular verbs. You can also find a list of the tracks that appear on the audio CD that comes with this book, so that you can find out where those dialogues are in the book and follow along.

Icons Used in This Book

You may be looking for particular information while reading this book. To make certain types of information more easily accessible, you find the following items in the left-hand margins throughout the book:

If you want information and advice about culture in the UK, look for these icons.

The audio CD included in this book gives you the opportunity to listen to English and non-English speakers. This helps you understand spoken English, which can often sound different to the way you write it. The icon marks the 'Straight Talking' dialogues that you can find on the CD.

This icon highlights tips and expressions that can make you sound like a very confident English speaker, even if your level of English isn't really that high.

The target highlights handy information to help you on your English-language journey.

This icon warns you about typical errors that non-English speakers can make using the language. It tells you what *not* to say, and it also warns you about words that you can easily confuse.

Where to Go from Here

Learning a language is all about getting out there and practising as much as you can, as well as reading about the language. So start now. You can start reading at the beginning, pick a chapter that interests you or play the CD and listen to a few dialogues. Try to repeat what you hear. In a short time you'll be confident enough to try out your English during a trip to the UK.

Part I
Getting Started

The 5th Wave — By Rich Tennant

"This will help you understand which words need more stress put on them."

In this part . . .

We show you that you probably already know a lot more English than you think! Even if you're thinking 'I don't know any English, because I didn't study it at school,' we bet you know lots of English words and phrases. Look around you – even in your home country, you can probably see English words in magazines and street advertisements, you hear English on TV and in films, and you may even have words that come from English in your own language.

In Part I we take a look at pronunciation English, give you a few survival phrases for a visit to the UK, review some of the basics of English grammar, and give you the language you need to meet and greet people, and to hold conversations. By the end of this part, you'll have learnt enough of the basics to go out and meet people in the UK!

Chapter 1

You Already Know a Little English

In This Chapter

▶ Taking a look at what you already know

▶ Avoiding linguistic embarrassment

▶ Using 'foreign' words in English

▶ Practising English pronunciation, stress and intonation

*W*elcome to the beginning of the adventure! If you're reading this then you may be living or working in Britain and speak some English already. Or perhaps you live in another country and plan to visit Britain at some point in the future. Either way, you're looking for a way to improve your level of English and to find out a little more about what makes Britain and the British tick. In that case, congratulations, you've come to the right place!

This book guides you through the complexities of everyday English language and teaches you a few things about life in Britain. By the time you finish you'll sound as if you've lived in the UK for years. You'll know how to talk the talk – not only the words and the grammar, but also the ideas and notions that make the British what they are. In short, Britain will feel a lot more like home! Amaze your friends with your grasp of pub etiquette and impress your boss with your telephone technique and meeting skills.

So, if you're ready, we'll get started. In this chapter we explore what you already know about the English language and look at some of the basics: false friends, international words and pronunciation, stress and intonation.

Realising that You Already Know Some English

It doesn't matter what age you are or where you come from, there's a very good chance that you know quite a bit of English already. Think of all those pop songs you've listened to over the years. Perhaps you're of the age of the Beatles and the Rolling Stones, or maybe something more recent like Coldplay or U2, but if you've spent time listening to music or watching MTV then you probably already have a big English vocabulary.

Of course, some vocabulary from songs may not be appropriate for your context. You'll be safe with 'Hello Goodbye' by the Beatles, but it's a good idea not to use too much of the language used in rap, as one example – it's not really appropriate for the workplace.

And you've probably seen some films in English over the years too, and have some words from those in your head waiting to spring forth. And perhaps you regularly use the Internet, which is still mostly in English. Or maybe you've used English at work on occasions, even just socially.

When you have a minute, listen to a popular song in English or take a look at a short English magazine or newspaper article online. How many words do you understand? The chances are you recognise quite a lot of individual words, even if you don't understand everything in the song or article. All of this is a result of having exposure to English: seeing it, hearing it, reading it. And, in fact, it's exposure that can help you become fluent more quickly. This is a good lesson to learn right at the start of the book – spend as much time as you can reading, speaking and listening to English. We hope you're fluent in no time.

Avoiding False Friends across the Languages

When we speak about *false friends* in terms of languages, we mean two words that look and/or sound similar in two different languages but have very different meanings. False friends have a lot of potential to embarrass the speaker and, ironically, often connect with more delicate matters.

A typical example is the English word *preservative*, which generally refers to chemicals for extending the life of substances such as food. Visitors from many European countries recognise this word, but for them it's usually a contraceptive device – a condom (*preservativo* in Spanish, *préservatif* in French). This might lead to some amusement in the local chemist.

Likewise, a Spanish speaker listening to someone talking about *embarrassing* another person will be surprised to discover that no babies are involved in the outcome – *embarazar* in some variants of Spanish is to impregnate.

A Portuguese speaker in a chemist asking for medicine because they are constipated will get something to help them go to the toilet, and not something for a cold – *constipação* in Portuguese is a cold.

There's no real way of learning these words or listing them all in a book like this, because they come from a wide variety of languages and contexts. You just have to keep an ear open for them and make a note when you hear them. You will probably, at some point, misuse a word from your own language that has an equivalent in English, but try not to worry about it, and learn from those events.

Meeting Some Differences between British and American English

Many words differ between American and British English. George Bernard Shaw said: 'England and America are two countries divided by a common language.' He was partially correct, particularly with reference to some vocabulary and some different uses of tenses. For example, British English often uses the present perfect tense to describe a recently completed action, while American English uses the past simple. Imagine that you've just finished breakfast. A British English speaker would ask 'Have you finished breakfast yet?'. An American English speaker, on the other hand, is more likely to ask 'Did you finish breakfast yet?'.

Here's a useful guide to the most common differences between American and British English:

British English	*American English*
Anywhere	Anyplace
Autumn	Fall
Bill (in a restaurant)	Check
Biscuit	Cookie
Bonnet (of a car, at the front)	Hood
Boot (of a car, at the back)	Trunk
Chemist	Drugstore
Chips	French fries
Cinema	Movies
Crisps	Potato chips
Crossroads	Intersection
Dustbin	Trashcan
Film	Movie

British English	American English
Flat	Apartment
Ground floor	First floor
Holiday	Vacation
Lift	Elevator
Lorry	Truck
Mobile	Cellphone
Motorway	Freeway
Nappy	Diaper
Pants	Shorts
Pavement	Sidewalk
Petrol	Gas(oline)
Post	Mail
Postcode	Zip code
Pub	Bar
Return (ticket)	Round-trip (ticket)
Rubber	Eraser
Shop	Store
Single (ticket)	One-way (ticket)
Sweets	Candy
Tap	Faucet
Taxi	Cab
Timetable	Schedule
Toilet	Bathroom, restroom
Trousers	Pants
Tube (train)	Subway
Vest	Undershirt
Wallet	Billfold
Zip	Zipper

Using International Words in English

International words or *loan words* are words that English has borrowed from other languages. You may find a word or two from your own language, because English has borrowed from almost all world languages at some point. Figure 1-1 shows the main influences on English vocabulary.

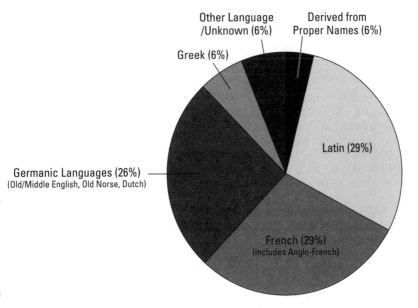

Other Language /Unknown (6%)

Derived from Proper Names (6%)

Greek (6%)

Latin (29%)

Germanic Languages (26%)
(Old/Middle English, Old Norse, Dutch)

French (29%)
(includes Anglo-French)

Figure 1-1:
The main influences on English vocabulary.

Words from 'other languages' make up only 6 per cent of English, but it's in this group that you may find something from your own language. Here are some examples:

Ketchup	Amoy (Chinese)
Robot	Czech
Paper	Egyptian
Igloo	Inuit (Eskimo)
Yeti	Tibetan
Walrus	Norwegian
Paprika	Hungarian
Karate	Japanese
Yoghurt	Turkish
Horde	Polish

In general, loan words usually come from first encounters with something new, and the words are often changed to sound more English. So, when the Czech writer Karel Čapek first used the word *roboti* to describe artificial people in one of his plays (*roboti* is Czech for 'work' or 'labour') it wasn't long before English-speaking people anglicised it into *robot*.

Listen out for words from your language – you may be surprised. There's a good chance that if you hear something from your country in everyday use in Britain then the word will probably sound quite familiar.

Perfecting Pronunciation and Stress

In general, *pronunciation* refers to the way you say words and *stress* refers to the emphasis you put on certain parts of words or sentences. In other words, pronunciation relates to *sounds* and stress relates to where you put the *accent* on a word when you speak. For example: 'This cake is delicious!'

✔ The *pronunciation* of the word delicious is de-li-shus. Notice how you write the last syllable of the word as '–cious', but when you *speak* you say 'shus'.

✔ Delicious consists of three syllables – de-*li*-cious. The second syllable (li) is the part of the word that you pronounce with most emphasis – in other words, where the *stress* of the word falls. You don't, for example, say *de*-li-cious, or de-li-*cious*.

Sussing out sounds

In this section, we show you the sounds of British English. In the left column of Figure 1-2 is the representation of the sound using the International Phonetic Alphabet (IPA). These are the sounds that you see next to an entry in a dictionary. For example:

/ju: nə 'vɜ: si ti: / university

Here's what you can tell from this example:

✔ The word has five syllables (there's usually a gap between each syllable).

✔ The stress is on the third syllable (you can usually see a ' sign on the stressed syllable). This means the word is pronounced uni*ver*sity.

Figure 1-2 shows you the IPA consonant and vowel sounds in English on the left, with an example word for each sound on the right, so that you know how to pronounce them.

/p/	pen	/ʃ/	shut
/b/	boy	/ʒ/	measure
/t/	ten	/h/	hope
/d/	door	/m/	man
/k/	king	/n/	no
/g/	goal	/h/	human
/f/	friday	/l/	lad
/v/	van	/r/	ring
/θ/	think	/w/	week
/ð/	that	/j/	yet
/s/	sip	/tʃ/	change
/z/	zip	/dʒ/	gin
/I/	pink	/p/	top
/e/	get	/ʊ/	measure
/æ/	tap	/ə/	potato
/ʌ/	shut		
/iː/	key	/uː/	shoe
/aː/	far	/ɜː/	girl
/ɔː/	law		
/eɪ/	may	/aʊ/	cow
/aɪ/	my	/ɪə/	here
/ɔɪ/	toy	/ɛə/	there
/əʊ/	no	/ʊə/	tour

Figure 1-2: The International Phonetic Alphabet (IPA).

Stressing words and sentences

Stress is the emphasis you put on particular parts of words, or on parts of sentences. Here we take a quick look at both word and sentence stress.

Word stress

When you say a word you don't pronounce every syllable the same. One syllable is louder or stronger than the others. This syllable is called the *stressed syllable* because it has more importance when you make the sound of the word. Take another look at the dictionary entry for *university*:

/ju: nə 'vɜ: si ti: /   university

From the way the entry is written you can tell it has five syllables (or sounds) and that the stress (the most important syllable) is the third one. You can see this because it is marked with a ' before it.

Look at these words and see how many syllables they have:

Word	Syllables	IPA
dog	one syllable	/dɒg/
quiet	two syllables	/'kwaɪ ət/
expensive	three syllables	/ek 'spen siv/
ceremony	four syllables	/'se rə mə ni:/
unexceptional	five syllables	/ ʌn ek 'sep ʃə nl/

Straight Talking

 Now listen to how the words are pronounced:

1. Dog
2. Quiet
3. Expensive
4. Ceremony
5. Unexceptional

Can you hear the stressed syllable?

One way to find out about syllables and word stress is to look up words in a dictionary. But sometimes it's easier to make your own records of word stress. One method that we particularly like is using lower and upper case letter 'o's. With this method, a lower case 'o' represents an unstressed syllable and an upper case 'O' indicates a stressed syllable. So:

Word	Syllables	IPA	Symbol
dog	one syllable	/dɒg/	O
quiet	two syllables	/ˈkwaɪ ət/	Oo
expensive	three syllables	/ek ˈspen siv/	oOo
ceremony	four syllables	/ˈse rə mə ni:/	Oooo
unexceptional	five syllables	/ ʌn ek ˈsep ʃə nl/	ooOoo

This is a quick way of remembering how a word sounds. Try to get used to keeping a note of word stress. See if you can find any patterns or rules that can help you to remember where the stress falls on your most frequent vocabulary items.

Sentence stress

Sentence stress puts emphasis on particular words in a sentence. English sentences consist of content words and structure words. *Content words* are the important words; generally, the words that communicate the meaning of the sentence. *Structure words* give the sentence form. Generally, the content words are the stressed words:

> I've *done* the *shopping*. Please *cook lunch*.

Here the content words are in italic type. You can remove the structure words and still understand the sentence:

> Done shopping. Cook lunch.

Of course, nobody really speaks like that – that's more like a written note to someone – but it does show that the sentence stress is on the content words. This is a very basic rule, but it helps you to think about how you apply sentence stress. In general, the following rules apply to an English sentence:

✔ You stress content words.

✔ You don't stress structure words.

✔ The time between stressed words is always the same.

The real exception to all this is when you really want to add emphasis to something:

> Have you seen the latest James Bond film? No, I haven't – but I *did* see the one before.

Here you stress *did* to emphasise some new information or to make a strong point.

Investigating Intonation

Intonation describes the *pitch* or tone of sentences. Here are some general rules about English intonation:

- ✔ For 'wh' questions (what, where, who) the pitch usually goes down at the end of the sentence:

    What are you doing ↘ tonight?

- ✔ For 'yes/no' questions the pitch usually goes up at the end:

    Are you coming to ↗ the cinema?

- ✔ For negatives, the pitch usually goes down at the end:

    No, I'm not ↘ coming to the cinema?

- ✔ For statements, the pitch usually goes down at the end:

    He's a ↘ doctor. He works ↘ in Manchester

Straight Talking

 Now listen to the intonation on these sentences:

1. What are you doing tonight?   [Falling intonation]
2. He's a doctor?   [Rising intonation]
3. Are you working on Saturday?   [Rising intonation]
4. No, I'm not working until next Monday. [Falling intonation]
5. I'm a teacher. I work in London. [Falling intonation]

Can you hear the small changes in intonation?

Fun & Games

Look for these words in a dictionary, or use www.dictionary.com if you have access to the Internet. Write out the stress symbol for each and practise saying them:

  1. Teacher   Oo

  2. Embarrassing   _____

  3. Tomorrow   _____

  4. Goodbye   _____

  5. International   _____

  6. Dictionary   _____

  7. Intonation   _____

  8. Pronunciation   _____

  9. Languages   _____

 10. Already   _____

 11. Shopping   _____

Key:

  1) Oo

  2) oOoo

  3) oOo

  4) Oo

  5) ooOoo

  6) Oooo

  7) ooOo

  8) oooOo

  9) Ooo

 10) oOo

 11) Oo

Chapter 2

Basic English Grammar

*L*ots of people – including many students and those who teach English – think that the grammar is the most important part of a language. And lots of people believe that by learning the grammar, you learn a language. We don't think this is completely true. Instead, we think of grammar as the basic building blocks of a language – when you know grammar, you know things like past tense verbs, how to use conditional forms, how to form questions and so on. But building blocks (the grammar) aren't much use unless you know how to put them together to create a useful object (communicating with others). Even if you know about all the rules in the English language, if you don't know how to apply them when talking to others, this knowledge isn't much use.

One very effective way to start communicating, even if you know very little grammar or have studied or heard very little English in the past, is to memorise 'chunks' or pieces of language, and to know when to use them. As early as the 1920s, Harold Palmer, who's often known as the father of linguistics, said that it would be better for students to spend time perfectly memorising phrases or chunks of language than simply studying grammar rules.

In this chapter we look at some of the basic rules of grammar. In the rest of the book, we give you chunks of language in phrases and questions that you can actually use in a variety of situations. So you don't need to start with this chapter, or read this chapter through completely, before you start speaking English. You can predict what situations you're going to be in, and look at and learn the English phrases in those chapters of this book first. Then you can always come back to this chapter about grammar to find out about the rules, which help you to generate more sentences in phrases with similar constructions.

Constructing Simple Sentences

In the affirmative, simple sentences in English look like this:

> subject (S) – verb (V) – object (O)

Here are some examples of simple sentences:

Subject	Verb	Object
Paul	works	in an office
I	love	pizza

In longer sentences you can add a complement and an adverbial phrase (adverbial) to the preceding structure:

> subject (S) – verb (V) – object (O) – complement (C) – adverbial (A)

Here are our original simple sentences made a little longer:

Subject	Verb	Object	Complement	Adverbial
Paul	works	in an office	that has no heating	in winter
I	love	pizza	made by my mother	with Granny's old recipe

You can describe the elements of a sentence like this:

- ✔ **Subject:** The main topic of the sentence (who or what).
- ✔ **Verb:** The action word.
- ✔ **Object:** Who or what is affected by the action word.
- ✔ **Complement:** Adds information about one of the elements in the sentence.
- ✔ **Adverbial:** Adds information about the time (when?), place (where?), or manner (how?).

Some languages use a double negative in the sentence. For example, Italian and French have a negation (*no* word) twice in the same sentence. In English the *no* word appears only once. You can say:

- ✔ I do*n't* know his name.
- ✔ We have*n't* got any bread in the house.

✔ We've got *no* bread in the house.

✔ Laura knows *nothing* about the phone call.

✔ Laura does*n't* know anything about the phone call.

 Even though the correct structure of a simple affirmative sentence in English follows the order S–V–O, you often hear native speakers using incomplete sentences or sentences that sound grammatically incorrect. You may hear sentences without a subject at the beginning, for example 'Went there, did she?' or 'Got the time?' or 'Likes his football, he does'. You may also hear sentences that are grammatically incorrect, such as 'He don't know nothing' (correct: 'He doesn't know anything'). Unless your English is of a very high level, don't deliberately use sentences that leave off the subject or are grammatically incorrect – native speakers can get away with it because they already know the correct forms in theory. Less proficient English speakers using these very informal forms simply sound like they're making a mistake.

Working on More Complex Sentences

Longer sentences are often more difficult to understand, especially if they have several *clauses* or parts.

Relative clauses are phrases you include in sentences to give extra information about something, for example 'This is the Japanese restaurant that Isabel recommended to me'. The relative clause in the sentence is *that Isabel recommended to me*. It gives extra information about the Japanese restaurant. Here are some more examples:

✔ I've got a new dress *that* my husband gave me for my birthday.

✔ The cafe *where* I have lunch every day is really cheap.

✔ This part of town, *which* has a fantastic market, is very difficult to get to.

✔ My brother, *whose* wife is Japanese, has recently moved to Tokyo.

✔ My boss, *who* lived in Greece for years, speaks really good Greek.

You often introduce relative clauses with the words *which*, *that*, *who*, *whose* and *where*. *Which* and *that* are to talk about things; *who* and *whose* are for people; *where* is for places.

Forming Questions

Knowing how to ask questions in English is extremely important. In all the chapters in this book you find examples of questions that you can ask in a variety of situations. In this chapter we review some of the basic rules involved in asking questions in English.

In English, you find different types of question:

> ✔ **'Wh' questions such as, Where do you live? What's your name? Who are your favourite singers? Which one did you want? How does Irene get to work?**
>
> Although 'how' doesn't start with the letters WH, it is still called a 'wh' question. These are the questions you ask to find out about things.
>
> ✔ **Yes / no questions such as, Do you live in Newcastle? Is your surname Jones? Are your favourite singers Elvis and Bono? Is this the one you wanted? Does Irene go to work by bus?**
>
> These are the questions you ask to get the answer 'yes' or 'no'. From the examples above, you see that some of the questions use the auxiliary verb *do*, or *does* (for the present tense) or *did* (for the past tense). But some of the questions don't. In the examples above, some of the questions use the verb *to be*. These are the questions that don't use an auxiliary verb. This how the question is formed:
>
> • **Sentence:** His name is Tom Jones.
>
> • **Questions:** Is his name Tom? / Is his surname Jones?

You invert the order of the subject (his name) and the verb (is) to form the question with the verb *to be*.

For questions that use auxiliary verbs, look closely at the examples again:

> ✔ **Sentence:** I live in Newcastle.
>
> ✔ **Questions:** Do you live in Newcastle? / Where do you live?
>
> ✔ **Sentence:** Irene goes to work by train.
>
> ✔ **Questions:** Does Irene go to work by train? / How does Irene go to work?

The verbs in the two example questions here are *live* and *go*. You use the auxiliary verb *do* or *does* to show that you're asking a question. You use *does* in the third person singular only – which makes sense, because the verb in the affirmative sentence also takes an 's': 'Irene goes to work by train becomes the question 'How does Irene go to work?' not 'How does Irene goes to work?'. You only have room for one third person 's'!

Remembering the word order for questions in English is important. Table 2-1 shows you how.

Table 2-1	Making Questions in English				
Questions with 'Do' and 'Does'	**Question Word**	**Auxiliary Verb**	**Subject**	**Main Verb**	**Object / Complement**
	How	does	Irene	go	to work?
	How much	does	this dress	cost?	
	Where	do	you	live?	
		Do	you	like	living in London?
		Does	Mike	work	in the same office as you?
Questions with 'to Be'	**Question Word**	**Verb 'to Be'**	**Subject**	**Verb + –ing**	**Object / Complement**
	What	is	his name?		
	Where	are	my glasses?		
		Are	you	coming	to the cinema?
		Is	Sue	living	in Hull now?

Subject/object questions

Using the auxiliary verb *do*, *does* and *did* (for past tense) depends on whether you ask a subject or an object question. Look at the two questions:

> Jenny likes Mario. Pietro likes Jenny.

> Who does Jenny like? Who likes Jenny?

Both of these questions are correct – but the answer to each is different. See whether you can put the correct name as the answer. Here it is:

✔ **Sentence:** Jenny likes Mario.

✔ **Question:** Who does Jenny like?

✔ **Answer:** Mario.

In this question, *who* refers to the object (Mario), so you use *does*. An object question asks for information about the object of the sentence.

✔ **Sentence:** Pietro likes Jenny.

✔ **Question:** Who likes Jenny?

✔ **Answer:** Pietro.

In this question, *who* refers to the subject (Pietro), so you don't need an auxiliary verb. A subject question asks for information about the subject of the sentence.

Here's another example:

Michelle lives in a blue house by the sea.

Look at the word order first: Michelle (S) lives (V) in a blue house (O) by the sea (A).

Here are some possible questions from the above sentence:

Who lives in a blue house? *Who* refers to the *subject* (Michelle).

Where does Michelle live? *Where* refers to the *object* (blue house).

Indirect questions

You can use indirect questions to ask for information politely. You can start an indirect question with an expression such as 'Could you tell me . . .?' or 'Would you mind telling me . . . ?' or 'Do you have any idea . . . ?' or 'I was wondering whether you know . . . ?'. The chapters in this book contain several examples of indirect questions to help you sound polite when you ask for information or help. Here are some examples to get you started:

Direct question: Where is the post office?

Indirect question: Could you tell me where the post office is?

Notice how the verb *is* (a form of 'to be') moves to the end of the question in the indirect question. If you imagine that the phrase 'Could you tell me . . .' contains the question, then the rest of the question (. . . where the post office is?) can take the affirmative form. Here's another example:

Direct question: Where does Michelle live?

Indirect question: Could you tell me where Michelle lives?

Notice how you drop the auxiliary verb *does* in the indirect question above –
you can see very clearly that 'Could you tell me . . .' is the question, and the
rest of the question (. . . where Michelle lives) is the affirmative form.

There are two main types of indirect question:

- ✔ 'Wh' questions
- ✔ Yes / no questions

In the earlier section on how to form questions, we discuss 'wh' indirect
questions. Here we discuss indirect questions of the yes / no type. A yes / no
indirect question looks like this:

Direct question: Is the post office near here?

Indirect question: Could you tell me if the post office is near here?

Direct question: Does Michelle live in this house?

Indirect question: Could you tell me if Michelle lives in this house?

So for an indirect yes / no question you simply add the word *if* or *whether*
after the question phrase (Could you tell me if . . . / Do you know whether . . .
and so on.)

Question tags

If you've ever studied English or bought an English grammar book then you
probably know about question tags. Question tags are top of the hate list for
many students of English. Question tags are very logical grammatically, but
using them correctly is difficult. The good news is that you can get away with
not using question tags at all yourself (see 'Sound Native', below). But you
do need to understand question tags when other people use them. Here are
some examples of question tags:

- ✔ Paulette is studying in France, isn't she?
- ✔ You're not looking very well, are you?
- ✔ He liked her a lot, didn't he?
- ✔ They didn't buy it, did they?
- ✔ Jack can't play very well, can he?
- ✔ I really should go, shouldn't I?

You can see the rule for question formation above, can't you? The rule is almost like a mathematical formula: a (positive or negative) statement + (negative or positive) auxiliary or modal verb + pronoun. The formula looks like this:

For the verb 'to be':

Positive statement	+ verb 'to be' (in negative)	+ pronoun
Paulette is studying in France,	*isn't*	*she?*
Negative statement	+ verb to be (in positive)	+ pronoun
You're not looking very well,	*are*	*you?*

For other verbs:

Positive statement	+ auxiliary verb (in negative)	+ pronoun
He liked her a lot,	*didn't*	*he?*
Negative statement	+ auxiliary verb (in positive)	+ pronoun
They didn't buy it,	*did*	*they?*

For modal verbs:

Negative statement	+ modal verb (in positive)	+ pronoun
Jack can't play very well,	*can*	*he?*
Positive statement	+ modal verb (in negative)	+ pronoun
I really should go,	*shouldn't*	*I?*

Don't worry too much about question tags. Although the rules are straightforward, remembering which auxiliary or modal to use in the tag (last bit) and which pronoun to use is difficult. You often use question tags for emphasis or to invite the listener to agree. The answer to a tag question is usually 'yes (+tag)' or 'no (+tag)', and it's often an introduction to a conversation. Imagine yourself standing at a bus stop and someone says to you 'Nice day, isn't it?'. This is an invitation to start a conversation on a safe topic such as the weather. Your answer could be: 'Yes, it is, and it was so cold yesterday . . .'

In some English-speaking countries, and in some parts of the UK, you hear different question tags. In London, for example, you may hear the tag *innit* (isn't it) as a generalised question tag. In India people use the same question tag (isn't it) as a tag, but pronounce it much more clearly! For example, you could hear 'He's just got a new job, innit?' or ' She's been on holiday, innit?'. Using this colloquial tag is not a good idea unless you're a native speaker from these regions – otherwise it just sounds strange! Another question tag that you may hear people use is simply *no*. For example, 'She lives here, no?' or 'Jack doesn't eat fish, no?' Technically, this form is incorrect, but you may hear even native English speakers use it.

Using Verbs and Tenses

Another of the basic building blocks of the English language is tense. Forming tenses in English is a fairly straightforward process – in this section we show you how to form the basic tenses in English.

Present tenses

The affirmative word order in English is subject – verb – object. To form a question in the present simple tense, you use the auxiliary verb *do* (or *does* in the third person singular). When you form a question with the verb to *be*, you invert the order of the subject and the verb. Below is a quick summary:

Basic present tenses

✔ **Affirmative:**

- Juan *comes* from Spain. (present simple)

- I often *go* to the cinema on Sundays.

- Juan *is living* in Glasgow at the moment. (present continuous / progressive)

- Just a moment, I'*m speaking* on the other line.

✔ **Negative:**

- Juan *doesn't* come from Poland. (present simple)

- I *don't* go to the cinema during the week.

- Juan *isn't living* in London at the moment. (present continuous / progressive)

- I'*m not speaking* on the other line.

✔ **Question:**

- Where *does* Juan come from? *Does* Juan come from Spain? (present simple)

- What *do* you do on Sundays? *Do* you go to the cinema?

- *Is* Juan *living* in London? (present continuous / progressive)

- *Are* you *speaking* on the other line?

You don't often use some verbs in English in the continuous form. Here are some of the most common verbs that you normally use in the simple rather than continuous form:

> like, dislike, hate, love, prefer, wish, want
>
> doubt, feel, know, remember, understand, believe, mean
>
> hear, taste, smell, sound, see
>
> please, surprise, impress, satisfy, appear, seem

Grammar books call these verbs *stative* or *state* verbs – the words refer to states. Verbs that you can use in a continuous form are called *dynamic* verbs – they refer to activities. These are just some examples of these state verbs. You can use some of them in the continuous form depending on context. For example, you can use the verb *think* to express an opinion such as 'I think Edinburgh is beautiful', or to express an activity as in 'I'm thinking about you'. When a well-known international fast food restaurant invented the slogan 'We're lovin' it', some people complained that this was not grammatically acceptable because you don't usually use the verb *love* in a continuous form.

Present perfect

You use the present perfect tense to talk about something that happened in the past but is related to the present. So although the structure looks like a past tense, it's called the *present* perfect. The present perfect is a tense that can be difficult to use correctly, and the rules given in books can be confusing. Also, some differences exist between USA and UK uses of the tense – North Americans tend to use the simple past instead of the present perfect, especially with the words 'yet' and 'already'. For example, in Britain you might hear the question 'Have you eaten breakfast yet?', whereas in the USA you may hear 'Did you eat breakfast yet?'. The good news is that even if you don't use the present perfect correctly and you use the present simple by mistake, if the context is clear, it's usually easy for your listener to understand what you mean.

Like the basic present tense described above, you have the simple form and the continuous / progressive form of the present perfect. Here are some examples:

> ✔ **Affirmative:**
>
> - I've seen that movie twice. (present perfect simple)
> - Juan *has been living* in Glasgow for two years. (present perfect continuous / progressive)

✔ **Negative:**

- I haven't seen a movie for ages. (present perfect simple)

- He *hasn't been doing* his homework, he's been reading the newspaper instead. (present perfect continuous / progressive)

✔ **Question:**

- Have you seen that movie yet? (present perfect simple)

- How long *has* Juan *been living* in Glasgow? (present perfect continuous / progressive)

The above examples show that the present perfect is formed by *have* (*has* for the third person singular) + participle of the main verb:

✔ **Present perfect simple:** have/has + past participle

✔ **Present perfect continuous/progressive:** have/as +been + –ing (present participle)

You use the present perfect to talk about events in the past but that are related to the present. When you say that something has happened, or has been happening, you usually include the present. For example, when you say 'I have seen that movie twice', you mean that you have seen it twice in the past, but you may see it again. When you say that 'Juan has been living in Glasgow for two years', you mean that Juan started living in Glasgow two years ago but he still lives there now.

There are two main ways to use the present perfect.

✔ You can use the present perfect to describe an action or situation which started in the past, but which continues up to the present moment; for example 'I've been waiting for 20 minutes', not 'I am waiting for 20 minutes'. I started waiting 20 minutes ago, and I'm still waiting now. You can also use this tense for a series of repeated actions in the past that continue up to the present; for example 'I have seen that movie twice'.

✔ You can use the present perfect to describe an action or situation that happened in the past but has importance in the present; for example 'I've spoken to my boss about the report'. If you say exactly *when* this happens, then you must use the past simple – 'I spoke to my boss about the report *yesterday*', not 'I've spoken to my boss about the report yesterday'.

You often use the words *since* and *for* with the present perfect tense. *Since* refers to a point in time, and you use it to say when something started; for example 'Juan has been living in Glasgow since 2007'. *For* refers to a period of time and you use it to say how long something has been happening; for example 'Juan has been living in Glasgow for two years'.

In British English, you often use the word *just* with the present perfect. For example:

> **Jan:** Have you got that report I need?
>
> **Isabel:** Yes, I've just finished it.

Here 'just' means that you finished the report only a few minutes ago.

The past

Compared to many other languages, the simple past tense is relatively easy to form in English. In many languages, such as Italian, French, Japanese, Greek or Russian (among others!), each verb has a different ending depending on which person you refer to (I, you, he, they and so on). English verbs, on the other hand, aren't highly inflected – this means that there are very few different endings for verbs. The previous section explains that you use an *inflection* (or ending) for verbs (verb + 's') for the third person singular in the present simple tense.

You use the simple past tense to describe situations or actions that happened in the past and are now finished. 'I lived in London' means that I don't live in London now, but lived in London in the past. You can also say when the action happened with the simple past, so 'I lived in London two years ago' or 'I lived in London for a while'. You also use the past simple to refer to the recent past, if the action is finished; for example 'I went to the bank this morning' or 'I finished the report five minutes ago'. (But as we explain in the earlier section on the present perfect, if you want to emphasise how recently this was finished and you don't state exactly when, you can use the present perfect for this example – 'I have just finished the report'. Notice how you don't say *when*.)

Regular verbs

Regular verbs in the simple past tense take the ending –ed, for all persons. You don't need to worry about the third person singular when you talk in the past tense. Here are some common regular past simple verbs:

Base Form of the Verb	Past Simple
live	lived
walk	walked
look	looked
want	wanted
use	used

Base Form of the Verb	Past Simple
ask	asked
work	worked
try	tried
call	called
seem	seemed

Forming the past simple of regular verbs in English is very easy: simply add 'ed' to the end of the verb. Watch out for the pronunciation though. In most of the verbs in the verb list above, the 'ed' that you add to the end of the word is pronounced like a 't'. So you pronounce *walked* as 'walkt' – as one syllable rather than the two syllables of 'walk-ed'. Similarly, you pronounce *looked* as 'lookt' and *asked* as 'askt'. There's a very slight sound change in the pronunciation of *lived* – you still pronounce it as one syllable, but instead of a 't' sound at the end, it's really a 'd' sound, so you pronounce it as 'livd'. The same happens with *used* (pronounced 'yoosd'), *called* (pronounced 'calld'), and *seemed* (pronounced 'seemd'). Hearing the difference between the 't' and 'd' endings on these verbs is quite difficult, so concentrate on making the past tense of these verbs *only one syllable*.

This being English, some exceptions exist! In a few regular past tense verbs you *do* pronounce the –ed ending as a separate syllable, for example *wanted* (pronounced 'want-ed'), *hated* (pronounced 'heit-ed') and *afforded* (pronounced 'afford-ed'). But each of these verbs ends in 't' or 'd' in the base form; it would be impossible to add the sound 't' or 'd' to make the past tense because you wouldn't be able to hear it! Try saying 'wantt' or 'heitt' – you can't hear the extra 't' on the end. In these verbs ending in the 't' or 'd' sound, you add the extra syllable –ed so that you actually hear that it's the past tense.

Irregular verbs

There are, of course, exceptions to adding –ed to form the past simple! Some of the most common verbs in English have an irregular past tense form. You need to memorise these! Here's a list of 16 common irregular past simple verbs and how you pronounce the trickier ones:

Base Form	Past Simple	Pronunciation
be	was / were	woz / wer
have	had	
do	did	
eat	ate	eit
put	put	

Base Form	Past Simple	Pronunciation
take	took	tuk
make	made	meid
know	knew	niu
go	went	
see	saw	saw (like 'door')
come	came	keim
think	thought	thawt
give	gave	geiv
find	found	faund
leave	left	
tell	told	

Apart from memorising these and other common irregular past tense verbs, you need to know how to pronounce them correctly so that people can understand you. We try to show you the pronunciation of some of the more difficult verbs in the table here, but the best thing to do is to *listen* to the verb and to practise, repeating it to yourself many times until you have memorised the correct pronunciation. The Internet has several free dictionaries where you can click on a word and listen to the pronunciation – www.dictionary.com, for example.

You make the positive or affirmative, negative and question forms of the past simple in the same way as in the present simple. And like the present simple, you also have a continuous / progressive aspect. Here's how that works:

✔ **Affirmative:**

- I *went* to the cinema at the weekend. (past simple)

- Heinrich *was reading* the newspaper when the phone rang. (past continuous / progressive)

✔ **Negative:**

- I *didn't go* to the gym at the weekend. (past simple)

- Heinrich *wasn't watching* TV when the phone rang. (past continuous / progressive)

✔ **Question:**

- *Did* you *go* to the cinema at the weekend? (past simple)

- What *was* Heinrich *doing* when the phone rang? (past continuous / progressive)

You use the past continuous / progressive to talk about an action or situation that was in progress when another shorter action happened. In the example above, Heinrich was reading the newspaper (a long, continuous action) when the telephone rang (a shorter action that happened during the longer action). You also use the past continuous / progressive to talk about an activity that was happening in the past at a certain point of time; for example 'Heinrich was reading the newspaper *at seven o'clock*'.

The future

You can talk about the future several ways in English. You can use the auxiliary verb *will*, but you can also use *going to*, the present continuous / progressive and the present simple. In this section we look at some examples of each of these and how they relate to the future.

Will

Many people who are learning English think that using *will* is the best way to talk about the future. This isn't strictly true. You use *will* in certain contexts, like that of predicting the future; for example 'Computers will take over the world one day'. You also use *will* to express future wishes or desires; for example 'I hope it will be sunny next week – we're going camping' or 'I'm sure you'll love York'. You can also use *will* to offer to help people, and to make promises. For example, if your flatmate is tired you can offer to do the washing up by saying 'I'll do the washing up tonight'. You can promise to do something, like telephone your friend, by saying 'I'll ring you tomorrow'.

Notice that when you speak fast, you can contract will to 'll, so you say 'I'll ring you tomorrow' rather than 'I will ring you tomorrow', although both of these forms are correct. With people's names, especially longer names, it's more difficult to contract *will*, so you may hear people using the complete form of *will*; for example 'Frederick will let us know'. It's also correct to say 'Frederick'll let us know', but you certainly need to *write* the full form because it looks strange contracted in writing – too many consonants are together in 'Frederick'll . . . '.

Will is an auxiliary verb, so you don't need to worry about the third person 's' and *will* remains the same for all subjects (I, you, he, we and so on). The negative form of *will* is *won't* (will + not). You use a main verb with *will* in the base form, so for example 'Where will you *be* at ten o'clock?', not 'Where will you are at ten o'clock?'.

  ✔ **Affirmative:**

  • I*'ll* ring you tomorrow.

  • Jane *will* get back to you as soon as she can.

✔ **Negative:**

- I *won't* ring you tomorrow.

- Jane *won't* be back in the office until late.

✔ **Question:**

- *Will* you give me a hand with the shopping?

- What *will* you wear to the party?

Going to

You use '[form of 'to be'] + going to' + base form of the verb to talk about future plans; for example 'We're going to drive around Scotland in the summer' or 'Jem is going to see what he can do to help with the project'.

If you aren't sure whether to use *will* or *going to* in a certain sentence, you may find it easier to use *going to*. People will definitely understand you.

✔ **Affirmative:**

- We *are going to* drive around Scotland in the summer.

- Jane *is going to* call them tomorrow about the order.

✔ **Negative:**

- We're *not going to* visit my aunt this year.

- Pol *is not going to* finish the report on time.

✔ **Question:**

- When *are* you *going to* let them know the results?

- *Is* Jane *going to* call them tomorrow?

With the verb to *go*, you normally use the present continuous, so instead of saying 'I'm going to go to York' you usually say 'I'm going to York'. Both of these forms are correct. The same thing happens with the verb to *come* – instead of saying 'I'm going to come to the party' you usually say 'I'm coming to the party'. Again, both of these sentences are correct, but the present continuous is more common.

Present continuous / progressive for future

You use the present continuous / progressive to talk about a definite arrangement in the near future. If you say 'I'm meeting Sergio at ten', it implies that you and Sergio have already arranged this. Here are some more examples:

✔ Hanna is catching the ten o'clock bus. (This implies that she has her ticket.)

✔ Secretary to boss: You're having lunch with the new head of department tomorrow. (This implies that the arrangement is fixed.)

✔ I'm flying to Singapore tomorrow morning. (This implies that I have my air ticket.)

You use the present continuous to ask people about their future plans. 'What are you doing next weekend / next Saturday / in the summer?' is a common way to ask people about their future plans. You can also use *going to* ('What are you going to do next weekend?'), but the present continuous is more common for this type of question.

Present simple for future

The present simple normally refers to the present, but sometimes you can use it to refer to the future when you're talking about actions or situations that are already on a programme or timetable. For example, when you talk about travel timetables, you use the present simple. Here are some examples:

✔ We fly to Belfast next Monday at 8am.

✔ What time does the bus leave?

✔ The train leaves from platform four.

✔ The 4.15 train from Victoria stops at Clapham Junction.

You also use the present simple to talk about the future after the word *when*. So you say 'I'll call you when I get home', not 'I'll call you when I will get home'. You also hear people use the present simple to refer to the future after the phrases 'I bet' and 'I hope'; for example 'I hope you have a great holiday this summer' or 'I bet he doesn't call tomorrow'.

Other expressions

Here are some other expressions you can use to talk about the future:

✔ [Form of 'to be'] + hoping + to. 'I'm hoping to visit the Lake District on my way to Scotland.'

✔ [Form of 'to be'] + planning + to. 'I'm planning to give him a call as soon as the meeting is over.'

✔ [Form of 'to be'] + looking forward to + –ing. 'We're all looking forward to having a holiday.'

✔ [Form of 'to be'] + thinking of + –ing. 'We're thinking of stopping at the Lake District on our way to Scotland.'

'Look forward to' is an expression that people use quite a lot in English. You often see the phrase in emails and letters; for example 'I'm looking forward to hearing from you soon'. Remember to use the verb with '–ing' after the expression 'look forward to' – this can be confusing because you normally put the infinitive after *to*. If you think of the expression 'look forward to' as one chunk or piece of language that stays together, then it's easier to remember. The difficult bit is to remember to use '–ing' after the expression. You always say 'I am looking forward to seeing you', and never 'I am looking forward to see you'. You can also use a noun or pronoun after 'look forward to'; for example 'I'm looking forward to the holidays' or 'I'm looking forward to it'.

Using Conditionals

You use conditional forms to talk about possible situations or actions in the present, future or past. You often use conditional forms with the word *if*. Here are some examples:

- ✔ If you take the number 19 bus, it will take you into the centre of town.
- ✔ If she doesn't arrive soon, she'll miss the start of the movie.
- ✔ If I pass the exam, I'll get a better job.

These three examples talk about possible events in the future or near future. Most English grammar books call this construction the *first conditional*.

'If' clause (if + present simple)	**Main clause (will / won't + base form of verb)**
If I pass the exam,	I'll get a better job

You use the present simple in the *if* clause. You don't say if 'I'll pass the exam, I'll get a better job'. You use a construction called the *second conditional* to talk about hypothetical, imaginary or unlikely events and situations. For example:

- ✔ If I had £1 million, I would never work again (but I am unlikely to have £1 million!).
- ✔ If I were him, I'd leave that job (but I will never be him).
- ✔ If I didn't have you, I don't know what I would do (but I do have you).
- ✔ If Elizabeth studied more, she would pass the exam (but she never studies).

'If' clause (if + simple past)	*Main clause (would / wouldn't + base form of verb)*
If Elizabeth studied more,	she would pass the exam

Our examples refer to imaginary or unreal situations – even though you use the verb in the *if* clause in the past simple, you're referring not to the past but to an imaginary situation. In the last example above, Elizabeth hasn't taken her exam yet, and the exam is at some point in the future. But it's clear that you think Elizabeth will not study more, and that she is unlikely to pass the exam. You could also say 'If Elizabeth studies more, she will pass the exam' – in this case it's possible that Elizabeth studies, and if she does, then she has a realistic chance of passing the exam.

You often use *were* after an *if* clause instead of *was* in the first and third person singular, especially in formal situations or in writing. For example, you may hear 'If he were smarter, he'd be the director by now' or 'If Jaime were to ask her, she'd probably say yes'. *Were* is especially common in the phrase 'If I were you . . .'. But you also hear people using *was* in these sentences. Although some people complain that this isn't grammatically correct, the truth is that in conditional sentences *were* is falling out of favour and native speakers are increasingly using *was*. So you're just as likely to hear 'If he was smarter, he'd be the director by now' or 'If Jaime was to ask her, she'd probably say yes'. You may also hear if 'If I was you . . .', but 'If I were you . . .' (the more 'correct' form) is still very common.

You also talk about possible or imaginary situations in the past using a construction called the *third conditional*. Here we talk about things that did not happen in the past, for example:

- ✔ If I had known you were coming, I would have brought Tim along (but I didn't know you were coming, so I didn't bring Tim).

- ✔ If he hadn't gone to Belfast, he wouldn't have met Shona (but he did go to Belfast, and he met Shona).

- ✔ If you hadn't called her, she would have missed the meeting (but you did call her, so she was able to come to the meeting).

'If' clause (if + had / hadn't + past participle)	*Main clause (would / wouldn't + have + past participle)*
If you hadn't called her,	she would have missed the meeting

You can use the second conditional to sound more polite. To ask someone politely for help you can say 'It would be great if you helped me with the washing up' (or 'It would be great if you could help me with washing up'). You can also ask permission politely using the second conditional; for example 'Would it be okay if I came round at about ten?'.

Chapter 3

Getting to Know People

. . . .

In This Chapter

▶ Talking to new people

▶ Discussing the weather

▶ Chatting about yourself and your family

▶ Telling stories and jokes

. . . .

Meeting new people in a new country can be difficult and stressful. In this kind of situation, *small talk* (informal chat in social situations) can help you establish relationships and find common interests to share with your new friends and colleagues. People like you to ask questions and show an interest in their lives, their family, pets and even – especially in Britain – the weather.

Chatting with Strangers

Most question words in English start with 'wh', as we discuss in Chapter 2. The following 'wh' words are very useful when you meet new people:

✔ Who . . . ?

✔ What . . . ?

✔ Where . . . ?

✔ When . . . ?

✔ Why . . . ?

To this list we can also add the following:

✔ How . . . ?

✔ How long . . . ?

✔ Which . . . ?

Here are some examples of these 'wh' questions in action:

- Who's that man over there?
- What do you do? [asking about a person's job]
- Where do you live?
- When does the train leave?
- Why is the bus late?
- How do I get to Baker Street? [asking for directions]
- How long does it take you to get to work?
- Which bus goes to London?

Straight Talking

 Maria is waiting at the station for a train. She has half an hour to wait, so she decides to have a coffee. The cafe is full, so she tries to find a seat.

Maria:	Excuse me, is this seat free?
Mike:	Sure.
Maria:	Thanks. [Maria sits down.]
Mike:	My name's Mike – nice to meet you.
Maria:	I'm Maria – nice to meet you too.
Mike:	Where are you from, Maria? I think I hear an accent.
Maria:	I'm from Portugal. I'm going to visit some friends in Manchester. How about you?
Mike:	I'm on my way to work, as usual!
Maria:	What do you do?
Mike:	I'm a teacher. How about you?
Maria:	I'm a banker, but I'm on holiday right now.

Initial conversations are often like the one here. Typically, people ask a person's name, where they come from and their job: you can ask for these three key pieces of information in many social situations to make small talk on public transport, in a café, at a party, in a pub . . .

If you meet someone new in a bar or pub, one question that it's *not* a good idea to use is 'Do you come here often?'. British people consider this to be one of the most unoriginal and stereotypical questions in the English language for trying to *pick someone up* (trying to get somebody interested in you in a sexual way)! Rather, try a sentence like 'Nice place this, isn't it?' or 'It's crowded in here, isn't it?' or 'What's that you're drinking?' (if it's not obvious!).

Sometimes you won't understand everything you hear. It's not always necessary to understand every word, but for those occasions when you think you're missing important information, these sentences may be useful:

- ✔ Can you speak more slowly, please?
- ✔ Pardon?
- ✔ Sorry, what was that?
- ✔ Could you repeat that, please?
- ✔ I'm sorry, I don't understand what you mean.

Native English speakers often use the following phrases to ask for clarification if they don't understand something:

- ✔ Come again?
- ✔ Sorry?
- ✔ You what?

Talking about the Weather

A popular subject in many English-speaking countries is the weather. This is especially true in Britain, where people like to talk about the weather a lot, often in optimistic terms, even if the weather is bad.

If you listen to strangers talking in a shop or at a bus stop or in other public places, you'll notice that they often use the topic of weather to start a conversation, or to pass the time. Here are some useful phrases connected with the weather:

- ✔ Lovely day!

- ✔ It's turned out nice again.

- ✔ Terrible weather, isn't it?

- ✔ Isn't this weather miserable?

- ✔ Isn't it cold today?

- ✔ I hear it'll clear up later.

- ✔ It's looking nice out today.

Often you add a question tag to end of the weather sentence. So you get 'It's turned out nice again, *hasn't it?*' or 'Lovely day, *isn't it?*'. You do this to invite a response, such as 'Yes, it is', and then conversation can continue from there. (Refer to Chapter 2 to find out more about question tags.)

One expression you probably *won't* hear from a British person is 'It's raining cats and dogs' – these days you only find that phrase in English grammar books. More common expressions are 'It's chucking it down' and 'It's tipping down', meaning that it's raining very hard.

Straight Talking

 Goran is buying a newspaper from a newsagent. Listen to how he makes small talk about the weather with the shopkeeper.

Goran:　　　Morning!

Newsagent:　Morning. How's it going?

Goran:　　　Not bad, thanks, you?

Newsagent:　Fine, apart from this rain! It's chucking down!

Goran:　　　Yes, it's terrible, isn't it? And so cold!

Newsagent:　They said it will brighten up later.

Goran:　　　They always say that! Still, it's warmer than back home.

Newsagent:　Really? What's the weather like in Zagreb now?

Goran: Freezing cold, and snowing.

Newsagent: Right! So this is like summer for you!

Goran: Right!

My Family and Other Animals

As Gerald Durrell, the author of the much-loved book *My Family and Other Animals* suggests, family can be quite special! Family is an area of life that people talk about a lot. You may show photographs of your family to friends, or share details of phone calls or emails. Families have different degrees of importance in different cultures. In English-speaking countries it's normal to ask one or two questions about a person's family the first time you meet them, but then wait until the person offers more information before delving any deeper. Family trees show people's relationships to each other.

- John is David's father [dad].
- Mary is David's mother [mum].
- David is John's son.
- Susan is John's daughter.
- David is Susan's brother.
- Susan is David's sister.
- Charlie is David's brother-in-law.
- Carla is Susan's sister-in-law.
- Charlie is Mary's son-in-law.
- Carla is Mary's daughter-in-law.
- Jamie is John's grandson.
- Rosa is John's granddaughter.
- Jamie and Rosa are Stuart's cousins.
- David is Stuart's uncle.
- Susan is Rosa's aunt.
- John is Rosa's grandfather [grandpa, granddad].
- Mary is Stuart's grandmother [grandma, granny, gran, nan].

Straight Talking

 Carla is showing photographs of a family barbecue to a new friend at work.

Carla: Well, that's me, obviously – and my husband, David. And our two kids, Rosa and Jamie.

Jane: They look lovely – how old are they?

Carla: Rosa's twelve now and Jamie's ten in September. They're good kids, but quite noisy sometimes.

Jane: And who are these two?

Carla: My in-laws, John and Mary – David's mum and dad. They're great – I get on really well with them and they're good with the kids.

Jane: And this must be David's sister?

Carla: Right – that's Susan and her husband, Charlie, and little Stuart.

Jane: How old's Stuart?

Carla: He was two last month.

Jane: He's very cute!

Telling Jokes and Anecdotes

Jokes and stories are very popular on social occasions and it's quite normal for people to take turns telling a story or explaining an incident from their lives. While you're listening it's a good idea to show that you're paying attention, and to seem interested!

A joke has an introduction, to get people's attention. The joke then continues and ends with a *punchline*, the funny part.

Every country generally targets another country in some of its jokes, and Britain is no exception. The British as a whole often make jokes about the English, Scottish and Irish, and you may hear jokes that begin with the line 'A Scotsman, an Englishman and an Irishman walked into a pub . . .'. Use this kind of humour with caution otherwise you may offend people. If you want to tell a joke, stick to a 'safe' topic and never tell a joke about another country or nationality except your own.

People in Britain often make jokes about themselves and laugh at silly things they do or mistakes they make. Comments such 'Oh, I'm hopeless at skiing / maths' or 'I'm useless when it comes to skiing / maths' aren't uncommon. People tend to say such things in a casual, throw-away tone. This kind of *self-deprecating* (laughing at oneself, or putting oneself down) comment is less common in other countries and can lead to cultural misunderstandings. Only make such comments for unimportant things – if you apply for a job as a maths professor, don't say 'I'm hopeless at maths'.

Straight Talking

Dan, Carla and Goran are having a drink in a pub before going to the cinema. Listen to Dan telling a joke.

Dan:	This'll make you laugh.
Carla:	What?
Dan:	A horse walks into a bar and asks for a whisky.
Goran:	Yes?
Dan:	And the barman says, 'Sure, but what's with the long face?'
Carla:	Ha, ha – that's a good one!
Goran:	I don't get it.
Carla:	Goran! Horses have long faces, right?
Goran:	Yes . . .
Dan:	And in English 'to have a long face' is to look sad. So if you say to someone 'What's with the long face?' you're asking 'Why are you so sad?'.

Goran:	Oh!
Dan:	Hmmmm . . . it's not so funny when you have to explain it!
Carla:	I've got one!
Goran:	No! No more jokes, please! Let's go and see the film.

Anecdotes – short stories about something that happened to you or someone you know – are a good way to make small talk. If you tell an anecdote try to use the present simple or progressive tense (refer to Chapter 2) because this makes the story more immediate for the people listening to you. It's also a lot easier than remembering to use all those irregular past tenses.

Straight Talking

Listen to Carla explaining how she started her holiday.

Carla:	So I get up at four in the morning and get a taxi to the station. It's freezing outside and the taxi driver is going too quickly. Of course, I know what's going to happen. Sure enough, we hit some ice and the car leaves the road.
Gina:	No!
Carla:	I'm not joking! We finished up next to the river, the car turns over and suddenly we're upside down.
Gina:	Seriously?
Carla:	Yes! And guess what the taxi driver does?
Gina:	What?
Carla:	He starts smoking a cigarette!
Gina:	You're joking!
Carla:	I'm not. So there we are upside down in the car!

Notice how people show interest and comment on jokes and anecdotes in the previous examples. In Britain, showing you're interested in the person and listening to the story is polite. Here are some useful phrases and interjections:

- ✔ Really?
- ✔ Seriously?
- ✔ No!
- ✔ No way!
- ✔ You're joking!
- ✔ I don't believe it!
- ✔ Unbelievable!

Fun & Games

1. Order the words to make correct questions. The first word is in bold, and the first example has been done for you.

1 you **Where** come say you from did?

Where did you say you come from?

2. been **How** country have in you long this?

3. that what was **Sorry**,?

4. have you any **Do** then kids?

5. **It's** nicely isn't clearing it up,?

6. it weather, **Terrible** isn't?

7. drink are to **What** having you?

8. quiet isn't here, it **It's** tonight in?

9. he says **And** what next guess?

10. heard **Have** one this you?

Now decide what context each question is used in. The first example has been done for you.

✔ Talking about the weather

✔ Making small talk in a pub or bar

✔ Asking about a person's background

✔ Asking for clarification

✔ Asking about family

✔ Telling a joke or anecdote

1 Where did you say you come from?

Asking about a person's background

Key:

Where did you say you come from? Asking about a person's background

How long have you been in this country? Asking about a person's background

Sorry, what was that? Asking for clarification

Do you have any kids then? Asking about family

It's clearing up nicely, isn't it? Talking about the weather

Terrible weather, isn't it? Talking about the weather

What are you having to drink? Making small talk in a pub or bar

It's quiet in here tonight, isn't it? Making small talk in a pub or bar

And guess what he says next? Telling a joke or anecdote

Have you heard this one? Telling a joke or anecdote

2. Put these sentences in order to make a conversation. The first two sentences are in the correct order, in bold.

In a pub:

Mick: **Crowded in here tonight, isn't it?**

Elena: **Sorry, what was that?**

Elena: I'm Brazilian. I'm here for a few months studying at the university.

Mick: Ah, I thought it was bloody Mary [tomato juice with vodka]. So where are you from? I thought I detected an accent?

Mick: Well your English sounds pretty good to me!

Elena: It's tomato juice – I don't drink much alcohol.

Mick [louder]: I said there are lots of people in this pub tonight!

Elena: Ah. Yes, loads. I've never been here before, but it's quite nice.

Mick: Really? What are you studying?

Elena: Actually, I'm studying English.

Mick: Yeah, it's usually pretty crowded on a Friday and Saturday though. What's that you're drinking? Looks interesting!

Key:

Mick: **Crowded in here tonight, isn't it?**

Elena: **Sorry, what was that?**

Mick (louder): I said there are lots of people in this pub tonight!

Elena: Ah. Yes, loads. I've never been here before, but it's quite nice.

Mick: Yeah, it's usually pretty crowded on a Friday and Saturday though. What's that you're drinking? Looks interesting!

Elena: It's tomato juice – I don't drink much alcohol.

(continued)

Mick: Ah, I thought it was bloody Mary. So where are you from? I thought I detected an accent?

Elena: I'm Brazilian. I'm here for a few months studying at the university.

Mick: Really? What are you studying?

Elena: Actually, I'm studying English.

Mick: Well your English sounds pretty good to me!

Part II
English in Action

"If body language is any indication, I'd say you needed work on your greeting."

In this part . . .

Do you want to improve your English? Then you need to get out and practise it! We show you how to communicate in lots of everyday situations – shopping, ordering a meal in a restaurant, arranging a night out, talking about your hobbies and what you do in your free time. What's more, we also help you to communicate in more formal settings such as the office. We show you how to talk on the phone, take messages at work and write good emails. Finally we take a look at the differences between written and spoken English.

This part helps you develop a good range of styles to express yourself in English, from informal spoken language in social situations, to polite language for shopping and restaurants, to more formal written language. Dive in!

Chapter 4

Shopping and Numbers

. . . .

In This Chapter

▶ Finding clothes and shoes to fit

▶ Shopping at the supermarket and the market

▶ Looking at numbers: money, phone numbers, dates and shop floors

. . . .

Going shopping in a new country can feel strange the first few times. You need to know how to ask for things, what times the shops open and what shop to go to for your needs. For example in some countries you can buy stamps, toys and even underwear in some tobacconists' shops. In the UK, visitors are often surprised by the amount of chocolate and sweets on sale in newsagents', which sell magazines and newspapers. And some large chemist chains in the UK sell things such as small electrical goods (irons or hairdryers), not just medicine!

Shopping in the High Street

The 'high street' is where most of the shops in many towns and cities are concentrated. London, for example, which was originally a collection of small villages, has many high streets.

Recently, British high streets have begun to look more and more alike, with the same large chain stores in all major towns and cities, selling clothes, shoes and electronic goods. You can still find smaller independent stores too, which specialise in certain goods and products, such as the butcher's shop or butchery (which sells meat), the baker's or bakery (for bread and cakes), the greengrocer's (for fruit and vegetables – also known simply as the 'grocer's') and the chemist's (for medicines and toiletries). People usually say 'I'm going to the butcher's' rather than 'I'm going to the butcher's shop' – you leave off the word 'shop', but because it's implied, you actually *write* the sentence with an apostrophe – so *butcher's* not *butchers* in the earlier sentence.

Some types of shops take their names from other languages, especially French, which supposedly sounds more sophisticated when it comes to food and drink or clothes, so you may find a 'delicatessen' – or 'deli' – which sells speciality food, or a 'boutique' for clothes.

Another shop you might see is the pawn shop, where people can sell things such as electronic equipment (TVs, stereos, CD players and so on) or jewellery to the shop owner, who then sells it on to the public for a profit. Probably more common than pawn shops are betting shops, where you can bet money on horse or dog races, on football matches and on many other sporting events.

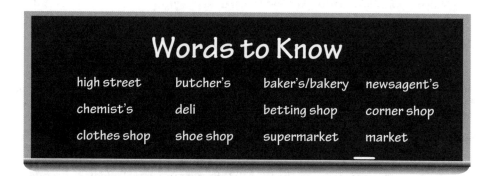

Words to Know

high street	butcher's	baker's/bakery	newsagent's
chemist's	deli	betting shop	corner shop
clothes shop	shoe shop	supermarket	market

Here are some useful phrases for asking for things in a shop:

- ✔ I'd like . . .
- ✔ Do you have . . . / Have you got . . .
- ✔ I'll have . . .
- ✔ I'll take . . . .

The shop assistant may say some of the following things to you:

- ✔ Can I help you?
- ✔ Here you go.
- ✔ Anything else?
- ✔ That'll be three pounds sixty-five.
- ✔ Cash or credit card?

Straight Talking

 Mario is at the baker's.

Mario:	Morning! I'd like a loaf of bread, please.
Shop assistant:	Certainly – white or brown?
Mario:	Brown, please.
Shop assistant:	We have several types of whole-wheat bread – with cereals or sesame seeds, or just plain.
Mario:	Plain, please. And I'd like half a dozen white bread rolls too, please.
Shop assistant:	Here you go – anything else?
Mario:	And one Danish pastry, to eat now.
Shop assistant:	Oh yes, these are freshly baked, just out the oven. That'll be three pounds sixty-five.
Mario:	Thanks.

You usually find different types of bread in a bakery. The main types are white bread and brown bread, although many types of each exist. Usually, you can find the name of each bread on the shelf, and information on what the bread contains (nuts, cereals and sesame seeds, for example) so that helps you know what to ask for.

Words to Know

whole-wheat bread	white bread	pastry
doughnut	baguette	cereals
seeds	freshly baked	rolls

Residential areas of larger towns and cities in the United Kingdom often have a small local *corner shop*, which stays open very long hours, seven day a week, and stocks essentials such as milk and bread, basic foodstuffs and toiletries (and even alcohol if the shop has a licence for this). A shop that sells only alcohol is known as an *off-licence*. You may hear a native speaker say 'I'm off down the offy', meaning she's going to the off-licence to buy something. You can also usually buy confectionary and cigarettes in an off-licence. No one under the age of 18 can legally buy either cigarettes or alcohol in the UK.

Straight Talking

Antonio is in the newsagent's buying a magazine.

Antonio: Hello. I'm looking for the latest copy of *Car Now* magazine. Do you have it?

Newsagent: Just a sec, I'll check. Look, the car magazines are here on this shelf.

Antonio: Oh, sorry, I didn't see that.

Newsagent: Okay, let's see. This one is last month's. No, sorry, this month's magazine hasn't arrived yet. It'll be here in a day or two.

Antonio: Alright, thanks.

Newsagent: Is there anything else you need?

Antonio: I'll have a bar of this dark chocolate.

Newsagent: Okay, that's ninety-five pence, please.

Instead of hearing 'I'm going to the shops', with the verb 'to go', you may hear phrases such as 'I'm off down the shops' or 'I'm just popping down the shops' from English-speaking friends or colleagues. Remember that unless your English is very good indeed, using a colloquial expression like this can sound strange, so it's fine for you to say 'I'm going to the shops'.

Shop opening times

High street shops in the UK are usually open from Monday to Saturday, from 9 or 10 a.m. to 5 or 6 p.m. Sunday shopping has become more common in recent years, and most big shopping centres in larger towns and cities are open on Sundays, although smaller independent shops usually close on Sundays. Pubs and restaurants are open much later. In theory pubs can stay open all night: after years of very strict licensing laws, the government recently introduced 24-hour licensing. The reality is that many pubs still close between 11 p.m. and 1 a.m. See Chapter 6 for more on pubs.

Shopping for clothes and shoes

The names of some types of shop are very easy to remember. You buy clothes from a clothes shop, and shoes from a shoe shop. You also find toys in a toy shop, and electronic goods in an electronics shop.

You also find *charity shops* or *second-hand shops*, which sell used clothes and other items and give most of the money they make to charity. Most British high streets have at least one charity shop, and many people in Britain aren't embarrassed about wearing second-hand clothes. However, modern Britain is a multicultural country, and not all people find it acceptable, or *cool*, to wear used clothes.

You can go shopping at the butcher's, the greengrocer's (or grocer's) and the newsagent's. But some shops are much easier to say – shoe shop, clothes shop, toy shop. There's no apostrophe (') in these, so you *never* say a shoe's shop, a toy's shop or a clothes' shop.

Try these basic phrases and questions in shops to ask about goods and prices:

- ✔ I'm looking for [a white jacket].
- ✔ Have you got / Do you have [any white jackets]?
- ✔ How much is [this jacket] / are [these jackets]?
- ✔ Can I try this on?
- ✔ Where are the changing rooms?

After you try something on, you may want to try a different size, colour or style. Or you may not like it. You can use these phrases:

- ✔ What size is this?
- ✔ This doesn't fit / These don't fit.
- ✔ This is too big / small. Have you got a [bigger / smaller] size?
- ✔ Do you have this in [a different colour / a brighter colour / black]?
- ✔ I'll leave this.

If the item is exactly what you're looking for and you want to buy it, use these phrases:

✔ This is perfect.

✔ This fits perfectly.

✔ Does this suit me? / That really suits you.

✔ I'll take it.

Straight Talking

 Mila goes to a clothes shop.

Shop assistant:	Can I help you?
Mila:	Hello, yes, I'd like to try on the black skirt I saw in the window.
Shop assistant:	Certainly, madam. What size are you?
Mila:	I'm not sure about the sizes here. I'm a European size forty.
Shop assistant:	Okay, let me see. I think that's a size fourteen here. Here you are.
Mila:	Thanks. Where are the changing rooms?
Shop assistant:	Over there in the corner.

[Mila tries on the skirt and goes back to the shop assistant.]

Mila:	I'm sorry, but this doesn't fit. The size fourteen is a bit too big for me. Have you got a smaller size?
Shop assistant:	You'll be a size twelve then. Let me check . . . No, sorry, we don't have any more black skirts in a size twelve. What about a different colour?
Mila:	I do like the style very much. What other colours do you have?
Shop assistant:	Dark grey, green and brown.

Mila:	This dark grey looks nice. I'll try that in a size twelve. And I'll also try that grey jumper with it, in a size twelve.

[Mila tries on the second skirt and jumper, and goes back to the shop assistant.]

Mila:	Okay, this skirt fits perfectly. I'll take it, but I'll leave the jumper: the style is a little too short.
Shop assistant:	Certainly, madam. Will you pay by cash or credit card?
Mila:	Cash, please.
Shop assistant:	Right. That's eighty-three pounds seventy-five in total.
Mila:	Here you go. Thanks.
Shop assistant:	Goodbye.
Mila:	Bye.

Giving compliments

To give someone a compliment on their clothes, you can use the following expressions:

- ✔ I really like [that skirt].
- ✔ It looks great / lovely / gorgeous / fabulous!
- ✔ It's great / lovely / gorgeous / fabulous!
- ✔ That's a great / lovely / gorgeous / fabulous [skirt]!
- ✔ Where did you get [that skirt]? I love it!
- ✔ That [skirt] really suits you!

If you compliment a person on her clothes, don't be surprised if she responds with a comment that seems negative. You may say 'That's a lovely jumper', and you may get a reply such as 'This old thing? Oh, I've had it for years' or 'Do you think so? I got it really cheap in the sales'. This is a cultural convention which, as a visitor, you don't need to follow. If someone compliments *you* on how *you* look, or on your clothes, you can simply say 'Thank you!' and smile. Much easier than trying to find a reason not to accept the compliment!

Checking the size of clothes and shoes

CULTURAL WISDOM

Shoe and clothes sizes use different numbering systems in different countries. You find S (small), M (medium), L (large) and XL (extra large) all over the world. However, Europe and the UK, for example, use very different size references, and it can be very confusing when a shop assistant suggests you're a size 12 dress, when in your country you've always been a size 40. Table 4-1 shows the different sizes.

Table 4-1	Knowing Your Size		
	International	*Europe (Inches)*	*UK*
Dress sizes	Small	36–40	8–10
	Medium	40–44	12–14
	Large	46–50	16–20
Shirt sizes (men)	Small		34–36 (inches)
	Medium		38–40 (inches)
	Large		42–44 (inches)
Shoe sizes		37	4
		38	5
		39	6
		40	7
		41	8
		42	9
		43	10
		44	11
		45	12

Words to Know

dress	skirt	shirt	blouse (for women)
trousers	jeans	suit	jacket
tie	shoes	boots	sandals
coat	jumper	jersey	tights

Straight Talking

 Mila wants to buy some shoes in a shoe shop.

Shop assistant: Good morning. Can I help you? Do you see anything you like?

Mila: Hello, yes, I'm looking for some black shoes to wear to work. Something formal, smart . . . These are nice. How much are they?

Shop assistant: Let's see . . . the price is on the back here. They're thirty-nine pounds ninety nine.

Mila: Nearly forty pounds. Right . . . and these are size six. Can I try them on?

Shop assistant: Yes, of course, madam. Please take a seat here.

[Mila tries on the shoes.]

Mila: Hmm. These are too small; they don't really fit. Have you got a bigger size?

Shop assistant: Right, I'll get you a size six and a half then.

Mila: Thanks. Oh yes, these are much better. They fit perfectly.

Shop assistant: Very nice. They suit you, especially with that skirt.

Mila: Okay, I'll take them. Can I pay by credit card?

Shop assistant: Yes, of course.

In the conversation shown here, you see the three key verbs to use when buying clothes or shoes: *try on*, *suit* and *fit*. To *try on* means to put the clothes on, and if it's the right size then the item *fits*. If the item *suits* you, then it looks good on you. So when you next go shopping for clothes, first *try on* the clothes to see whether they *fit*, and then look in the mirror to see whether they *suit* you!

Going to the Supermarket

When visiting a foreign country, it's often tempting to go to a supermarket for your food shopping. In a supermarket you don't need to speak to anyone, and you can take products off the supermarket shelves without asking for help or worrying about asking for a different size jacket! In fact, some of the larger supermarket chains now sell not only food, but also toys and clothes.

You may need help in a supermarket if you want to find something or at the checkout till when you pay. The following phrases may be useful:

✔ Have you got / Do you have [any shoe polish]?

✔ Which aisle is the [shoe polish] in? [Note that 'aisle' is pronounced the same as 'I'll']

✔ Can I pay by credit card?

✔ Can I have a plastic bag, please?

Straight Talking

Pierre is in the supermarket.

Cashier: Hello, sir, nice to see you.

Pierre: Hi.

[The cashier totals Pierre's purchases.]

Cashier: Reward card? No? Then that's forty-eight pounds and sixty-three pence, please.

Pierre: Can I have two plastic bags please?

Cahier: Yes, they're two p each. Is that alright?

Pierre: Okay. And can I pay by credit card?

Cashier: Yes, of course – just put your card through here, please.

Pierre: Okay. Oh, the machine won't accept my card. Maybe because it's from France?

Cashier: That's alright, it's probably not chip and PIN. You can sign for your shopping. I'll put your card through here. And here's your receipt. Have a nice day!

Pierre: Thank you.

Credit cards and 'chip and PIN'

In the UK large shops such as supermarkets usually use a credit card payment system called 'chip and PIN'. 'Chip' refers to an electronic microchip in the credit card, and 'PIN' means 'Personal Identification Number'. Chip and PIN credit cards need you to key in your personal identification number instead of signing for a purchase, so they are more secure than credit cards that need only a signature. However, many visitors to the UK don't have chip and PIN credit cards, so supermarkets also have the older style credit card terminals, which allow you to sign for your shopping.

Words to Know

shopping trolley

shopping basket

aisle (pronounced 'I'll')

checkout

cashier

reward card

receipt (pronounced 're-SEET')

to sign (pronounced 'sihn')

Shopping bags and reward cards

Some large supermarket chains charge you a few pence for a plastic bag, and many people take their own plastic or cloth bags to the supermarket to carry their shopping home. The cashier at the checkout may also ask you if you have a 'reward card'; this is a supermarket card the same size as a credit card, and it gives you a discount on your shopping, or gives you extra 'points' that can count towards discounts. You usually need to be resident in the UK, with a UK address, to apply for a reward card. When you pay for your shopping in a large supermarket chain, the cashier usually asks if you have a reward card, but she will often refer to the card by name – a 'Nectar' card is one of the most common reward cards, and you can use it in several different shops. Some supermarkets even give you a few points on your reward card if you take your own bags for your shopping and don't use their plastic bags.

Visiting the Market

More interesting than supermarkets are markets, either open air or covered. Some markets operate every day, some only at weekends and some on special dates. You can buy almost anything in a market, from food to furniture, chips to china.

Buying fruit and vegetables

To buy fruit and vegetables, you need to know your weights and volumes, which we explain in the later section 'Measuring up – weights and volumes'. Useful words and phrases for buying fruit and vegetables at the market are:

- I'd like a pound / kilo of [oranges], please.
- I'll take some of [those strawberries].
- How much are [the strawberries]?

Buying meat and fish

Like fruit and vegetables, vendors may sell meat and fish in pounds or in kilos, although by law shop owners must always display the metric weights. You can usually ask the butcher to cut your meat for you, or the fishmonger to clean the fish.

Meat

Here are some of the meats you may find at a butcher's stall at a market – and in a butcher's shop in the high street:

- Meat: beef (from a cow), pork (from a pig), lamb (from a sheep), liver, tripe (the intestines of an animal), sausages, bacon
- Poultry: chicken, duck
- Steak: cooking steak, rump steak, T-bone steak
- Mince or mincemeat (very finely ground meat)
- Chops: lamb chops, pork chops

Fish

Fish comes from a fishmonger's (the name of the shop). Some of the most commonly eaten fish in the UK are:

- Trout
- Salmon
- Plaice
- Cod

Shellfish

Shellfish also comes from the fishmonger and is more expensive than fish. You usually find the following shellfish at a fishmonger's:

- Shrimp/prawns
- Lobster
- Crayfish
- Mussels
- Cockles
- Oysters

Measuring up: weights and volumes

Like other European Union countries, the UK officially uses kilos and grams, but you still see the *imperial* weight system of pounds and ounces on signs, and hear many people using this system. Even if the sign on a pile of oranges says '£1.50 per kilo', you may hear a customer asking for 'two pounds of oranges'. (A kilo is about 2 pounds in weight). This can be confusing as the currency is in 'pounds' too! In the case of these oranges, they're about £1.50 for half a pound!

 Many shops and market stalls use both the newer metric system and the imperial system on the same sign. So if you're more familiar with the metric system, you can do all your food shopping in kilos and grams, and you don't need to puzzle over the intricacies of 16 ounces to the pound.

The metric martyrs

The 'metric martyrs' were a group of traders in Britain who were given large fines for using imperial weights only on signs for food they were selling. The law says that imperial weight *can* be put on signs, but metric weights *must* always be shown. The newspapers called this group of men the 'metric martyrs' after a politician said they could martyr themselves if they wanted to, but the law was the law.

Car boot sales

Car boot sales are unofficial markets that take place in a public open air location such as a car park, often on Sundays. Anyone can bring anything that they no longer want, and sell them to others, from the boot (or trunk) of their car. At a car boot sale you find interesting ornaments, old electrical goods, watches, jewellery, second-hand books, furniture . . . really anything that's been lying around in someone's house for years, and that they no longer want. Beware – car boot sales usually have a lot of old, unwanted junk, although you may be lucky and find a bargain!

A similar thing happens when you buy liquids. Although you may buy a litre of orange juice in a carton in a supermarket, milk is usually measured in pints (1 litre is about 1.8 pints). And when you buy beer in a pub, you can order a pint or half a pint of beer, but not a litre.

Words to Know

A bunch of grapes / bananas / radishes

A packet of peas / nuts / crisps

A box of strawberries   A dozen / half a dozen eggs

A pint of milk   A carton of orange juice   A tin of tuna

Straight Talking

 Gina is at the market, buying food for the week. She first goes to the fruit and vegetable stall.

Trader 1:   Hello, love, what would you like?

Gina: Let's see . . . I'm making a salad for eight tomorrow, so two lettuces, I think, and a bunch of radishes . . .

Trader 1:	Okay, I've got some lovely tomatoes here . . .
Gina:	Right, I'll take two pounds of tomatoes, and that cucumber. Oh, and half a dozen eggs. Those grapes look nice too – I'll have two bunches.
Trader 1:	Is that all then?
Gina:	Just a pound of potatoes and that's it.
Trader 1:	Here you go, love. That'll be six pounds forty.
Gina:	Thanks. Bye.
[Gina goes to the butcher's stall.]	
Trader 2:	Can I help you?
Gina:	I'll take some of those nice looking lamb chops. How much are they?
Trader 2:	Five ninety-nine a pound.
Gina:	Oh! Right, that's more than I thought! Okay, so I'd like two pounds of mince, please.
Trader 2:	No problem. Here you go. Anything else I can help you with?
Gina:	I need some chicken too, so five chicken thighs, please, and that's it.
Trader 2:	Right, that's three pounds fifty.
Gina:	Here you go. Thanks.

Practising Your Numbers

We're not going to teach you how to count in English, because you probably know how to do that already. Instead, we're going to look at how you use numbers to talk about certain things, such as prices and phone numbers.

Money

The UK currency is pounds and pence, with 100 pence in one pound. How do you say prices, though? It's pretty easy really – just say the pounds first, followed by the pence, so:

- £4.99: four pounds, ninety-nine
- £18.75: eighteen pounds, seventy-five

Notice that when you say these prices, you don't put 'and' between the pound and pence (not 'four pounds *and* ninety-nine'), and you usually don't add *pence* at the end (not 'four pounds ninety-nine *pence*').

What about when you talk about pence only? You often shorten the word 'pence' to just 'p' (pronounced 'pee').

- 59p: fifty-nine pence, or fifty-nine p
- 16p: sixteen pence, or sixteen p

Here are some more examples:

- £19.99: nineteen pounds ninety-nine
- £50: fifty pounds
- £3.89: three pounds eighty-nine
- 25p: twenty-five pence (or twenty-five p)
- 75p: seventy-five pence (or seventy-five p)
- 10p: ten pence (or ten p)

When you talk about larger numbers, you often round them up or down, so instead of saying 'The car cost me three thousand, one hundred and twenty-two pounds' you say 'The car cost me about three thousand pounds'. Other phrases you use for this are:

- Three thousand and something
- Nearly five hundred
- Just under six thousand
- Over ten thousand

You use these phrases with numbers in the hundreds and thousands, not with smaller numbers.

Be careful of the difference in pronunciation between tens and teens. For example, look at the difference between how you say 60 (sixty) and 16 (sixteen). With the tens, you put the emphasis on the first syllable – so you say 'SIX-ty'. With the teens you put the emphasis on the second syllable, so you say 'six-TEEN'. Say it aloud and you'll hear the difference! Even native speakers need to ask for clarification sometimes, and you can do this by saying 'Sorry, was that SIXty or sixTEEN', exaggerating the emphasis.

Like many languages, English has several slang (or colloquial) words for money. The best known are 'quid' for a pound (British English) and 'buck' for a dollar (American and Australian English). So you may hear someone saying 'That cost ten quid!' meaning £10, or 'Give us a tenner!' meaning 'Give me a ten pound note'. The word 'fiver' for a five-pound note also exists, as in 'It's only a fiver' – it only costs £5.

Dates

Always use ordinal numbers in English to say dates. So you can write 28 December or 28th December, but always say 'the twenty-eighth' of December' or 'December (the) twenty-eighth'. So, 1 May is 'the first of May' or 'May (the) first' but never 'one of May' or 'May one'.

For years before 2000, you divide up the first part into teens and the second into normal numbers, so 1985 is 'nineteen eighty-five'. For dates after 2000, you say 'two thousand and . . . ', so 2010 is 'two thousand and ten'. You can also say 'twenty-ten' for 2010, although this is less common.

Here are some more examples:

- ✔ 1964: nineteen sixty-four
- ✔ 1992: nineteen ninety-two
- ✔ 2001: two thousand and one (or twenty-oh-one)
- ✔ 2012: two thousand and twelve (or twenty-twelve)

Only use the word 'and' in dates with the word 'thousand'. So say the date 2011 like this: 'two thousand *and* eleven'. But to say 1985, you say 'nineteen eighty-five', not 'nineteen and eighty-five'.

Shop floors

Large shops with several floors that sell many different goods are called 'department stores'. London, especially, has some very famous department stores such as Harrods and Fortnum & Mason.

In buildings in the UK, the floor at street level is the 'ground floor', and the floor above it is the first floor. Then you get the second, third, fourth floors and so on. Remember that when you get into the lift to go back downstairs, street level is at G (for ground floor) on the lift panel, not 1!

Straight Talking

 Goran rings Dan about an order for a clothes delivery to a shop that is late.

Goran:	Hi, Dan, I'm just calling to check what's happened to that order for three hundred jackets for the fourteenth of June. Today's the sixteenth and it's still not here.
Dan:	Yes, you're right, sorry. I meant to call you and tell you there's been a problem at the factory. They say they can get the order to you by the twentieth.
Goran:	The twentieth is a little late, but if you can give me Steve's phone number, I'll ring him and tell him about this. Have you got his number handy?
Dan:	Just a sec. Yes, here you go, it's oh two oh seven five eight three two double nine three.
Goran:	Sorry, was that double nine or double three?
Dan:	Double nine, then three.
Goran:	Okay. I suppose that if he's only paying a fiver for each jacket, he can hardly complain . . .
Dan:	Exactly. A few days won't make that much difference. Thanks, Goran.
Goran:	No problem. Cheers.

 *Fun & Games*

1. In what type of shop would you say the following? Match the sentence to the shop.

butcher's / market, market, shoe shop, clothes shop / boutique, supermarket, department store, pub, newsagent's, baker's / bakery, off-licence

1. I'd like a dozen brown bread rolls, please.

2. I'm looking for the latest copy of *Home Owner's* magazine.

3. Where are the changing rooms?

4. These trainers don't fit – can I try on a bigger size?

5. Which aisle is the frozen food in?

6. I'll take that box of strawberries and two bunches of grapes.

7. I'd like a pound of cooking steak, please.

8. Two pints of lager, please.

9. Which floor for soft furnishings, please?

10. Is this white wine on offer a chardonnay? Okay, I'll have two bottles.

Key:

1. baker's / bakery

2. newsagent's

3. clothes shop / boutique

4. shoe shop

5. supermarket

6. market

7. butcher's / market

8. pub

9. department store

10. off-licence

2. Paula is in a clothes shop. Put the dialogue between Paula and the shop assistant below in the correct order. The first line is in bold.

Shop assistant:	Can I help you?
Shop assistant:	Over on that side of the shop.
Shop assistant:	Okay, I think a European size forty-two is a twelve or fourteen here. Why don't you try on both a twelve and a fourteen?
Paula:	Good idea. Where are the changing rooms?
Paula:	Yes, I'd like to try on these jeans, but I'm not sure what my UK size is. In Portugal I'm a size forty-two.

Key:

Shop assistant:	Can I help you?
Paula:	Yes, I'd like to try on these jeans, but I'm not sure what my UK size is. In Portugal I'm a size forty-two.
Shop assistant:	Okay, I think a European size forty-two is a twelve or fourteen here. Why don't you try on both a twelve and a fourteen?
Paula:	Good idea. Where are the changing rooms?
Shop assistant:	Over on that side of the shop.

3. Paula tries on the jeans and goes back to the shop assistant. Put the rest of their conversation into the correct order. The first line is in bold.

Paula:	The size twelve jeans fit fine. I'll take them.
Paula:	Okay, that's great. Where can I pay?
Paula:	No, I'll just take the jeans, thanks. These are on sale, right?
Shop assistant:	You can pay at the cash till over there, in cash or by credit card.
Shop assistant:	Yes, there's a ten per cent discount on these.
Shop assistant:	Okay, can I help you with anything else?

Key:

Paula:	The size twelve jeans fit fine. I'll take them.
Shop assistant:	Okay, can I help you with anything else?
Paula:	No, I'll just take the jeans, thanks. These are on sale, right?
Shop assistant:	Yes, there's a ten per cent discount on these.
Paula:	Okay, that's great. Where can I pay?
Shop assistant:	You can pay at the cash till over there, in cash or by credit card.

Chapter 5

Eating In and Out

In This Chapter

▶ Understanding British meal times

▶ Staying at home to eat

▶ Eating out at pubs and restaurants

*W*hen you think of food in Britain, do you imagine dull, tasteless and unimaginative things to eat? Nothing could be farther from the truth. Britain today is a multi-cultural society with a long tradition of immigration from all corners of the globe. Because of this, in many towns and cities you find excellent food from all over the world – Italian food, Indian food, Chinese, Mexican, Polish . . . in the large capital cities you find food from almost any country you can name! And apart from the excellent range of international foods, you can eat good-value traditional British cooking in many pubs and small local restaurants. There's a lot more to food in Britain than fish and chips!

Taking a Look at British Meals

The three main meals in a day are breakfast, lunch and dinner (or supper). Lunch is at about 12 or 1 p.m. and dinner is early, between 5 p.m. for children to about 8 or 9 p.m. for adults. Don't arrive at a restaurant for lunch at 2 p.m. or for dinner at 10 p.m. – you probably won't get any food!

Confusingly, lunch is sometimes called dinner. Children, for example, have their school dinner at school, at lunch time. And people in the north of England, Scotland and Ireland sometimes call dinner *tea*. Thankfully, breakfast is always called breakfast!

Breakfast

You probably know about the typical 'English breakfast' of eggs, bacon, sausage, toast, tea . . . Many hotels offer this huge breakfast as part of your stay. You also find small local cafes offering full English breakfasts. But most people in Britain don't eat this every morning. For a start Britain has people from many cultures and countries, so there are as many different kinds of breakfast as there are cultures. Second, Britain's increasing contact with Europe means that a European or 'continental' breakfast is often on the menu too. Many adults and children just have a bowl of cereal before they go to work or school.

Words to Know

English breakfast	Continental breakfast
scrambled eggs	toast
beans	butter
fried eggs	jam
bacon	croissant
sausages	orange juice
cooked tomatoes	coffee and tea
toast	

Lunch

Most working people in Britain have a very short lunch break – usually not more than an hour. This means that lunch time meals during the week are usually small. A lot of people have a sandwich or a light pub lunch (see 'Where to eat' for more on pub lunches). In good weather you see parks and benches full of office workers having a sandwich or a snack at lunch time.

The one day in the week that people often have a large lunch is on a Sunday – the *Sunday lunch* – but otherwise dinner is the main meal of the day. A typical Sunday lunch is a *roast* – meat or poultry cooked in the oven and usually eaten with potatoes and vegetables. You pour *gravy*, or meat juice, over the meat. Not everyone eats this kind of Sunday lunch of course, but you can often find it in pubs on a Sunday, if you'd like to try it.

Dinner

People in the UK eat dinner relatively early (between about 6 pm and 8.30 pm) because it's the largest meal of the day, so you need time to digest it. People are more likely to eat out in a restaurant at dinner time, when they have more time to relax and enjoy the meal, without rushing to get back to work.

Before your start your meal, you can wish your companion a good meal by saying 'Bon appétit'. Yes, this is French, not English – the English language has no specific words for wishing you a pleasant meal. You can, however, drink to people's health in English by raising your glass, touching their glass with yours (not too hard) and saying 'Cheers!'.

Words to Know

Bon appétit!	Cheers!	a roast
dinner	lunch	supper

Eating In

You don't need to go to an expensive restaurant to eat well in the UK. People often prefer to eat in (at home). If you don't want to cook yourself, you can always order takeaway food, which can be inexpensive and very tasty!

Ordering takeaway food

Apart from international hamburger takeaway places, which are almost the same all over the world, you have other options for cheap and fast takeaway food in Britain. The UK's large Middle Eastern population means that lamb *kebabs* (meat on a stick) are easy to find, and so are fish and chip shops. You usually eat chips from a fish and chips shop with salt and vinegar, but most places let you add your own vinegar, so if you don't like it that's no problem. Fish and chips shops are more common in holiday areas of Britain such as the south coast of England, and local people sometimes call them the *chippie* rather than the *chip shop*.

Straight Talking

 Jorge is at a chip shop.

Jorge:	Can I have one plaice and chips, and some pickled onions, please.
Chip shop owner:	Eat here or take away?
Jorge:	Take away, please.
Chip shop owner:	Do you want vinegar on your chips?
Jorge:	No, thanks. Just salt.
Chip shop owner:	Anything else for you?
Jorge:	I'll also have a can of that apple juice, please.
Chip shop owner:	Here you go then. That'll be six pounds thirty-five.

You can eat takeaway food that's easy to carry, like fish and chips, a hamburger or a kebab, in the street. But you can also get full meals as a takeaway, especially pizzas and food from Indian or Chinese restaurants. Many pizza places and takeaway restaurants bring the food to your house, and you pay when the meal arrives. You can even order online from some restaurants these days.

Eating at a friend's house

If someone invites you for a meal at their house, it's normal to talk a little about the food at some point in the meal. Compliment the food, even if you don't like it. Here are some phrases you can use:

- This is delicious!
- How did you make it?
- Can I have the recipe [re-si-pee]?
- Thank you so much for a wonderful meal!

Straight Talking

Natalya is having dinner at a friend's house. Her hostess is Jane.

Natalya: This meat is delicious, Jane!

Jane: It's an old recipe of my mother's. The secret is to add soy sauce to the gravy.

Natalya: Well, it's fantastic.

Jane: I'm so glad you like it. It's really easy to make, you know.

Natalya: Really? Well, you must give me the recipe then!

If a friend invites you for dinner at his house, it's common to take a small gift such as flowers, chocolates or a bottle of wine. If you smoke, you must ask permission, and you usually go outside the house to smoke. It's bad manners to leave immediately after eating. People normally stay sitting at the table after the dessert to chat for a while.

During dinner you can talk about most things: travel, friends, family and even politics if you're all more or less in agreement on the topic – but avoid controversial politics. The one topic you *don't* talk about is how much money people earn in their jobs. See Chapter 3 for more on how to make small talk.

Words to Know

eat in	takeaway	plaice	cod
chips	picked onion	kebab	recipe

Going Out to Eat

One of the best things about visiting a foreign country is trying the food, and the UK is no exception! From traditional British dishes with strange names such as Welsh rarebit or haggis to well-known international foods such as pizza or curry, you can find them all in Britain.

Choosing where to eat

Like anywhere, where you decide to eat depends on your *budget* – that is, how much money you want to spend. The cheapest eating places are fast food restaurants such as McDonalds and Burger King, which you find all over the world, with very small local variations in the menu. This means that you understand the menu easily, and you usually find pictures illustrate what you're ordering. But you probably want to try local food too – and one of the best places to find local food cheaply in Britain is in a pub.

Pubs

Pubs are a good place to try fresh local food at reasonable prices. Some pubs have a more formal 'restaurant' section, with tables already set out with cutlery (knives and forks), but most pubs have an informal eating area, often in the main part of the pub where people drink. Here you usually order your pub meal directly from the bartender, at the bar, and you pay when you order, not after the meal. Some pubs have a printed menu and some have a board near the bar listing the food on offer that day.

Figure 5-1 shows a typical pub menu.

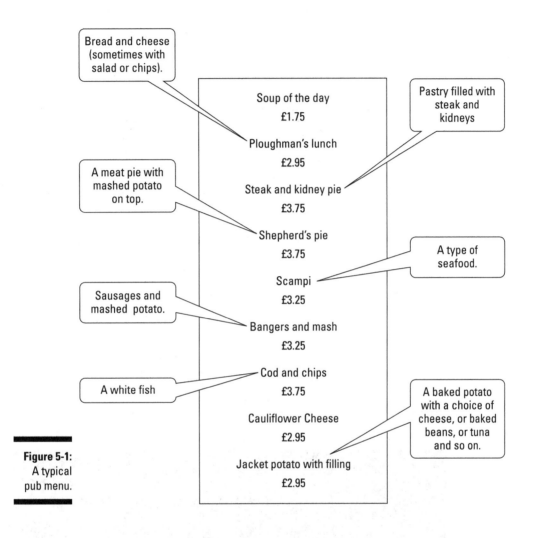

Bread and cheese (sometimes with salad or chips).

Pastry filled with steak and kidneys

A meat pie with mashed potato on top.

A type of seafood.

Sausages and mashed potato.

A white fish

A baked potato with a choice of cheese, or baked beans, or tuna and so on.

Soup of the day
£1.75

Ploughman's lunch
£2.95

Steak and kidney pie
£3.75

Shepherd's pie
£3.75

Scampi
£3.25

Bangers and mash
£3.25

Cod and chips
£3.75

Cauliflower Cheese
£2.95

Jacket potato with filling
£2.95

Figure 5-1:
A typical
pub menu.

Straight Talking

Pierre and Goran are having lunch in a pub.

Goran: Hello, I'd like to order lunch and a drink, please.

Bartender: Okay, what can I get you?

Goran: What's scampi?

Bartender: It's a type of seafood. It's covered in breadcrumbs, deep-fried and served with a slice of lemon. You can have it with salad or with chips.

Goran:	No, I think I'll have cod with chips then. What about you, Pierre?
Pierre:	Do you have anything for vegetarians?
Bartender:	Yes, we have cauliflower cheese or jacket potatoes with baked beans, or cheese. The ploughman's lunch is also vegetarian – bread, cheese and chutney.
Goran:	Chutney?
Bartender:	It's a kind of thick pickle sauce, sort of like tomato relish . . . Well, you'll have to try it.
Pierre:	Okay, I'll have the ploughman's lunch then.
Bartender:	Right, and what would you like to drink?
Pierre:	Orange juice for me, please.
Goran:	A pint of Guinness for me.
Bartender:	Okay, just take this number and we'll bring the food over to your table when it's ready. You'll find cutlery and napkins on the side table over there. The condiments are there as well.

Words to Know

cutlery	knife	fork
napkin	condiments	salt
pepper	mustard	relish
tomato sauce / ketchup	mayonnaise	pickle

These days you often find international food on pub menus. You may also find some traditional British foods with very strange names, such as *toad in the hole* (sausages in batter), *bubble and squeak* (mashed potatoes fried with cabbage), *black pudding* (sausage made with animal blood) and *bangers and mash* (sausages and mashed potatoes).

Regional food

Like all counties, Britain has regional variations in its food. Scotland, for example, is famous for *game* (wild animals such as deer [venison]) and *salmon* (a pink river fish). You may also have heard of *haggis* – sheep's innards cooked with spices and served with *neeps* (turnips). From Ireland, we have *Irish stew* (meat, potatoes and vegetables in gravy) and the famous *Irish coffee* (coffee with whisky). Wales has given us *Welsh rarebit*, which is a special cheese sauce on toast, served hot. Be careful of Welsh rarebit, because the word *rarebit* sounds a bit like *rabbit* so it might confuse you! The north of England is famous for its *chip butties* – sandwiches of fried potato chips – not recommended if you're on a diet!

Although the regional tourist boards may imply that everyone in a certain region eats only regional food, the most popular dish in Britain remains the curry, which is an integral part of British life.

In the UK, *dessert* is also sometimes called *pudding*, so you can say 'What's for pudding?' meaning 'What's for dessert?'. You could also say 'What's for afters?' although this is less common.

Restaurants

Britain has an excellent range of international food, and you can try the best of it in restaurants. Italian, Indian, Indonesian; Turkish, Thai, Tunisian; Mexican, Malaysian, Moroccan . . . the major capital cities of Britain have most of these international foods on offer. Especially popular are Italian and Indian restaurants.

Restaurants vary a lot in terms of price. Some are expensive, and some are inexpensive. Here are some useful phrases to use when asking about restaurants and pricing:

✔ Do you know of a good [Thai] restaurant around here?

✔ How expensive is it?

✔ That's a bit out of my price range / That's a bit beyond my budget.

✔ That's a bit pricey for me.

✔ Is there anywhere else more economical / cheaper nearby?

The best way to find a good restaurant is to ask a friend or colleague to recommend one. You can also look at a tourist guide book, or a local newspaper or magazine, for restaurant reviews and recommendations.

British desserts

Some traditional British desserts have very strange names. You might see 'spotted dick', 'trifle', and 'apple crumble and custard' on the menu. *Spotted dick* is a steamed pudding made with dried fruits and often served with hot *custard*, a thick sweet yellow-coloured creamy sauce. *Trifle* is a dessert with layers of cake, jam or fruit, custard and cream; people often eat trifle at Christmas time too (see below). *Apple crumble* is a dish of baked apples with a top of crumbled baked biscuits, also often eaten with custard or cream.

People eat special desserts and sweets at Christmas time: *Christmas cake* (a fruit cake with marzipan and white icing), *Christmas pudding* (hot pudding often soaked in alcohol and eaten with brandy butter) and *mince pies*, which aren't made of meat but of a sweet filling of raisin and sultanas.

Britain as a multi-cultural society also offers desserts from other cuisines, of course. Some of the best known are Indian sweets such as *barfi* (a sugary, fudge-like confectionery), *gulab jamun* (a small dough ball deep-fried and soaked in syrup) or the Middle Eastern *halwa* (a solid sugary sweet made with nuts). From the Middle East people also eat *baclava* (small light pastries with a filling of nuts) and from Italy *tiramisu* (layers of cake, white cheese, cream and coffee), which can be found on many restaurant menus.

Straight Talking

Goran asks his friend Mike about eating out in the area.

Goran: Mike, can you give me a minute? I need some advice.

Mike: Sure, what is it?

Goran: I have some friends from Croatia coming to visit me next week, and I want to take them to a Thai restaurant. I don't think they've tried Thai food before. Do you know of a good Thai place around here?

Mike: Right, let me think . . . Well, there's a really good Thai restaurant on Lever Street, but it's not cheap.

Goran: How expensive is it?

Mike: About forty pounds a head if you have wine . . .

Goran: Forty pounds! That's a bit beyond my budget! Is there anywhere else cheaper you know of?

Mike:	I can't think of one. But take a look in *Time Out* magazine. They usually have restaurant recommendations, and they tell you the price range.
Goran:	Okay, good idea. I'll see what I can find in that.
Mike:	Good luck, mate. You can always take them to the local chippie [fish and chips shop]!

Booking a table

If you want to go to a popular restaurant, try to make a booking a day or two in advance. For some restaurants you can book (make a reservation) online, but you still need to telephone most restaurants in Britain.

Useful phrases include:

✔ I'd like to make a booking.

✔ I'd like to make reservation.

✔ I'd like to book a table for [Friday night].

✔ A table for two, please.

International food

Here are some of the international main course dishes you might see in restaurants or pubs:

✔ Lasagne: An Italian pasta dish

✔ Moussaka: A Greek dish made with aubergines (eggplants)

✔ Chicken / lamb tikka: An Indian curry

✔ Tandoori chicken / lamb: A dry Indian curry

✔ Chilli con carne: A Mexican dish made with spicy meat with beans

✔ Nachos: Mexican corn chips covered with cheese and/or meat

✔ Moules frites: A French dish of mussels with chips

✔ Chicken teriyaki: Chicken served with a Japanese soy sauce

Straight Talking

 Maria wants to book a table at The Lamb's Tail restaurant. She telephones to make the booking the day before.

Waiter:	Good afternoon, The Lamb's Tail, can I help you?
Maria:	Yes, please, I'd like to book a table for tomorrow evening, please.
Waiter:	Right, we're very busy on Saturday nights, let me check. A table for how many people, please?
Maria:	Just two people.
Waiter:	Oh yes, that's fine. For what time?
Maria:	Eight-thirty.
Waiter:	Certainly. And could you give me your name, please?
Maria:	Yes, it's Maria Gonzalez.
Waiter:	Sorry, how do you spell your surname?
Maria:	G-O-N-Z-A-L-E-Z.
Waiter:	Right, you have a table for two booked for tomorrow evening, at eight-thirty, in the name of Maria Gonzalez.
Maria:	Thank you.
Waiter:	You're welcome.

 If you make a reservation by phone, you may need to spell out your name or surname. Check you know how to pronounce the letters of the alphabet in English.

Arriving at a restaurant

When you arrive at a more expensive restaurant, and especially if you have a reservation, you wait until a waiter shows you to your table.

Straight Talking

 Maria arrives at a restaurant with her friend, Gina.

Maria: Good evening. We have a reservation for two, for eight-thirty.

Waiter: In what name, please?

Maria: Maria Gonzalez.

Waiter: Ah yes. Can I take your coats?

Gina: Yes, please.

Maria: That's okay, I prefer to keep my jacket on.

Waiter: Thank you. Right this way, please.

[Maria and Gina follow the waiter to their table.]

Ordering food and drink

When you order food in a pub or restaurant, it's common to order only one dish – the main course. In more expensive restaurants you can order a starter or appetiser, and then your main course. If you like sweet things, you can order a dessert; you usually place your order for dessert after you've finished your main course.

If a restaurant has an alcohol licence, you can order wine, beer or *spirits* (strong alcoholic drinks like whisky, vodka or rum). Many restaurants offer a *house* wine (the cheapest wine). On the menu you'll see *soft drinks* (drinks with no alcohol) and also wines, beers and spirits. You can also order bottled mineral water which is *still* (no gas) or *sparkling* (with gas). Some restaurants offer *cocktails* (fruit juices with alcohol).

Here are some useful phrases for ordering a meal:

- ✔ I'd like / We'd like [a bottle of wine].
- ✔ Can I have [the soup of the day], please?
- ✔ We'll have [some sparkling mineral water], please.
- ✔ I'd like my steak rare / medium / well done.

Note: If you order a steak, the waiter usually asks you whether you want it *rare* (bloody, so not very cooked), *medium* or *well done* (very well cooked).

✔ What exactly is in [the chef's salad]?

✔ Does it come with [chips / salad]?

✔ Could I have the bill, please?

Straight Talking

 Gina and Maria are ordering dinner in a restaurant.

Waiter: Good evening. Are you ready to order?

Gina: Yes, please. As a starter, I'd like the deep fried scampi, please.

Maria: And I'll have a tuna salad.

Waiter: Certainly. And what would you like for your main course?

Gina: Can I have the lamb chops with mint sauce, please?

Waiter: I'm sorry, madam, we've just run out of the lamb chops. Would you like to order something else? [*To run out of* means *to finish*.]

Gina: Ummm . . . I'm not sure. What do you recommend?

Waiter: Today's chef's specials are on the board over there. I recommend the braised lamb in red wine if you like lamb.

Gina: Okay, that sounds lovely. Does it come with salad or vegetables?

Waiter: With vegetables or salad – which would you like?

Gina: With salad, please. What are you having, Maria?

Maria: The same for me, please, but with vegetables. Oh, and we'd also like a bottle of wine, please.

Waiter: Red or white?

Maria:	The house red, please. And a bottle of sparkling mineral water.
Waiter:	Certainly, madam, anything else?
Maria:	No, that's all for the moment, thank you.

Words to Know

starter	main course	a bottle of house red / white
still mineral water	sparkling mineral water	salad
vegetables	braised / roasted [lamb]	chef's specials
today's specials		

Complaining about the food

If you're unlucky and get a meal with food that is especially bad or *off* (rotten), you can complain to the waiter or the restaurant manager. In general, people in Britain prefer not to complain, but if you have a good reason to complain, then you can certainly do so. You need to use a respectful tone of voice, say 'please' a lot and refrain from shouting. Explaining clearly and reasonably why the meal was not okay is the best way to complain. If your complaint is reasonable, the manager may decide not to charge you for the food that was not good enough, or to bring you another plate of the same food, but this depends on the restaurant.

Some useful words and phrases for complaining about a meal are:

✔ Excuse me, waiter, but my meat is underdone [not cooked enough] / overdone [cooked too much] / burnt.

✔ There's something wrong with this [wine / meat / dessert].

✔ This food is cold / off [rotten; used especially for meat or fish].

✔ This food is too salty / greasy / sweet / cold.

✔ This bread is stale [old; bread or cake].

✔ This beer / sparkling water is flat [with no gas; used for drinks with gas only].

✔ Please could you heat this up for me?

✔ Please take this back to the kitchen.

✔ Please call the manager.

Straight Talking

Maria and Gina aren't happy with their main course in a restaurant.

Maria:	Excuse me, waiter.
Waiter:	Yes, madam?
Maria:	I'm sorry, but this lamb is underdone.
Waiter:	Are you sure? Nobody else has complained about the lamb tonight. It looks all right to me.
Maria:	But look – the inside is almost raw. Could you call the manager, please?
Waiter:	All right, one moment.

[The manager comes over.]

Manager:	Can I help you?
Gina:	Yes, we're not happy with the braised lamb. It's completely underdone – look!
Manager:	Well, some people like their lamb rare, but if you're not happy with this, of course we can put it back in the oven for you, or we can offer you a different main course – but that will take at least twenty minutes to prepare.
Gina:	Well, I'd prefer a different main course now; this looks horrible. I'll have the T-bone steak instead – well done not rare!
Maria:	Please put mine back in the oven to cook for another ten minutes, and I'm sure it will be fine.
Manager:	Of course, madam, and I'm sorry about this. I'll have a word with the chef.

'Waiter, there's a fly in my soup . . .'

This is the start to one of the best-known jokes in English. Hundreds of versions of this joke exist that begin with this line. Here are a few:

Waiter, there's a fly in my soup!
> Don't worry, sir. That spider on your bread will soon get him.

Waiter, there's a fly in my soup!
> Don't worry, sir. They don't eat much.

Waiter, there's a fly in my soup!
> There can't be, sir. The cook used them all in the raisin bread.

This joke is a common cultural reference in many English-speaking countries.

Ordering dessert and coffee

When you've finished the main course it's time to order dessert or coffee. The dessert menu often includes a selection of ice creams or sorbets, cakes and other sweet things. Some restaurants might have cheese and biscuits (crackers) on the dessert menu, a custom adopted from France. Many people move from the main course straight to coffee or tea. Espresso coffee is fairly common in restaurants in the UK.

Straight Talking

 Maria and Gina have finished their main course and are ready for dessert.

Waiter:	Would you like some dessert?
Gina:	Yes, can I see the dessert menu, please?
Waiter:	Here you are. We also have some dessert specials today, which are up on that board on the wall. I especially recommend the apple crumble and the tiramisu.
Maria:	I think I'll just have coffee; I'm full. An espresso, please.
Waiter:	Certainly, madam – and for you?
Gina:	I think I'll try the apple crumble – as long as it's cooked enough!

| Waiter: | Would you like that with cream, ice cream or custard? |
| Gina: | Cream, please. And I'll also have an espresso coffee, but with a little bit of milk, please. |

Words to Know

dessert	cream	custard
ice cream	sorbet	espresso
cake	pastry	crumble

Be careful of the difference in pronunciation between *dessert* (the sweet that you order at the end of your meal) and *desert* (a hot place full of sand, like the Sahara). You pronounce dessert 'de-ZERT', with the emphasis on the last syllable. You pronounce places like the Sahara 'DEZ-ert', with the emphasis on the first syllable. Say the two words aloud and you'll hear the difference.

Asking for the bill and tipping

Some restaurants bring your bill along with the coffee, but in some restaurants you need to ask for the bill. *Tipping* (giving the waiter some money for his work) is lower in Britain than in many other English-speaking countries. In some cases the restaurant adds a service charge of 10 to 20 per cent to the bill – the *service charge* is for the workers in the restaurant. If is the bill includes a service charge on your bill, you don't need to tip, but if there's no service charge then it's a good idea to leave about 10 per cent of the bill yourself, as a tip.

You also see a 15 per cent charge on your bill for *VAT* (value added tax), a UK government tax that is on all bills.

Your restaurant bill may look something like that in Figure 5-2.

14/02/10	22.19

THE LAMB'S TAIL

Waiter 09

Tuna salad	£4.50
Scampi	£6.75
Braised lamb	£18.00
Braised lamb	£18.00
House red	£12.50
Sparkling mineral water	£3.00
Subtotal	£62.75
10% Service charge	£6.28
VAT (12.5%)	£7.84
Total	£76.87

Figure 5-2:
A typical
restaurant
bill in
the UK.

Straight Talking

 Maria and Gina have finished their meal at a restaurant, and ask for the bill.

Maria: Excuse me, could I have the bill, please?

Waiter: Yes, of course, madam. Just a moment. Here you are.

[The waiter goes away.]

Gina: Let me get this.

Maria: No, no, this is my treat. I promised I'd take you out for your birthday, so I'm paying!

Gina: Well, all right. That's really nice of you, Maria.

Maria:	Not at all. Okay, let's see. Hmmm . . . there's a twelve per cent service charge on the bill, so we don't need to leave a tip. I'll pay by credit card.
[The waiter comes back.]	
Maria:	[Gives the waiter her credit card.] Here you go.
Waiter:	Thank you, madam. I hope you enjoyed the meal.

When someone gives you something, they often use these expressions as they hand it to you:

✔ Here you go.

✔ Here you are.

If you want to offer to pay for the meal, the following expressions are useful:

✔ It's on me.

✔ Let me get this.

✔ It's my treat.

✔ It's my turn to treat you.

When you offer to pay for a round of drinks only, not food, you can use these expressions:

✔ It's my round.

✔ Whose round is it?

To thank someone who has paid for your meal or drinks, you can say:

✔ Thanks so much.

✔ That's really kind / nice of you.

✔ I'll get the next one.

In the UK you often hear people say 'ta' instead of 'thank you'. 'Ta' is the short form of 'thank you' and is very informal. The word is used mainly in the UK: you won't hear it in the United States. All English-speaking countries use the informal 'thanks', which is also less formal than 'thank you'.

Fun & Games

- -

1. Look at the pub menu in Figure 5-3. Put the words into the correct place on the menu:

Cod, carne, lunch, whole wheat, mash, soup, salad, cauliflower, bread, beans

The King's Head Pub
Lunch Menu

Light meals

_____ of the day (see board)	£3.25
BLT club sandwich	£4.75
Cheese and chutney sandwich	£2.95
Ploughman's _____	£5.25
[on your choice of white or _____ bread]	
Jacket potatoes with filling [all served with a side _____]	£3.75
Your choice of: tuna mayonnaise / cheese / baked _____ / brie and onion	
BBQ spare ribs	£4.75

Extras:

Garlic_____	£1.75
Chips	£2.00
Baked beans	£1.75

Main meals

Scampi with chips and peas	£7.95
_____ with chips and peas	£7.95
Lasagne with garlic bread	£1.75
Chilli con _____	£6.95
Bangers and _____	£6.95

Vegetarian:

Mushroom risotto	£6.95
Veggie pasta bake	£6.95
_____ cheese	£6.95

15% VAT not included

Figure 5-3:
Put the
words in
the correct
place on the
menu.

Key:

soup, lunch, whole wheat, salad, beans, bread, cod, carne, mash, cauliflower

2. Natasha and Vassily order lunch at The King's Head pub. Put the verbs into the correct place. You use some of the verbs more than once.

want, like, have, get

Natasha: We'd _____ to order lunch, please.

Bartender: Okay, what can I _____ you?

Natasha: What's in the BLT club sandwich?

Bartender: BLT is bacon, lettuce and tomato.

Natasha: Oh, okay. I'll _____ that please.

Bartender: Do you _____ it on white or whole wheat bread?

Natasha: On white bread, please.

Vassily: I'll _____ a jacket potato with tuna mayonnaise.

Bartender: Sure. Would you _____ anything to drink?

Natasha: We'll _____ two half pints of lager, please.

Key:

like, get, have, want, have, like, have

3. Imagine you are invited to eat at a friend's house in the UK. Are these statements true (correct) or false (incorrect)? Write **T** for true and **F** for false.

1. It's important to arrive on time.

2. Your host expects you to bring dessert.

3. It's nice to take your host a small gift, such as chocolates or flowers.

4. You can take a bottle of wine for your host.

5. You can shake hands with people you meet for the first time.

6. It's normal to smoke at the table.

7. You don't need to ask permission to smoke.

8. Don't ask people how much money they earn.

9. You can talk about things like your friends and family.

10. You should leave immediately after you finish your meal.

Key:

1T, 2F, 3T, 4T, 5T, 6F, 7F, 8T, 9T, 10F

Chapter 6

Out on the Town

. . . .

. . . .

*A*sking out that special someone can be quite difficult in your own language, and you may find it a challenge in English, but we help you out in this chapter. We look at finding the right words to ask someone out, making arrangements for the first date and choosing a place to go. We also suggest some simple conversation topics to make the first few minutes a little easier. And we look at other social occasions too – going to the pub and visiting friends at home, for example.

Asking Someone Out

Most people meet potential partners at work, because work is where you spend most of your time. Perhaps you have your eye on someone in the same department as you, someone you spend time with at work? In the UK it's quite common to go for a drink after work, and this can be the ideal opportunity to get to know someone better. If you don't drink alcohol or simply don't like pubs then you can always invite somebody for a coffee or some lunch.

When asking someone out it's always a good idea to be prepared. When are you going to invite him or her? Where will you take her? What sort of things does she like? If you can choose the perfect place and time then you have a better chance of the person accepting your offer. And, of course, it's always good to be prepared for a negative answer. Your potential date may just be busy, but you need to be able to understand what she's saying if she doesn't want to go.

You may want to take your time to get to know a person before you invite her out. If a group of people go for a drink after work some days, ask if you can join them and become part of the group before making your move.

Here are some useful phrases for asking someone out:

✔ [Do you] fancy a drink after work?

✔ Are you busy later?

✔ I was wondering if you're doing anything tonight?

✔ How about a coffee?

✔ Do you want to get some lunch in a while?

You may hear some of the following answers to these questions:

✔ That would be lovely, thanks!

✔ No, nothing special tonight. Why?

✔ Sorry, I can't right now. How about later?

✔ Oh sorry, I'm busy tonight. Some other time, maybe?

Straight Talking

 Goran is at work.

Goran:	Hi, Carla! How's it going today?
Carla:	Oh, hi, Goran! Not bad – as busy as always, you know . . .
Goran:	Anything I can help with?
Carla:	Not really, thanks – but thanks for offering; I appreciate it!
Goran:	No problem. If you change your mind, you know where to find me.
Carla:	Thanks, Goran.
Goran:	So will you be working late again?
Carla:	Oh no, I'll have all this finished by five-thirty.
Goran:	Great! How about a drink after work then?
Carla:	Okay, that sounds good – I'll need one after all this!

Goran:	Excellent! I'll come and get you when I'm leaving.
Carla:	Good! See you later, Goran.

The pub is the perfect place to invite a potential date to because people who work together often go to the pub after work for a social drink before going home for dinner. The British have quite a reputation for drinking too much, but social drinking after work is quite normal. Claire is happy to accept Goran's invitation for a drink because it doesn't necessarily mean anything else. It's important to know that when someone accepts an offer of a drink it doesn't mean they're ready to have a relationship with you. The situation can change, of course, after a while.

Straight Talking

 Pierre and Helen are in the pub on Friday night, as usual, with their colleagues.

Pierre:	I'm so glad it's Friday at last!
Helen:	Me too, what a week!
Pierre:	I don't think I have the energy to cook. How about some dinner?
Helen:	Oh, I'd love to, but I'm going to see a film with my sister.
Pierre:	No problem. Some other time, maybe?
Helen:	Absolutely! How about next Friday?
Pierre:	I'll look forward to it.
Helen:	Me too! Another drink before we go?

Arranging to Meet

Whether it's with the man or woman of your dreams or just friends or colleagues, you may well have to arrange a social meeting or get-together. This can be complicated: a combination of days, places and times that are often difficult to navigate in a foreign language.

If you're like us, you may find this stressful on the phone in another language. Thankfully, in the modern world you have all kinds of other ways of organising social meetings and it's not uncommon to arrange things by email, text message (SMS) or online chat. Having said that, we suggest you don't arrange your first amorous meetings like this – it might make you seem a bit too cold and businesslike!

Here are some basic phrases and questions you can use to arrange a date and time:

- ✔ Are you doing anything [on Friday / at the weekend]?
- ✔ Are you free [on Saturday morning]?
- ✔ How about [Sunday afternoon] then?
- ✔ Friday's out for me, sorry – I've already made plans.
- ✔ Saturday morning's good for me. How about you?

After you arrange a day and a time, you need to agree on a location. Start with agreeing on the kind of thing you want to do (a drink, dinner) and then move on to the specific place.

- ✔ Do you fancy [a film / a bite to eat / a quick drink]?
- ✔ A drink and a bit of dinner sounds great!
- ✔ I thought we could go to the pub, then maybe have some dinner?
- ✔ What about skipping the drink and going straight for something to eat?
- ✔ How about trying that new [Italian / Chinese / Indian] near the station?
- ✔ Pizza sounds good to me!
- ✔ The new Bond film has opened at the Odeon – how about that?
- ✔ How about a film we'll *both* enjoy?
- ✔ Coldplay are playing at the Arena if you fancy that?
- ✔ If you can get tickets that sounds fantastic!

Then you just need to make the final arrangements:

- ✔ Great, I'll meet you there at seven, okay?
- ✔ Okay, I'll make a reservation at the Italian for eight o'clock then.
- ✔ Shall we meet outside the cinema at six-thirty?
- ✔ I'll see if I can get some tickets and let you know, okay?

Straight Talking

 Gina is on the phone to her friend Dan.

Dan:	Hello?
Gina:	Dan? Hi, it's Gina! Are we still going for dinner later?
Dan:	Sure! I'll be finished by about seven.
Gina:	Where are we going?
Dan:	Oh . . . um . . . I thought you were choosing?
Gina:	Oh . . . well . . . how about that new place in Westfield?
Dan:	The Italian?
Gina:	Yes, they say it's very good.
Dan:	Sounds good to me. Shall I book a table?
Gina:	Could you? Eight o'clock?
Dan:	Perfect! Do you know where it is?
Gina:	Not really. I don't know that area very well.
Dan:	Okay, get the number nineteen bus and get off at the sports ground.
Gina:	Right . . .
Dan:	I'll meet you there at seven forty-five, okay?

[Dan is waiting for Gina when she arrives at eight o'clock.]

Gina:	Sorry, Dan, there was loads of traffic and it took ages on the bus.
Dan:	It's fine – we're just in time, I think.

In the past UK it was considered okay for a woman to be late, but not a man – and this left lots of men standing outside pubs and restaurants in the cold and the rain waiting for their date to arrive! Of course, these days people have mobile phones and mobile email and it's much easier to tell someone if you're going to be late. It's polite to do this, so don't forget if you're running late. And don't forget to apologise when you finally arrive.

You can make arrangements by email and mobile phone – mobiles are probably the form of communication people use most commonly these days and we discuss them in Chapters 8 and 14. In the meantime, here are some common abbreviations that you may use when arranging a meeting by mobile phone:

Pub?	Do you want to meet in the pub?
CU @ 8	See you there at eight o'clock.
R U there yet?	Are you there yet?
Sorry. Going 2 B L8 :-(	Sorry, but I'm going to be late!
Where R U?	Where are you?

Deciding Where to Go

Depending on the size of the town you are in, you have several choices about where to go. The larger the town, the more options you have. The cinema, the theatre, the pub, a restaurant, a concert . . . you can find something to do any night of the week in medium sized and large towns. And even the smallest villages usually have a pub, even if they have no cinema.

The cinema

The cinema is a popular place to go on social occasions, if you can all agree on a film to see. People often go in groups to see new films when they first come out, and you can also take a partner on a date to the cinema. Popular places to take a first date also include the pub, a restaurant or a concert (which we talk about in the following sections). Cinemas in big cities in Britain are open most of the day, so you can usually find a time to suit you. You can find out what films are on by phoning the cinema or by looking in the local newspapers or online.

If you're planning a date then you need to know what sort of films your partner likes before moving on to organise something – and you need to share your interests too:

✔ So what sort of films do you like?

✔ I don't suppose you like action films, do you?

✔ Do you like [horror films / comedies / foreign films / Brad Pitt / Angelina Jolie]?

✔ I like anything apart from those chick flicks [a *chick flick* is a film supposedly made for female audiences, often romantic].

✔ I prefer films with subtitles, personally.

In bigger groups you're often with people who share the same interests as you, so it will be easier to arrange:

✔ Anybody fancy catching a film later?

✔ I was thinking of seeing the new Bond film tonight – interested?

Straight Talking

 Franz is having lunch with his colleagues.

Franz: Anybody fancy the cinema later?

David: It's Friday, isn't it? There must be something new on . . .

[David opens the local newspaper to see what's on.]

David: There's the new comedy with Jim Carrey where he plays a pilot.

Karen: Oh, not Jim Carrey, please! I can't stand him!

David: Fine! How about the new thriller with Matt Damon?

Franz: Definitely not – that man can't act at all!

[David gives the paper to Franz.]

David: Well, it was your idea – you suggest something.

Franz: There's the new Tim Burton film. How about that?

Karen: I love Tim Burton! I'm up for that.

David: Sounds good to me. How about a drink before we go?

Franz: Great – let's meet in the pub at six.

People are generally very quiet in cinemas in the UK and you won't find a lot of mobile phones ringing during the film, so don't forget to turn yours off before you go in. You can't smoke or drink alcohol in the screen area of the cinema, but it's quite common to buy some popcorn and a big soft drink before you go in and enjoy them as you watch the film.

Traditionally, the back rows of the cinema are reserved for naughty adolescents and young couples wanting more 'intimate' space, so if you really want to concentrate on the film, we recommend not sitting there!

Concerts

Concerts and comedy evenings are very popular in the UK. In big cities such as London you can find lots of events, from small gatherings in rooms above pubs and clubs right up to the biggest bands playing in stadiums and rock venues.

You can usually find information about these events in local newspapers and magazines or by looking online. Tickets to see big groups and famous comedians often sell out very quickly, so you need to know when they are going to be playing and try to book tickets well in advance.

Smaller clubs often sell tickets 'on the door' until they're full – this is particularly true of comedy clubs and small bands playing in pubs and clubs.

Some people buy more tickets than they need and then go to concerts and try to sell the tickets outside for a lot of money. These *ticket touts* are often operating illegally and there's a chance that the venue won't accept your ticket, especially for the very big events. 'Caveat emptor' (buyer beware) is good to bear in mind if you buy from touts. If you really want to see a group, you could also try buying a ticket online. In bigger cities you find small shops specialising in tickets for the big shows and you can often get very good prices on tickets there.

Pubs

For some people the pub is a kind of second home where they like to spend a lot of their free time, and the place where they can always find some of their friends and a friendly smile from the *publican* or owner. As we mention in Chapter 4, Britain now has 24-hour licensing for pubs, but many pubs still close between 11 p.m. and 1 a.m. before opening the next day.

History of the pub

Pubs came to Britain along with the Romans who used to hang bunches of grapes outside wine bars to attract drinkers inside. When the Romans arrived, they found the climate too cold for vines, so they started hanging bushes outside taverns. One of the oldest pub names in Britain is 'The Bush' or 'The Bull and Bush'.

Pub names are often of historical importance, though modern pubs tend to have slightly more surreal names. Odd pub names currently in the UK include The Ship and Shovel, The Pickled Liver, The Pump and Truncheon and The Burning Plague.

Closing time is affectionately known as *chucking-out time* by regulars, although lots of regulars often get invited to a *lock-in*, where the owner closes the pub to the general public but allows close friends and regular customers to stay on for a while. When the owner wants you to go she may shout 'Time, ladies and gentlemen, please!' or ask 'Can I see your glasses now, please?'. This is not a request (as a Spanish friend of ours once thought) to examine your spectacles, but rather a polite way of telling you to drink up and return your empty glass to the bar.

Pubs are often full at around 5.30 p.m. as people leave work and go for a drink and a social chat with their friends and colleagues. This time is an ideal opportunity to get to know people better, and – perhaps – invite that special someone for dinner or a film. Another popular time is Sunday late morning where you often find people reading the Sunday newspapers over a coffee or a beer and then staying on to sample the food at lunchtime.

The pub is one of the most common social areas in the UK and you'll probably get to know one or two very well. Most people have a *local* – a pub near them where they regularly go. In your local you may make and meet friends, you may sometimes eat there and you may even play in a sports or games team organised by the pub.

Pubs vary from old, traditional places which you are more likely to find outside city centres, to modern spaces full of noise and fruit machines (be careful not to lose all your money playing these electronic games!) and, increasingly, 'gastro pubs' which specialize in food as well as drink. Gastro pubs are often much quieter and ideal places for romantic encounters. Most pubs sell snacks, from peanuts to crisps, pies and sandwiches and, sometimes, odd things such as pickled eggs.

Smoking is now prohibited in pubs in Britain, so you often find a lot of the customers outside in the cold and rain smoking and chatting. If you're a smoker, this is a good opportunity to *smirt* – a combination of smoking and flirting that can be a lot of fun if you can forget the weather!

Drinks in British pubs are in 'pints' and 'half pints' for beer, and in 'measures' for spirits such as whisky, vodka and rum. A pint is just over half a litre. A 'measure' or 'shot' of vodka is very, very small – particularly if you come from continental Europe where measures are often poured by hand by generous bar staff! You can buy wine by the glass (the bartender usually asks whether you want a small or large glass) or by the bottle. Soft drinks are often as expensive as alcoholic drinks.

You also find lots of bottled beers, *alcopops* (brightly coloured combinations of alcohol and fruit juices) and a large variety of foreign beers: Spanish and Polish ones are very popular in the UK these days. If you're feeling adventurous you can ask for *shots*, small measures of exotic drinks such as tequila.

Most drinks are easy to order, but if you find yourself working behind a bar, be prepared for people asking for 'a pint of lager top' – a pint of beer with a small drop of lemonade on the top – or any other number of strange beverages. And remember, if a customer asks you for 'sex on the beach', look at the cocktail menu before doing anything else!

Small groups of people often buy *rounds* of drinks, with each person taking a turn at buying a drink for everyone else. In bigger groups you usually buy your own or buy only for your closest friends.

The pub is a complex place and it takes time to learn the culture, but here are a few expressions to get you started. We start with your group:

- Okay, who's for another drink?
- It's my round, I think – what's everyone having?
- Do you want a top up? [usually used when offering wine from a bottle]
- Fancy another?
- I'm all right, thanks.
- Oh, go on then – but just a half!

And some useful phrases at the bar:

- Could I have a [pint of lager / glass of house white (wine) / gin and tonic] please?
- Let's see . . . two pints of [lager / bitter], a [dry white wine / red wine / cola / orange juice], please.
- And one for yourself. [British people generally don't tip in pubs, but if you're feeling generous, you can offer to buy the bartender a drink.]

    ✔ Do you have any snacks?

    ✔ I'd like to order some food as well, please.

    ✔ Yes, it's table twelve. [When ordering food in a pub, you usually tell the bar tender which table you're sitting at.]

The easiest way to sound native in a pub is to order your beer by the brand name, rather than using the generic terms 'lager', 'bitter' and so on. If you like trying new things, you could ask for a pint of 'Old Speckled Hen' or 'Theakston's Old Peculiar', but don't blame us if you don't like them.

Straight Talking

Gina is in the pub with some friends.

Gina: Okay, it's my round. Same again for everybody?

Helen: Another bottle of red?

Gina: Why not? It's the weekend!

Mike: I'll stick to the orange juice, thanks – I'm driving. But you go ahead.

Gina: Goran?

Goran: Another pint of lager, please?

Gina: What kind?

Goran: I don't really mind to be honest – it's all beer!

Gina: Right, so that's another bottle of the house red, an orange juice – do you want ice and lemon, Mike?

Mike: No, thanks.

Gina: And a pint of lager . . . crisps or anything else?

Mike: Packet of cheese and onion, please.

Gina: Anyone else?

[Gina takes their empty glasses over to the bar.]

Gina: Hi, another round, please!

Bartender:	Hmm . . . let's see – a bottle of the house red, an orange juice and . . .
Gina:	. . . a pint of lager, please.
Bartender:	Any particular type?
Gina:	Not really – whatever you have.
Bartender:	Ice and lemon in the orange juice?
Gina:	No, thanks. Oh, and could I have a packet of cheese and onion crisps, please?
Bartender:	Sorry, we only have salt and vinegar.
Gina:	That's fine, I think.
Bartender:	Here you go. That'll be twenty-one fifty, please.

Visiting Friends

Another popular social occasion is visiting friends for drinks or dinner, to watch a film on DVD or just for a *cuppa*, or a cup of tea. Many people hold small dinner parties in their houses because this is often cheaper than eating out and easier to organise if you have children – affectionately called *kids* – to look after. In the UK kids aren't too popular in a lot of restaurants, so having a dinner party at home is often easier than going out to eat. Events like this aren't usually formal – but check with your host, just in case.

If someone invites you to a special occasion at their house, find out what kind of occasion it is – is it dinner, a drink . . . ? The most likely event is a small dinner among friends, and this is quite easy to plan for. The dinner may be what Americans call a *potluck dinner*, where each guest takes part of the meal with them, and usually this is planned in advance. The safest thing to do is to ask the simple question 'Can I bring anything?' or 'Do you need anything?'.

At the very least, take some wine with you or beer if you're sure that people will want to drink it. For the host you may also consider taking a small present such as some flowers or some chocolates, although this gesture is not as common in the UK as it is in many countries in continental Europe. If the hosts have kids it's often nice to take them a small gift, particularly if you haven't seen them for a long time.

Dinners and other meals may not last as long as they do in other countries, particularly if they are in the middle of the week, but people commonly spend some time after eating chatting and relaxing, so allow time for that. Helping with the cooking and clearing away of plates – and even with the washing up – is considered polite and you'll be a popular guest if you follow some simple rules.

You need to be careful when accepting or rejecting invitations to people's houses. Note that *come* to dinner always means going to someone's house, unlike *go out* to dinner.

Invitations include:

- ✔ John and I were wondering if you would like to come to dinner on Saturday?
- ✔ We'd love to have both of you round for dinner at the weekend if you're free?
- ✔ How about coming over for lunch on Saturday?

Depending on whether you're free you can reply:

- ✔ Oh, I'm sorry, but I already have something on this Saturday. I'd love to come over at some point, though.
- ✔ Thanks, that would be lovely! Can I bring anything?

Note that the polite answer to this last question is usually 'just yourself' unless it's a potluck dinner.

Straight Talking

Mike is talking to Pierre on the phone.

Mike: Helen and I wondered if you'd like to come to dinner on Friday?

Pierre: That would be great, thanks!

Mike: And your wife, of course.

Pierre: I'll have to check with her, but I think that'll be okay.

Mike: We're having a few friends over for dinner – nothing formal, okay?

Pierre: That's great, Mike, I'll look forward to it. Do we need to bring anything?

Mike:	Just yourselves! And a bottle of wine if you like.
Pierre:	No problem – see you then!

[Pierre and Gina arrive at Mike's house on Friday.]

Pierre:	Mike! This is Gina. Gina, this is my boss, MIke.
Gina:	Hi, Mike, what a beautiful house!
Mike:	Please, come through to the dining room. This is my wife, Helen.
Helen:	Hello, Pierre . . . and you must be Gina. I'm Helen. Please, take off your coats and relax and I'll get you both a drink. Is wine okay?
Pierre:	Juice for me, please – I'm driving.
Gina:	A glass of red would be great, thanks! And these are for you!
Helen:	Flowers? How thoughtful. Thanks, Gina.
Gina:	You're welcome. Can I help in the kitchen?
Helen:	No, it's fine, thanks. Mike has it all under control.

Knowing What to Talk About

Making conversation with new friends or colleagues can be difficult at first, but if you listen to people at most social occasions you'll see that they usually talk about the same subjects: work, family, television, the weather, politics, sport and so on. The secret to taking part in this kind of thing is to know a few phrases in each area and use them when you have the opportunity. And, of course, it helps to ask questions and take an interest in the person you're talking to. See Chapter 3 for more on making small talk and telling stories, jokes and anecdotes.

Try to read an English-language newspaper every day – you can usually get free ones on public transport and at train and bus stations. These have the most popular stories in them and each story is usually short. Newspaper stories are a great way of getting some things to talk about for social occasions. If you really want to impress, try reading one of the so-called quality newspapers, or watching the news on television each day. Programmes such as the news are perfect for increasing your vocabulary too!

Fun & Games

1. Complete the sentences by putting one word in each gap.

doing	round	book	suppose	this
fancy	free / busy	trying	wondering	about

1. Do you _____ a drink after work?

2. Are you _____ anything tonight?

3. Are you _____ on Saturday morning?

4. How about _____ that new Italian in the High Street?

5. Shall I _____ a table for eight o'clock?

6. I don't _____ you like horror films, do you?

7. How _____ a drink before we see the film?

8. It's my _____. Same again for everybody?

9. I was _____ whether you'd like to come to dinner on Friday?

10. _____ is John. John let me introduce you to Sarah.

Key:

1. fancy

2. doing

3. free / busy

4. trying

5. book

6. suppose

7. about

8. round

9. wondering

10. this

(continued)

2. Carlos is inviting his colleague out for a drink. Put the dialogue in order:

Carlos: Hi, Susan, how's it going?

Susan: No plans, why?

Carlos: Fine, thanks. Listen, are you doing anything after work?

Susan: Not bad, thanks. You?

Carlos: No problem, me neither! Just a quick beer.

Carlos: I wondered if you fancied a quick drink?

Susan: Okay, great – see you then.

Susan: Sounds good, but I can't stay long.

Carlos: I'll come and meet you here at five-thirty then, okay?

Susan: Sure, why not?

Key:

Carlos: Hi, Susan, how's it going?

Susan: Not bad, thanks. You?

Carlos: Fine thanks. Listen, are you doing anything after work?

Susan: No plans, why?

Carlos: I wondered if you fancied a quick drink?

Susan: Sounds good, but I can't stay long.

Carlos: No problem, me neither! Just a quick beer.

Susan: Sure, why not?

Carlos: I'll come and meet you here at five-thirty then, okay?

Susan: Okay, great – see you then.

• •

Chapter 7

Hobbies and Free Time

*L*ife isn't all about working and then going home and spending the evening watching TV (although for some people that is their favourite hobby!). In this chapter we look at some things to do in your spare time – from hobbies to a selection of indoor and outdoor leisure activities and sport, perhaps one of the most popular topics of conversation in most countries.

So, what sort of person are you? Are you a *night owl* – someone who likes to go out to pubs and clubs at night? Or are you an *early bird* – someone who gets up early in the morning to get on with the day's work or perhaps go for a jog or a swim before going to the office? Or maybe you're a *couch potato* – someone who likes to sit on the sofa at home watching TV or listening to music. Whatever kind of person you are, we include something for everyone in this chapter, from going out to the cinema and eating out in restaurants, to staying in and having a quiet evening at home.

Talking about Your Hobbies

Hobbies exist all over the world, and the UK is no different – you find children collecting stamps and stickers and adults playing golf and *rambling* (walking in the countryside). But in the UK you also see train and plane *spotters* (people who obsessively record the movements of different kinds of transport) and birdwatchers, cyclists, painters . . . the list is endless.

People often talk about hobbies more than they actually do them. So, after you choose your hobby, you may want to share it with your friends and colleagues.

Popular hobbies

A poll carried out in 2002 found the top ten most popular hobbies in the UK to be:

- Reading
- Watching TV
- Fishing
- Gardening
- Playing team sports
- Going to the cinema
- Swimming
- Golf
- Socialising with friends / neighbours

If you want to choose a popular British hobby, try one from this list – but make sure it's one that's a little more social than reading or watching TV if you want to meet people. The best thing to do when choosing a hobby is to pick something you actually enjoy – and something you have the money to pay for.

I know what I like!

You can say what you do and don't like doing in lots of ways in English. We suggest you stay away from the extreme examples such as *love* and *hate* until you know how the person you're speaking to feels about these things.

Here are some useful phrases for likes and dislikes. The symbols after each sentence indicate likes (+) and dislikes (–). One + indicates mild liking, two ++ indicate liking something quite a lot and three +++ indicate liking something very much. In the same way, one – indicates mild dislike, two – – indicate disliking something quite a lot and three – – – indicate disliking something very much. A nought (0) indicates no strong feelings either way (*neutrality*).

- I love going to the cinema. (+++)
- I'm a big fan of [football / reading / travel]. (++)
- I quite like [watching films / eating out / cooking]. (+)
- I don't mind [knitting / watching sports]. (0)
- I don't really like [going out / taking photos]. (–)
- I'm not into [sports / the pub] at all. (– –)
- I can't stand [staying in / going to the gym]. (– – –)

In my experience . . .

When you want to talk about your experiences, you use the present perfect. This is made up of the present tense of the verb *have* and the past participle:

✔ I've never been skiing – is it difficult?

✔ I've been on holiday to Spain twice.

✔ Haven't you seen the new *Harry Potter* film yet?

✔ Have you read anything by Peter Carey?

Notice how you often shorten or contract the verb:

I have = I've

You have = You've

She has = She's

We have = We've

They have = They've

Not as often as I'd like . . .

You use adverbs of frequency to say how often you do things. You'll find a lot of these words, but here are some to get you started:

✔ Every [morning / day / weekend / Easter]

✔ Most [evenings / weekends]

✔ Some [weeks / weekdays]

✔ Once / twice / three times . . . [a day / a week / a month]

✔ Always

✔ Often / usually

✔ Sometimes

✔ Hardly ever

✔ Never

Just in time . . .

You may also need some of the following expressions around time periods:

✔ In [the morning / afternoon / evening / my free time]

✔ On [Saturday / Tuesday evenings / Mondays / holiday]

✔ At [four o'clock / the weekend]

Straight Talking

Bettina is being interviewed for a feature called 'New in Town' in the company magazine, which aims to help to introduce new people to their colleagues.

Sara: So, Bettina, welcome to the company. It's my job to introduce you to your colleagues in this magazine feature.

Bettina: Thanks, Sara – I'm really excited about starting work here and I can't wait to meet everyone.

Sara: Okay, everyone knows you're starting in the marketing division, but what about the real Bettina – what do you like doing when you're not working?

Bettina: Well, I have a few hobbies that I hope to keep doing now I've moved to the UK.

Sara: What sort of things do you like?

What about the grammar of using the verb *like*? Why is it that sometimes you hear a sentence such as 'I like *skiing*', where you use like plus the –ing form of the verb, but other times you hear a sentence such as 'I like *to ski*', where you use like plus the infinitive form of the verb? There's a very small difference between these two example sentences, although they're both correct. Here's a general rule to help you. When people speak about hobbies and interests in general, they usually use like plus –ing: 'I *like* ski*ing*, but I hate mountain climbing.' When they talk about particular occasions or regular events they usually use like plus to: 'I *like to* walk in the mornings before I start work.'

Bettina: I love skiing.

Sara: (laughing) Well, there's not much chance of that here! Where do you like to ski?

Bettina: I've never skied in Europe, but I used to go a lot in Argentina.

Sara: Okay, so, skiing. Anything else?

Bettina: I'm a big fan of the cinema, and I usually try to go most weekends when I have the time. I like to go on a Saturday morning when it's quiet. Oh, and I love cooking.

Sara: Really? What type of food do you cook?

Bettina: Lots of different types. I cook for myself every evening and I like to have friends round for lunch or dinner at the weekends.

Sara: Great! I look forward to an invitation! Anything else for our readers?

Bettina: Let me see . . . oh yes, I'm going to Japanese classes at night school.

Sara: Wow! Is it as difficult as people say it is?

Bettina: It is quite difficult. I go twice a week, on Tuesdays and Thursdays, for two hours each lesson, but I'm not progressing very quickly!

Sara: Well, good luck with the Japanese and thanks for talking to us.

Bettina: Thank you!

Enjoying Yourself Indoors

You probably know the reputation of the weather in the UK, and that's why lots of British people spend a large part of their leisure time indoors – visiting museums, art galleries, theatres or cinemas, studying at night school, going to the gym or simply staying at home and watching television.

Straight Talking

 Goran is visiting London for the first time and spending a day with a friend, Dan. It's cold and raining, so they're trying to plan what to do for the day . . .

Dan: I think we should try to visit some galleries or museums, Goran. London's full of them, and because of this rain . . .

Goran: I'm not a big fan of museums and galleries, but in this weather I really don't mind visiting a couple of them. Any suggestions?

Dan:	Well, there's the Natural History Museum, which is excellent, and the National Portrait Gallery. And perhaps the Tate Modern, which is an amazing building down by the river.
Goran:	I hate portraits – all those serious people looking down at you – but the Natural History Museum sounds good. How about going there this morning and the Tate this afternoon?
Dan:	Great! What about food?

In most big towns and cities you can eat at any time of the day – sandwiches, fish and chips and fast food. If you want to sit down and have lunch or dinner, though – perhaps in a restaurant or a pub – then you need to check the times. A lot of places serve lunch only between certain times, and restaurants may close earlier in the evening than in lots of other countries. You can find out more about food and eating out in Chapter 5.

Goran:	I'd like to try a pub for lunch – everyone tells me the food is excellent.
Dan:	Okay, let's go to the Natural History Museum this morning, then have lunch in a pub down by the river and then go to the Tate Modern.
Goran:	That sounds good. What are you up to this evening?

'What are you up to . . .?' is a good way of asking what someone is doing, as in the example: 'What are you up to this evening?' Note that if a policeman asks 'What are you up to?' it may have a very different meaning – so just make sure you're not doing anything bad when policemen are around!

Dan:	I usually go to my French class on Tuesdays, but I'm not going today so if you want to have dinner or something . . .?
Goran:	Great! How about a film first?
Dan:	Okay, let's see how tired we feel when we've done the museum and gallery.

On the box

Television is one of the most popular topics of conversation in Britain at work and between friends. Watching TV is actually the second most popular hobby in the UK after gardening. The first thing you need to know is what sort of programme you like – have a look at Table 7-1 and see what best describes your interests.

Table 7-1	Different Types of Television Programme
Soap opera	A regular drama series featuring the same group of people and their regular lives
The news	A current affairs programme with the top stories of the day, the weather and so on
Cartoons	Animated drawings, often for children
A music programme	News from the music world with the latest groups and hits
A documentary	An in-depth look at a topic or issue
A comedy	A funny programme
The weather forecast	A look at the weather for the next few days
A film	This could be a drama, a comedy, a thriller . . .
A reality show	A show usually featuring members of the public rather than famous people
A quiz show	A show where people compete to win prizes

Try using the adjectives in the 'Words to Know' box nearby to talk about TV programmes.

Soap operas

Many people say that British people call popular drama series 'soap operas' because of the first advertisements played on the radio during shows. Soap companies sponsored a lot of these early commercials and when the radio shows eventually moved over to TV they kept their name (and, often, their soap sponsors!).

Words to Know

Positive	Negative
fantastic	terrible
amazing	awful
interesting	boring
hilarious (very funny)	rubbish
brilliant	pathetic
outstanding	dull

Many of the television programmes that you can watch in the UK are the same as the types of programme you can watch all around the world. You can find an enormous selection of soap operas such as *Eastenders* and *Coronation Street*, reality shows for people who want to become famous pop stars or dancers, shows about gardening or home decoration and quiz shows like the popular *Who Wants to Be a Millionaire?*.

Straight Talking

Carla and Goran meet at the coffee machine at work in the morning . . .

Carla: Did you see *EastEnders* last night?

Goran: Yes! Wasn't it amazing? I had no idea John was Susan's dad.

Carla: Oh really, Goran! It was so obvious.

Goran: Well, I haven't watched it for very long, so I still get confused with all the characters' names. I don't know who's who yet.

Carla: Oh, I've watched it for years – I love it! What about *Pop Star*, did you see that too?

Goran: *Pop Star*?

Carla:	The reality show where they try to find the next sing-ing star.
Goran:	Oh no, I can't stand reality shows! How can you watch them?
Carla:	They're really very funny, especially the auditions.
Goran:	No, I watched *News Time* – I like to keep up with cur-rent affairs.
Carla:	Oh! Anyway, fancy a coffee then?

Read all about it

Book clubs are very popular in the UK. In a book club, people get together to discuss a book they've all read in the previous week or two. Book clubs usually happen in people's houses, perhaps with some food or drinks. The clubs are an ideal way to meet new people.

Here are some useful phrases for talking about books you liked:

    ✔ I really enjoyed it. I thought . . .

    ✔ I liked the part where . . .

    ✔ I liked the character of . . .

    ✔ I thought it was very well-written.

Try the following phrases for comparing books:

    ✔ It's not as good as . . .

    ✔ I didn't enjoy it as much as . . .

    ✔ I preferred . . .

    ✔ This was much better than . . .

If you don't like a book, try some of these phrases:

    ✔ I found it difficult to get into.

    ✔ I didn't like the character of . . .

    ✔ I didn't enjoy it as much as . . .

    ✔ I didn't enjoy it at all.

Heading Outside

The sun does shine sometimes in Britain, and then it's time to get outside and take part in some outdoor leisure pursuits. With lots of beautiful countryside, the UK is ideal for hiking and trekking and camping in the middle of nowhere. Camping is an especially popular way to spend holidays in the summer.

Other popular outdoor activities include picnics when the weather is good: you often find families picnicking in parks on the weekends in the summertime. If you go for a drive in the British countryside in the spring or summer you often see people riding bicycles. So even though Britain is famous for rain and grey weather, people in Britain do know how to take advantage of good weather to do things outside!

People often go to the beach (even though it's seldom warm enough!) or skiing in Scotland (even though it's seldom cold enough!) or for a walk by the sea, a river or a lake. You need some equipment before you do most of these activities . . .

Words to Know

camping	trekking	the beach
a tent	walking boots	a swimming costume
a sleeping bag	a waterproof coat	sunscreen
a gas stove	maps	sunglasses
a first-aid kit	a compass	flip-flops
a torch	a mask and snorkel	food and water

Getting Involved in Sports

A popular joke is that the British invented lots of the world's best-loved sports but aren't very good at playing any of them. However, the UK is still a nation of sport lovers, whether they're talking about sports, watching them or – sometimes – playing them.

Making it all up

Popular history says that football was invented in the 19th century (1863) in the UK. Britain also invented the following: cricket (1787), rugby (1871), golf (1502), hockey (1860), badminton (1887), tennis (1859) and snooker (1875). Unfortunately, as we note elsewhere, there's a big difference between inventing a sport and being good at it!

Playing sports

Finding the right location to play your sport is important. Here's a list of the names of the different places where you play sport.

- ✔ On a court: tennis, basketball, badminton, squash
- ✔ On a pitch: football, rugby, hockey
- ✔ On a course: golf, horse racing
- ✔ In a ground: cricket, polo
- ✔ In a pool: swimming, diving, water polo
- ✔ In a stadium: athletics, cycling
- ✔ On a table: pool, snooker, billiards
- ✔ In a ring: boxing, wrestling
- ✔ In a rink: ice skating

Do you play boxing? The simple answer to this question is 'no' – you don't *play* boxing, you *do* boxing. You can talk about the different kinds of sports you play in a variety of ways:

- ✔ Play: football, rugby, cricket, tennis, squash
- ✔ Do: judo, karate, boxing
- ✔ Go: swimming, sailing, jogging

A simple rule works most of the time: you use *play* with ball games or competitive games where you play against another person or team (or even a computer!). You usually use *go* for sports and activities that end in –ing. You use *do* for recreational activities, non-team sports or games and activities without balls.

Straight Talking

 Maria gets a phone call from Helen.

Helen: Hi, Maria, it's Helen.

Maria: Hi, Helen, how's it going?

Helen: Fine, thanks. Listen, I had a game of tennis organised for tomorrow but my partner has cancelled. Do you play?

Maria: I haven't played for years, but I used to.

Helen: Well, it's not a serious match – just some fun and exercise. Do you want to join me?

Maria: Sure, that sounds great! What time?

Helen: I booked the court for seven.

Maria: In the morning?

Helen: No, after work!

Maria: Perfect. Perhaps we can grab a bite to eat afterwards?

Helen: Absolutely. Have you got all the gear you need?

Maria: I think so – but if you can bring me a tennis racket that would be good.

Helen: Okay, I'll pick you up from work at six then.

Maria: Fine – see you tomorrow.

Joining a gym or health club

If you want to do regular exercise then you might think about joining a gym or a health club. Some of these can be very expensive and you have to pay a lot of money every month to be a member. Other clubs are cheaper and you can often pay a small amount of money each month and then pay an additional amount for what you use.

You can take part in plenty of activities at gyms and health clubs, such as those in the following 'Words to Know' box.

Words to Know

do yoga	do aerobics
lift weights	have a massage
play squash	go dancing
use a running / rowing machine	have a swim
have a sauna	have a spa treatment

Watching sports

Watching sports is another popular leisure activity in the UK, whether you prefer to sit at home shouting at the referee on the television or like to sit in the sun in the summer watching a slow game of cricket. Tickets for popular football games can be very expensive, but you can find plenty of local opportunities to watch smaller games and matches – look in the local newspaper for more information.

Straight Talking

Jim and Georges are in the pub.

Jim: Did you see the match last night?

Georges: Yes, what a disaster!

Jim: Well, we played all right in the first half.

Georges: And the second – but that ref [referee] was rubbish!

Jim: Agreed! That was never a penalty!

Georges: Anyway, the United player was offside.

Jim:	If we don't win next week then we're finished.
Georges:	Are you going?
Jim:	To the match?
Georges:	Yes – we're playing at home next week.
Jim:	I don't know – the tickets are so expensive, and what if we don't win?
Georges:	Well, with fans like you, I'm surprised we win anything.
Jim:	Oh go on then. Will you get the tickets?

As in most countries, British football supporters are very loyal to their teams and are usually not happy when their team loses, or when someone says something bad about their team. Be careful at football matches to avoid the more lively fans and don't get involved in discussions at the match about which team is the best or who's playing better.

Odd sports

Of course, the British didn't simply invent sensible sports! If you plan to travel around the UK, why not try to see the British World Marbles Championships in Sussex, bog snorkelling in Wales, the cheese rolling race in Gloucester or the World Toe Wrestling Championship in Fenny Bentley? Find out more at www.visit.britain.co.uk.

Fun & Games

• •

1. Match the sports with the verbs

GO   PLAY   DO

Football, skiing, judo, rugby, horse racing, tennis, boxing, hockey, skating, swimming, gymnastics, squash, cycling, cricket

Key:

GO: skiing, horse racing, skating, swimming, cycling

PLAY: football, rugby, tennis, hockey, squash, cricket

DO: judo, boxing, gymnastics

2. Basia is talking to a colleague. Fill in the gaps with the following words:

lunch / nothing / like / museum / see / doing / love / meet / great

Basia: What are you _____ at the weekend?

Sam: _____ special, why?

Basia: I'm going to the Modern Art _____. Would you like to come?

Sam: That sounds _____. When are you going?

Basia: In the afternoon, after _____.

Sam: Okay, what time shall we _____?

Basia: Well, we could have lunch together and then go. Do you _____ Japanese?

Sam: I _____ it!

Basia: Okay, _____ you at the station at twelve!

Key:

Basia: What are you doing at the weekend?

Sam: Nothing special, why?

(continued)

Basia: I'm going to the Modern Art Museum. Would you like to come?

Sam: That sounds great. When are you going?

Basia: In the afternoon, after lunch.

Sam: Okay, what time shall we meet?

Basia: Well, we could have lunch together and then go. Do you like Japanese?

Sam: I love it!

Basia: Okay, see you at the station at twelve!

• •

Chapter 8

Talking on the Phone

*W*hen you're not confident in a language, talking on the phone in that language can be a challenge. On the phone you can't see the person you're speaking to, so the clues you usually get from a person's body language and facial expression aren't there to help you. Knowing a few useful phrases for talking on the phone, and predicting what the person on the other end of the telephone may say to you, can help you feel a lot more confident when talking on the telephone in English.

In this chapter, we divide phone calls into the different types of call you can make.

Making Different Sorts of Phone Call

You can make phone calls for a variety of reasons. You can make a *social phone call* to a friend, for example to have a chat or to arrange to meet for dinner or to go to the cinema (see Chapter 6 for more on going out with friends). You can make an *enquiry phone call*, where you ask for information about something such as train times, you book a service such as calling for a taxi or you buy a product such as theatre tickets. Finally, you can make a *work phone call*, related to your job, or have a *conference call* with work colleagues in the UK or in other countries.

Depending on the type of phone call you're making, the language you use may be more formal or more informal.

Understanding language in a phone call

You may have difficulty understanding the person you talk to on the phone, especially if you aren't familiar with the accent or if the person speaks very fast. You can do a couple of things to help yourself understand fast speech, and to slow the conversation down. You can prepare the phrases and questions you'll probably need to use in advance. You can ask for clarification, or ask the speaker to repeat information (see the useful phrases in the section 'Dealing with Communication Problems', later in this chapter). You can slow the conversation down by using fillers such as 'um . . .', 'well . . .', 'er . . .' and 'you know . . .' followed by a short pause. This gives you time to think and to prepare what to say next! Remember also that in spoken language words link together, so sometimes it's difficult to hear when one word ends and the next begins. You can always ask the speaker to speak more slowly.

You *make* a call when you're the person who rings someone else. You *take* a call when you receive the phone call. So if you're sitting with friends in a cafe and need to ring someone from your mobile phone, you may say 'Excuse me, I just need to make a quick phone call'. If your phone rings while you're with friends or work colleagues, you may say 'Excuse me for a moment while I take this call'. Instead of the verb 'to telephone' you usually say to *phone*, to *call* or to *ring*, as in 'I'm going to ring / phone / call Miguel'. You can use these verbs interchangeably – they mean exactly the same thing. British people generally talk about 'mobile phones' or 'mobiles', and people in other English-speaking countries such as the USA tend to call them 'cell phones' or 'cells'.

Words to Know

to phone, call or ring	to make a phone call
to take a phone call	mobile phone / cell phone
land line	answering machine
answering service	voicemail
dial tone	receiver
engaged (busy) signal	telephone directory / phone book

Social phone calls

When you call a friend, you probably use informal language. The first thing you do is check who's answering the phone, or ask for your friend by name. You can also say your own name if your friend doesn't immediately recognise your voice. You can then make some general comments, asking how your friend is, before you move on to the reason for calling. Finally, you say goodbye.

Here are some phrases you can use for each of these stages when you make an informal social phone call:

Say who's calling:

- ✔ Hello, this is Mark.
- ✔ Hi, it's Mark here.
- ✔ Hi, this is Mark calling.

Ask for your friend:

- ✔ Is that Maria?
- ✔ Is Maria there?
- ✔ Is Maria around?
- ✔ Can I speak to Maria, please?

Ask your friend how she is:

- ✔ Hi, Maria, how's it going?
- ✔ Hi, Maria, how are things?
- ✔ Hi, Maria, how are you?

Get to the point:

- ✔ Listen, I'm calling about . . .
- ✔ I'm ringing to ask . . .
- ✔ I was wondering whether . . .

Give a contact number:

- ✔ My mobile number is . . .
- ✔ I'm on . . .

Say goodbye:

▶ Okay, I've got to go.

▶ Okay, see you soon then. Bye.

▶ Take care. Bye.

▶ Catch you later. Bye.

When you receive a phone call, you answer the phone by saying 'Hello?', not 'Good day'. If the person calling you asks 'Is Maria there?' and you are Maria, you reply by saying 'Speaking' or 'Yes, speaking', not 'I am Maria' or 'Here is Maria'.

When you call someone on the phone, you may want to say who you are at the beginning of the conversation. You can say 'This is Maria' (most formal), 'It's Maria' (less formal) or 'Maria here' (most informal). But you never say 'I'm Maria'.

Straight Talking

  Carla rings Maria. The phone rings and Maria answers.

Maria: Hello?

Carla: Hello, is Maria there, please?

Maria: Speaking.

Carla: Hi, Maria, it's Carla. How's it going?

Maria: Oh, hi, Carla. Fine, thanks – and you?

Carla: Not too bad, thanks. I'm ringing to see if you'd like to come to the cinema on Saturday. There's a new Spanish movie on at the Plaza, and I thought you might like to see it with me.

Maria: Yes, I'd love to. What time on Saturday?

Carla: It starts at seven, so how about if we meet there at six-thirty?

Maria: Yes, that sounds great. Why don't you give me your mobile number in case I'm late.

Carla: Okay, sure, it's seven double-oh nine, three three six, five nine nine [7009 336 599].

Maria:	Okay, thanks – see you there! Bye.
Carla:	See you on Saturday then. Bye.

The red telephone box is one of the stereotyped images many visitors to the UK know well. The Brits originally designed these telephone boxes in the 1920s and painted them red to make them easy to see. In recent years you find fewer of these red boxes around, although you still see them in Britain and in ex-British colonies such as Malta, Bermuda and Gibraltar.

Enquiry phone calls

You may need to ring a person or place to get information. If you prepare what you're going to say, and what the person at the other end of the phone line may say to you, this can help you a lot. If you know what subject or product you're ringing about, you can usually predict the kind of questions you need to ask and what the person might say in response to your questions. Being prepared in this way helps you understand a phone conversation much more easily.

If you're in the UK for a short time, you may want to ring an organisation for information about train or bus times, to book a hotel or to buy theatre or concert tickets. If your stay is longer, you may want to enquire about renting a room or flat, to apply for a temporary job or to sign up for a language class. The language you use in an enquiry phone call is more formal than in a social call, and you may need to use several question forms, such as 'Who?', 'When?', 'What?', 'How long?' and 'How much?' If you don't understand an answer to your question the first time, ask the speaker to repeat the answer or to explain what she means. In the list of useful phrases below, when you ask for clarification you usually start with the phrase 'Sorry . . .' or 'I'm sorry. . .' and you use 'please' and 'thank you' a lot.

Phone (home) cheap

Telephone calls from the UK to countries outside the UK aren't expensive, often only a few pence a minute (depending on the country). As well as using a phone in your home or office, you can call from a telephone box (phone booth) or from an Internet cafe. Internet cafes use the Internet to make very cheap calls. Internet cafes are also often quieter than trying to call from a phone box in the street. Another disadvantage of a phone box is that you won't be given any change if you put in a large coin (such as a one-pound coin) but only use up say 20 pence on a call. Many telephone boxes accept credit cards or special phone cards, though, which means you pay for the time you spend on a call.

Give the reason for your call:

> ✔ Hello, I'm ringing to enquire about . . .
>
> ✔ Hello, I'd like some information about . . .
>
> ✔ Good morning, could you tell me about . . .

Ask specific questions:

> ✔ Could you tell me . . .
>
> ✔ . . . what time trains to Glasgow leave on Sunday morning?
>
> ✔ . . . how much the pay is?
>
> ✔ . . . how much the room is per month?

Ask for clarification:

> ✔ I'm sorry, what was that?
>
> ✔ I'm sorry, could you repeat that, please?
>
> ✔ Sorry, what time was that again?
>
> ✔ Sorry, I didn't get that – could you repeat it, please?
>
> ✔ I'm sorry, could you say that a little more slowly, please?
>
> ✔ Could you spell that for me, please?

Signal that you've finished the conversation:

> ✔ Okay, thanks, I think that's everything I need.
>
> ✔ Okay, I think I've got all the details now.

Thank the speaker and say goodbye:

> ✔ Thank you for your help. Goodbye.
>
> ✔ Thank you, you've been very helpful. Goodbye.
>
> ✔ Thanks, that's very helpful. Bye.

Some enquiry phone calls can be very informal, such as this one here:

Straight Talking

 Goran wants to rent a room in a flat, and has seen this advertisement in the newspaper (see Chapter 10 for more help on how to understand *small ads* – the advertisements that appear in newspapers and magazines):

Bayswater W2. Single room in shared flat. Near tube. Non-smoking. £450 per month + bills. 02089784 pms only.

Goran rings the phone number in the ad.

Dan: Hello?

Goran: Hello? I'm ringing about the room in a shared flat. I saw the ad in the newspaper.

Dan: Yes. Dan here. Okay, what would you like to know?

Goran: It says that the room is four hundred and fifty pounds per month plus bills. What are the bills?

Dan: You need to pay part of the electricity and water bills for the house. It's not that much a month, maybe another fifty quid tops.

Goran: Oh, okay. And it's near the Underground, right? Which tube station?

Dan: It's just around the corner from Queensway Tube. That's the Central Line.

Goran: The ad also says 'Bayswater W2' – what is this W2?

Dan: Ah! That's just the postcode for this part of London.

Goran: Oh, okay. How many rooms are there? How many people are living in the house?

Dan: There are three of us living here now, so four with the room for rent. Four rooms. Two of us study, and the third person, Anne, works. Where are you from?

Goran: I'm Croatian.

Dan: Well, Sergey is Russian and Anne's Scottish. Why don't you come over and see the place for yourself? Then you can decide if you want the room.

Goran: Okay, I could come over tomorrow evening around six o'clock?

Dan: Yeah, that's fine, I'll be here. See you then.

Not all enquiry phone calls are as informal as the conversation between Goran and Dan. If you ring a public office, such as rail enquiries, a theatre or a government office, you need to be much more formal. Here's an example of a more formal telephone enquiry call:

Straight Talking

 Goran rings the rail service enquiry line to find out whether there are any train delays expected.

Enquiry desk:	South-eastern Rail Service Enquiries. How may I help you?
Goran:	Hello. I need to get a train from London to Tunbridge Wells this Sunday. Are there any possible delays?
Enquiry desk:	Yes, sir. We often carry out engineering work on the tracks on Sundays. The Sunday trains run as far as Tonbridge. From there you need to get a replacement bus service through to Tunbridge Wells.
Goran:	Sorry, the trains run only as far as where?
Enquiry desk:	Tonbridge.
Goran:	And how long does the bus take from there?
Enquiry desk:	About another twenty minutes.
Goran:	How regular are these buses?
Enquiry desk:	They run to coincide with the train times. When you arrive at Tonbridge there will be a bus waiting to take you on to Tunbridge Wells.
Goran:	Okay, thank you for your help.
Enquiry desk:	You're welcome.

Automatic answering services

Sometimes when you ring a public place for information an automatic answering service is in operation, with a recorded voice that asks you to put in numbers so that you're connected to the department that can best answer your enquiry. Some enquiry numbers, such as ringing an airport to enquire about flight arrival times, are fully automatic and you don't need to speak directly to anyone. The recorded voice asks you to *dial* or press certain numbers or symbols though, such as the star / asterisk (*) or the hash sign (#).

Straight talking

 Sergey calls Heathrow Airport to find out what time Natasha's flight from Moscow arrives. He hears the following recorded message:

> Welcome to BAA Heathrow Airport automated answering service. For the latest security measures, please press nine. Please select one of the following five options. You may press star at anytime to hear the options again. For flight information, press one. For car parking and transport, press two. For lost property and baggage, press three. For hotel reservations, press four. To confirm a flight, press five. Press zero for the operator.

[Sergey presses 1.]

> Welcome to Heathrow Airport's automated flight information system. You'll need your flight number or arrival time to use this service. For flight arrivals, press one. For flight departures, press two. To hear the options again, press star.

[Sergey presses 1.]

> If you know the flight number, press one. If you know the flight arrival time, press two. To hear the options again, press star.

[Sergey presses 1.]

> Enter the flight number. Please omit any letters . . .

[and so on . . .]

Britain and the USA increasingly outsource enquiry phone calls to other countries. This is especially true of the computer industry but also large companies such as rail transport providers and even some passport enquiries! Nowadays, if you need technical help with your computer and you ring the computer company's help line, you're likely to talk to someone in India. India has large call centres, especially in the Bangalore region in the south, with hundreds of staff answering calls from the UK and the USA.

Work phone calls

You probably use more formal language when you make work phone calls, but the structure of a work phone call is similar to that of a social call, which we talk about earlier in this chapter.

1. **Ask for the person you need to speak to.**

2. **Say your own name and the name of your company.**

3. **Talk about the main reason for the phone call.**

4. **Signal the end of the conversation, for example by summarising what you've discussed or decided.**

5. **Thank the person you called, and say goodbye.**

You can see all these elements in the work phone call that follows.

Straight Talking

 Carla Stevens rings Mike Saunders about a work order.

Secretary:	Good morning, Saunders and Levy Suppliers. Can I help you?
Carla Stevens:	Hello, can I speak to Mike Saunders, please?
Secretary:	Who's calling, please?
Carla Stevens:	This is Carla Stevens of the Consultants-E.
Secretary:	Hold on one minute, please. [Pause] I'm putting you through now.
Mike Saunders:	Hello, Carla, thanks for calling.
Carla Stevens:	Hello, Mike. I'm ringing to see if we can arrange a conference call with Lisbon for Friday at ten a.m. We need to discuss the order with them, I think.

Mike Saunders:	Hang on one minute, let me check my appointments for Friday. Yes, that's fine. Ten a.m. I'll note it down.
Carla Stevens:	Okay, thanks. I'll set up the call and let you have the details before then. I've got another call coming in, so need to go. Good to talk to you.
Mike Saunders:	Yes, we'll speak again on Friday. Thanks for organising that. Bye.
Carla Stevens:	Bye.

Conference calls

Conference calls are meetings held on the phone. They involve three or more people in different locations. Usually, one person sets up and runs the conference call, which is scheduled for a certain time. The callers often have an *agenda* – a list of items to discuss. The person running the conference call usually asks for contributions and manages the conversation. You may need to know how to ask for clarification and repetition in a conference call if you don't understand something. It's also important to know how to interrupt politely, so that you can add your opinion. You can find several useful phrases for asking for clarification in the section 'Dealing with Communication Problems', later in this chapter. Here are some phrases for interrupting politely:

✔ I'm sorry, can I just say that . . .

✔ Sorry to interrupt, but what about . . .

✔ That's a good point. Can I just add that . . .

✔ Talking of which, can I just add that . . .

English speakers often use the word 'just' to sound less direct and more polite, especially when they ask for something or interrupt a conversation. *Just* isn't stressed or emphasised in the sentence, you say the word normally. Here are some examples of *just* in telephone phrases:

✔ Could you just tell her I called?

✔ Sorry, could you just repeat that number for me?

✔ I'll just have a look at the documents and get back to you.

✔ I just wanted to ask whether Susan will be at the meeting.

Straight Talking

 Mike Saunders, Carla Stevens and Maria Aapo are holding a conference call. Mike is in London in the UK, Carla is in Brighton in the UK and Maria is in Lisbon, Portugal.

Carla: Thanks for making time for this conference call. You received the agenda I sent by email yesterday, I hope? Okay, let's get started then. Maria, can you tell us the situation in Lisbon?

Maria: Morning, Mike. Morning, Carla. Yes, we've had some problems with the distributor here, but they say the order will be ready by early next week.

Carla: Okay, that's good to know . . .

Mike: [Interrupts] Sorry, can I just ask if he's going to offer us a discount on the late delivery of this order? This is the second time this month, and my customers aren't that happy about it.

Maria: I'll ask him about that, Mike. It sounds fair to me.

Getting the Message

Sometimes when you make a phone call, you have to leave a message on an answering machine or voicemail or with another person. Sometimes you need to take a message for a person who isn't there. In this section we look at the language you use to do each of these things.

Voicemail

Most telephones have a voicemail service, with a recorded message, after which you can leave your own message. Some people record their own voicemail message and some people prefer to use the default voicemail recording that the telephone company provides. Here's an example of each:

Hi, you've reached Sergey and Olga on oh-seven-nine-six-three, four-two-eight. We can't take your call right now, so please leave your name and number after the tone, and we'll get back to you as soon as we can. [Beep]

Welcome to BT Answer One-five-seven-one. The person you're calling is not available. Please leave a message after the tone. [Beep]

To leave an informal message on voicemail for a friend, you can say something like:

Hi Sergey, Misha here. I just wanted to see if you're coming with us to the cinema this Saturday. Give me a call when you can. I'm on seven-six-nine-eight, four-two-seven-eight. Thanks. Catch you later.

Leaving a voicemail for a business contact or work colleague is usually a little more formal, and might sound like this:

Hello, Mike, this is Carla Stevens calling from the Consultants-E. I'd like to check the new order for next week with you – could you give me a call back sometime today? My mobile number is seven-nine-eight-three, seven-six-nine-eight, or you can find me in the London office this afternoon on oh-two-oh-seven, six-double nine, nine-five. Thanks, and I hope to speak to you later.

When you leave a voicemail for a business contact, try to include the following information:

✔ Your full name and phone number

✔ Why you called (keep this short!)

✔ When and how the listener can contact you

Leaving and taking a phone message

You may need to leave a message with another person if the person you're ringing isn't in. If you ring an office to speak to somebody and a secretary answers the phone, the secretary normally first asks for your name ('Who's calling please?') and then asks you to wait ('Please hold') while she checks that the person you're calling is available. If the person you're calling *is* available, the secretary passes on the call ('I'll put you through'). If the person you're calling is *not* available, the secretary uses an expression such as 'I'm afraid he's / she's not available right now' and asks you to leave a message with your name and phone number. Be prepared to leave a message when you ring somebody in case they're not available – you can practise saying the message before you ring!

You may answer the phone when it's not for you, and need to take a message for somebody else. Certain set phrases can help you:

✔ Who's calling please?

✔ Please hold.

- ✔ I'll put you through.

- ✔ I'm sorry, he's in a meeting.

- ✔ I'm afraid he's not in the office today.

- ✔ I'm afraid he's not available right now.

- ✔ Shall I tell him you called?

- ✔ Can I take a message for you?

- ✔ Would you like to leave a message?

- ✔ I'd like to leave a message, please.

- ✔ No, I'll call back later, thanks.

- ✔ This is [Carla Stevens] here.

- ✔ Please ask [Mike] to . . .

- ✔ Please tell [Mike] I called.

- ✔ Please ask him to call me back.

Straight Talking

Sergey rings Misha and leaves a message with Misha's flatmate, Paul.

Paul:	Hello?
Sergey:	Hi, is Misha there? This is Sergey.
Paul:	Oh, hi, Sergey, Paul here. How's it going? Misha's out at the moment. Can I take a message?
Sergey:	Yes, please. Can you ask him to call me back on my mobile when he gets in? It's seven-zero-nine-eight, three-four-two-seven.
Paul:	Okay, hold on one second, let me get a pen to note this down. Sorry, what was that number again?
Sergey:	Seven-zero-nine-eight, three-four-two-seven.
Paul:	Okay, no problem, I'll tell him when he gets home, and I'm sure he'll get back to you as soon as he can.
Sergey:	Thanks. Bye.

Here's the note that Paul left for Misha:

> 7pm Sergey ph - pls call mob no 709 83427 whn u r back

Often when you take messages you use abbreviations and leave out words. Paul's message written out in full would say:

> 7pm Sergey phoned - please call him on mobile number 709 83427 when you're back.

Straight Talking

Carla Stevens rings Mike Saunders on a business matter, and leaves a message with Mike's secretary.

Secretary:	Good morning, Saunders and Levy Suppliers. Can I help you?
Carla:	Hello, can I speak to Mike Saunders, please?
Secretary:	Hold on one minute, please. [Pause] I'm sorry, he's not available right now. Can I take a message?
Carla:	Yes, please. This is Carla Stevens . . .
Secretary:	[Interrupts] I'm sorry, just a moment, let me get a pen to note this down. Okay, go ahead.
Carla:	Right. This is Carla Stevens from the Consultants-E. We have a meeting arranged for tomorrow at nine, and I wondered whether we could move the time forward a little to ten.
Secretary:	Certainly, I'll pass on the message. Is that Stevens with a 'v' or with a 'ph'?
Carla:	Stevens with a 'v'.
Secretary:	Right, could I have a contact phone number, please?
Carla:	Yes, best if he calls me back on my mobile. It's seven-nine-eight-three, seven-six-nine-eight. But if my mobile is off, he can get me on the office number in Brighton – oh-one-two-seven-three, five-nine-eight, three-two.

Secretary:	Thank you. I'll make sure he gets the message as soon as possible.
Carla:	Thanks. Bye.

The secretary leaves Mike Saunders this note:

> From: Carla Stevens
> Company: Consultants-E
> To: Mike S
> Phone: m 7983 7698 / 01273 598 32
> Message: Move tmrw's 9am meeting fwd to 10? Pls call & confirm.

The secretary's message written out in full says:

> Move tomorrow's 9 a.m. meeting forward to 10 a.m.? Please call and confirm.

You may hear people on the phone using various *phrasal verbs* (verbs with a preposition or adverb). These verbs include *hold on* (which means 'wait one moment'), *note down* (which means to write on a piece of paper), *call back* (which means to return a phone call), *go ahead* (which means 'please continue speaking') and *get back to* (which means 'to get in touch with again'). The tricky thing about these verbs is to remember where to put a pronoun, if the verb needs one. If you look at the conversations in this chapter between Sergey and Paul, and between Carla and the secretary, you see all of these phrasal verbs in use. Notice you say 'Ask Mike to call *me* back' – not 'call back me'. We use 'Go ahead' and 'Hang on' as individual phrases, and so you don't need to add prepositions.

Words to Know

hold on	hang up	note down
call back	pick up	go ahead
get back to		

Phone numbers and spelling

When you leave a message, you often leave your phone number so the person you're ringing can call you back. When you give your phone number, you say the numbers one after another. So 257839088 is 'two-five-seven-eight-three-nine-oh-double eight'. You hear both 'oh' and 'zero' used for 0. If two consecutive numbers in a phone number are the same – 257839*088* – you can say 'double eight' or 'eight eight'.

When you say a phone number, you usually pause after two or three numbers to give the person listening time to write it down. So 257839088 is 'two-five-seven [pause] eight-three-nine [pause] oh-double-eight'. If there is an area or country code before the number, we say these numbers all together. For example the code for Brighton in the UK is 01273, so we say the Brighton phone number 01273 784 933 like this: 'oh-one-two-seven-three [pause] seven-eight-four [pause] nine-double three'.

With international country codes, you often say 'plus' before, because this is how you write, with a plus sign (+). You say the country code, then pause, then the city code, and then pause again. So you can say the German phone number + 44 89 39582 like this: 'plus four-four [pause] eight-nine [pause] three-nine-five-eight-two'.

In some languages you say telephone numbers together in groups of decimals (twenty-five, seventy-eighty . . .) but this sounds very strange in English. In English you always say the numbers one by one, so two-five-seven-eight . . .

Telephone tips

Speaking on the phone in a foreign language can be difficult, so here are some tips to make it easier for you.

- ✔ If you don't understand the other speaker, ask for clarification or ask them to speak more slowly. It's better to do this than to not understand! Try to call from a quiet place with no background noise to distract you.

- ✔ Prepare and practise the phrases you need to telephone. You can often predict 60 to 90 per cent of the content of a telephone call and have the necessary language ready. A lot of telephone calls, especially work or enquiry calls, use set phrases. Make sure you have phrases ready to ask for clarification.

- ✔ Be polite in telephone calls and use 'please', 'thank you' and phrases like 'May I . . .' or 'Could you . . .' often. Foreign language learners can seem very direct to English speakers, and people can feel you are being rude.

- ✔ Practise dates, telephone numbers and spelling if you may need them in a phone call. This is especially useful for enquiry or work phone calls.

When you leave a message, or make a phone enquiry, you may also need to spell your name, so make sure you know the necessary letters of the alphabet for your name! The person taking the message may ask just for clarification of a few letters, if she can already guess how to spell the name; for example, 'Is that Stevens with a "v", or Stephens with a "ph"?'

Text messages

Texting, or sending a text message by mobile phone, is very popular in many countries, and the UK is no exception. In fact, many people send more text messages from their mobile phones than they make phone calls! Most languages have text spelling conventions, with short forms and symbols. You can read more about texting in Chapter 10, but here are some of the most common text abbreviations in English:

- **C u l8r:** See you later
- **Gr8:** Great
- **Thx:** Thanks
- **Lol:** Lots of love or laugh out loud

Dealing with Communication Problems

You can prepare yourself for talking on the phone by having a good collection of phrases and strategies to use when communication breaks down, or when you don't understand something. Here are some phrases for asking for clarification, put in order from more formal to less formal:

- I'm sorry, could you repeat that, please?
- Sorry, what was that again?
- Sorry, what did you say?
- Sorry, what was that?
- Pardon?
- Sorry?
- Say again?
- Eh?

The last two phrases are *very* informal and you use them only with people you know well.

Sometimes you may understand most of what someone says but need her to repeat a part of the information. One way to do this is to repeat the sentence and add a question word, which you stress (emphasise) to show that this is the information you need:

✔ She'll be away until *when*?

✔ She's in a meeting with *whom*?

✔ The new communications manager is *who*?

✔ She's the new buyer for *which* company?

✔ She's arriving on *which* flight?

✔ She's arriving at *what* time?

Straight Talking

 Goran rings Sergey, but the line is bad.

Sergey:	[answers phone] Hello?
Goran:	Hi, it's Goran. I'm just ringing to find out what time Olga's flight from Zagreb is arriving.
Sergey:	Sorry, this line is terrible! What did you say?
Goran:	Olga's flight is arriving at what time?
Sergey:	Oh, right. I rang Heathrow to check, and it's been delayed for six hours because of snow.
Goran:	Sorry? Delayed because of what?
Sergey:	Snow!
Goran:	Ah, okay. I was thinking of coming with you to the airport to fetch her.
Sergey:	Okay, we can meet at Queensway Tube at eleven then?
Goran:	Say again?
Sergey:	Eleven o'clock! Queensway Tube!
Goran:	Okay, see you there then. Bye!
Sergey:	Bye.

Fun & Games

1. Stavros calls the National Express bus service to ask about buses to Heathrow Airport. Put the following conversation in the correct order. The first line is in the correct place.

Employee: Good morning, National Express enquiries. May I help you?

Employee: Eleven-fifteen in the morning.

Employee: You're welcome.

Employee: Then the morning bus would be best for you. It leaves Canterbury bus station at eleven-fifteen, and arrives at Heathrow at about one o'clock depending on traffic.

Employee: Certainly, sir. What time would you like to leave Canterbury?

Stavros: Right. Thank you for your help.

Stavros: I need to be at Heathrow by one-thirty.

Stavros: Hello. Yes, I'd like to know about bus times from Canterbury to Heathrow Airport on a Sunday.

Stavros: Sorry, it leaves Canterbury at what time?

Key:

Employee: Good morning, National Express enquiries. May I help you?

Stavros: Hello. Yes, I'd like to know about bus times from Canterbury to Heathrow Airport on a Sunday.

Employee: Certainly, sir. What time would you like to leave Canterbury?

Stavros: I need to be at Heathrow by one-thirty.

Employee: Then the morning bus would be best for you. It leaves Canterbury bus station at eleven-fifteen, and arrives at Heathrow at about one o'clock depending on traffic.

Stavros: Sorry, it leaves Canterbury at what time?

Employee: Eleven-fifteen in the morning.

Stavros: Right. Thank you for your help.

Employee: You're welcome.

2. What happens when you make a phone call? Put the phrasal verbs from the list into the summary below.

noted down   hung up   go ahead   picked up   call her back   hang on

Yesterday Carla rang the London office to speak to Mike Saunders. His secretary_____ the phone and told her to _____ while she called through to Mike. Mike was not available, so the secretary told Carla to _____ and leave Mike a message. Carla asked Mike to _____ later that day, and the secretary _____ Carla's name and number on a piece of paper. Carla thanked the secretary and _____.

Key:

Yesterday Carla rang the London office to speak to Mike Saunders. His secretary *picked up* the phone and told her to *hang on* while she called through to Mike. Mike was not available, so the secretary told Carla to *go ahead* and leave Mike a message. Carla asked Mike to *call her back* later that day, and the secretary *noted down* Carla's name and number on a piece of paper. Carla thanked the secretary and *hung up*.

3. How do you say these numbers?

1. Prices: £14.99 / £4,000 / £16.50 / 20p / 59p

2. Telephone numbers: 020 894382 / 01273 66988 / +34 93 424 200

3. Dates: 22 November 1952 / 1 March 2010 / 3 June 2002

4. Tens and teens: 15 – 50 / 18 – 80 / 17 – 70 / 13 – 30

Key:

1. fourteen pounds ninety-nine / four thousand pounds / sixteen pounds fifty /

    twenty pee (or pence) / fifty-nine pee (or pence)

2. oh-two-oh [pause] eight-nine-four [pause] three eight two /

    oh-one-two-seven-three [pause] double six-nine [pause] double eight /

    plus thirty-four [pause] nine-three [pause] four-two-four [pause] two-double oh

3. twenty second of November nineteen fifty-two / first of March two thousand and ten / third of June two thousand and two

4. fif*teen* – *fif*ty / eigh*teen* – *eigh*ty / seven*teen* – *seven*ty / thir*teen* – *thir*ty

Chapter 9

At the Office and Around the House

. . . .

In This Chapter:

▶ Looking at British working life

▶ Finding a job in the UK

▶ Investigating British houses

▶ Searching for accommodation

. . . .

*T*ourism isn't the only reason to visit an English-speaking country. In these days of increasing globalisation, you may need to visit an English-speaking country on a business trip, or for a longer work or study visit. Or you may have a longer work placement stay, in which you live in the UK and work in a UK-based company for a period of time, from several weeks or months to even years. Or you may come to the UK as a European Union national, looking for temporary or casual work for a period of time, before returning to your country of origin. You need to have the correct visa to study or work in the UK, although for visitors from some countries in the European Union, a work visa isn't always necessary. You can check with the British Consulate or Embassy in your own country to find out what you need.

Working in an Office

Offices and businesses in the UK are usually open from 9 a.m. to 5 p.m. This can be a shock to visitors from countries where shops and offices stay open much later. The lunch break for office workers in Britain is usually about an hour, from 12 p.m. to 1 p.m., or from 1 p.m. to 2 p.m. Many people either take food from home to work, or buy a sandwich or light meal from a nearby cafe or restaurant at lunch time. Very few people in big cities have time to go home for lunch. In good weather, and especially in summer, you see many office workers sitting in parks at lunch time eating their takeaway lunch.

Getting a job

Many European and other nationals spend time in the UK working in offices, where their additional languages are an advantage. This is especially true of large multinational companies, or UK companies that do business with other countries.

You find several typical jobs in an office, from secretaries to sales staff and managers. Depending on the type of work the office does, you may see some of these departments: sales, marketing, translation, R&D (research and development), logistics and operations.

Words to Know

office staff	secretary	sales representative (or 'rep')
designer	advertising executive	
marketing director	project director	
manager	director	CEO (chief executive officer)

If you need to find a job, you have several places to look. You can find jobs advertised in 'small ads' (see Chapter 10) in the newspaper, or with employment agencies. These employment or 'recruitment' agencies often have temporary, or short-term, casual work available. This work can be non-skilled, such as kitchen work in bars or restaurants, or working on building sites, to more skilled secretarial or managerial positions. Of course, you need to have the necessary visas or residential permits to be able to work in the UK, before you look for work. You also usually need to have some experience in the sector you're hoping to work in.

Straight Talking

 Costas is at the employment agency looking for short-term, part-time work.

Agent:	Morning. Can I help you?
Costas:	Yes, please. I saw the ad in your window for a part-time kitchen porter at the Heights Hotel. Is that position still available?
Agent:	Yes, it is. The hotel needs someone to help in the kitchen, with washing up and general cleaning duties.
Costas:	Okay, can you tell me more about it? What about the hours?
Agent:	Well, it's part-time, so sixteen hours a week, but only on Saturdays and Sundays.
Costas:	Yes, that's perfect. I'm here doing a degree in computer science, so I'm busy with classes during the week. What about the pay?
Agent:	Well the pay is seven pounds an hour, because it's weekend work. There are two eight-hour shifts: one on Saturday and one on Sunday.
Costas:	Is the pay net or gross?
Agent:	It's gross, so you need to pay tax and national insurance out of that. What nationality are you? Are you an EU national?
Costas:	Yes, I am.
Agent:	Okay, well, that's no problem then. You'll also get your meals on Saturday and Sunday at the hotel, during your shift.
Costas:	Okay, well, I need the work, so when can I start?
Agent:	This weekend if you're ready. We can do the paperwork now if you like.

Words to Know

go for an interview	go on a training course
get a job	get made redundant
get fired	get promoted
look for a job	lose your job
write a CV (curriculum vitae)	fill in an application form
earn a good salary / wage	shift work
a gross or net salary	

In the UK, if you lose your job then in some cases you may be able to claim unemployment benefit. The colloquial term for this is 'the dole'. You may hear people talking about being 'on the dole' or 'going on the dole'.

Travelling to work

Rush hour in the UK is between 8 a.m. and 9 a.m., when schools and offices open, and between 5 p.m. and 6 p.m., when offices close and people go home. At these times, public transport in big cities can be very crowded, and car traffic can be very slow.

Some people travel fairly long distances to get to work, especially in big cities like London. Comparing how long it takes you to get to work is often a topic of conversation when you first meet someone. Here are some useful phrases for talking about how you travel to work:

- How do you get to work?
- I go by [bus / train / Underground / bike].
- How long does it take you to get to work?
- It takes about [an hour / 40 minutes].
- How far is it?
- It's about 20 kilometres.
- It's on the other side of Glasgow.

> ✔ How much does it cost?
>
> ✔ It costs about 30 pounds a week.
>
> ✔ Which [bus / Underground line] do you take?
>
> ✔ I take [the number 24 bus / the Central line Tube].

Arriving at reception

If you're in the UK for a business meeting, or you're on your first day of a new job, you first go to the reception area of an office to announce your arrival.

Straight Talking

Maria Sanchez is visiting the UK office from Spain. She has a meeting at 10 a.m. with two UK colleagues.

Receptionist: Good morning. Can I help you?

Maria Sanchez: Yes, please. I have a meeting at ten o'clock with Mike Sanders. My name is Maria Sanchez.

Receptionist: That's right. If you'd like to take a seat. I'll call through to Mr Sanders and let him know you're here.

Maria Sanchez: Thank you.

Arriving on time for a meeting in the UK is important. Arriving late is seen as rude, and it will have a very negative effect on any business you want to do with UK colleagues. Arriving five minutes late is okay, but being any later than that isn't a good idea. It's best to arrive a few minutes early for your meeting, and wait in the reception area for the secretary to take you to your meeting. Punctuality (being on time) is seen as a sign of seriousness and reliability in the UK. Make sure you leave home or your hotel in plenty of time to arrive at a business meeting punctually. If you see you're going to be late, call ahead to let the office know.

In some large office blocks, you need to pass through security on the ground floor to enter the building. You usually need to 'sign in' to a visitors' book, leaving your name and possibly your postal address. Security may give you a special name tag, or guest tag, to put around your neck or to fasten to your jacket. You may also need to pass any bags you're carrying through a scanning machine. Levels of security vary depending on the office block you're visiting. Make sure you leave plenty of time to get through security before your meeting, although this usually doesn't take more than a few minutes.

Talking about your work

Talking about your personal life and about what you do are two useful topics of conversation in many social situations (see Chapter 3). People may ask you about your work life in the UK, or you may meet other visitors to the UK and want to ask them about their work. Asking and answering general questions about what you do is a useful social skill, and here are some phrases to help you. We start with asking others about their work:

- ✔ What do you do?
- ✔ What do you do for a living?
- ✔ What's your job?
- ✔ What's your job like?
- ✔ Are you looking for work / a job?
- ✔ Is this a business trip or are you on holiday?
- ✔ Are you here for work or pleasure?
- ✔ Is this your first trip to the UK?
- ✔ Have you been here before?
- ✔ Is this the first time you've [worked here / been to London]?
- ✔ Do you do a lot of travelling for work?
- ✔ How long are you planning to stay?

To describe what you do, and to talk in general terms about your work life, here are more useful phrases:

- ✔ I'm [retired / unemployed / looking for a job / freelance].
- ✔ I have a temporary job.
- ✔ I work [full time / part time / in shifts].
- ✔ I'm in training to be a [nurse / translator / lawyer / electrician].
- ✔ I work for a multinational company.
- ✔ I work in the [computer / building / catering / hotel] industry.
- ✔ I run my own business.
- ✔ I earn my living by working [in construction / with computers].

In any conversation, it's important to show that you're listening, and to show interest in what the other person is saying. When listening to people talking about their work or job, you can respond with interest by using expressions like 'Really? How interesting!' or 'That sounds really interesting' or 'How fascinating!'. Of course, if the job is *not* particularly interesting, then respond with phrases like 'Right', 'Uh-huh' or 'Okay', otherwise you sound very false!

Be careful of the difference between the words *career* and *degree*. You study for a degree at university (not a career!). Your career is your work life in a chosen area; for example, you may decide on a career in sales, so you do a degree at university in business studies. Your career only starts when you start your work life.

Meeting work colleagues

You can do a few things to make a business meeting go more smoothly. First impressions are important, and here are some tips for meeting business colleagues for the first time:

- ✔ Stand up when you meet someone, smile and make eye contact.

- ✔ Introduce yourself immediately, and explain who you are or what your job is, if necessary.

- ✔ Shake hands.

- ✔ Make sure you know who the most important person is in the meeting.

- ✔ Pay attention to names when you meet people. If they introduce themselves with only their first name ('Hi, I'm Mike'), you can use that to address them ('Nice to meet you, Mike').

It's common in a business context for a third person to introduce you or the person you are meeting, and to use both your first name and surname to do this. Imagine you are Maria Sanchez, and you are meeting Mike Sanders (whom you know) and Daniel Wilson (whom you don't know). Mike Sanders can introduce you by saying 'Maria Sanchez, may I introduce Daniel Wilson'. You don't usually use titles such as Mr or Mrs in introductions, so you *won't* hear 'Ms Maria Sanchez, may I introduce Mr Daniel Wilson' in the UK. But you may hear an honorary title like Dr (doctor) in an introduction, just so you know that the person you're dealing with is a doctor. Using full names in introductions gives people the opportunity to use first names if they want to address each other more informally. Using first names in business settings is common practice in English-speaking countries such as the USA, Canada, the UK and so on, but if you aren't sure whether to use first names, then copy what your business colleagues do.

Straight Talking

Maria Sanchez is visiting the UK office from Portugal. She meets Mike Sanders and Daniel Wilson for a business meeting. She knows Mike Sanders from a previous meeting, but she's meeting Daniel Wilson for the first time.

Mike Sanders:	Good morning, Maria. Nice to see you again.
Maria Sanchez:	Morning, Mike. Good to see you too.
Mike Sanders:	May I introduce Daniel Wilson. Daniel, this is Maria Sanchez. Daniel is the new marketing director of the Western Europe division.
Daniel Wilson:	Pleased to meet you, Maria.
Maria Sanchez:	Pleased to meet you too, Daniel.
Mike Sanders:	Right, I've reserved a room for our meeting. Shall we go through?
Daniel Wilson:	After you, Maria.
Marta Sanchez:	Thank you.

When you're first introduced to someone, it's important to greet them. The following phrases for greeting someone are in order from the most informal first, to the most formal last:

✔ Hi, how are you?

✔ Nice to meet you.

✔ Glad to meet you.

✔ Pleased to meet you.

✔ How do you do?

Sometimes it's difficult to hear a new colleague's name, especially if it's a name from another country or culture or a name that you aren't familiar with. To get someone to repeat his name, you can say 'Sorry, I didn't quite catch your name'. The person then repeats his name, hopefully more clearly.

Looking at Housing in the UK

In your own country, you may live in a flat or a house, but some types of housing are peculiar to the UK, with special words to describe them.

Suburbia

The *suburbs* is the area in the outskirts of a large city, where houses are usually a little bigger than in the centre of the city. People sometimes use the word 'suburbia' to refer to this area. In some countries, the 'suburbs' often refer to the poorer areas of town, but in Britain this isn't usually the case, and people feel that the quality of life in the suburbs can be better than in the city centre, with less pollution, more parks and woods and less traffic. Of course, a negative side exists, and people often use the word *suburbia* to refer to the dullness and monotony of the suburb, with identical houses, and no vibrant city centre or interesting mix of cultures. Some parts of suburbia are called the *commuter belt* where office workers live and *commute* (travel every day to work and back home).

In the UK, a house may be a semi-detached house (or 'semi') or a detached house. A *semi-detached house* is one that has another (often identical) house attached to it. You see many of these semis in the suburbs around large cities, often with a very small front yard and a straight narrow garden in the back, divided from the neighbours by a fence. The front yard can be a small concrete driveway where you can park your car, and it often has the rubbish bins standing in it. The British built many of these suburban semis in the 1920s and 1930s. A *detached house* isn't attached to any other houses.

In many places in the UK, especially big cities such as London, Birmingham and Edinburgh, you see rows of identical houses all joined together. These are *terraced houses* and were built earlier than the semis of suburbia. People first built terraced houses in Europe, and they appeared in the UK in the early 1700s. Many terraced houses you see today in Britain's cities are *Victorian* – from the nineteenth century.

In the centre of large towns and cities many people live in flats, because property is usually quite expensive and smaller flats are cheaper to rent or buy than larger detached or terraced houses. Note that the British use the word *flat* more than *apartment*. British people talk about a 'block of flats' rather than an 'apartment block'. Apart from modern blocks of flats, you also find older terraced houses, of two or three *storeys* (levels) that have been divided into individual flats.

When describing where you live, you can mention some of the public areas or buildings nearby. So, perhaps you live across the road from a pub, or next to a car park, or near a park, or just off the high street. Your flat might be in a 'nice' or a 'run down' (poorer) part of town. If you live in a block of flats, the ground level of the flat is the 'ground floor' and then the first level up is the 'first floor' – unlike in the USA, where the ground floor is called the first floor!

Housing estates

Some cities in Britain have large 'housing estates' on the outskirts of town, which were built from the 1950s on. These estates often have blocks of *high-rise* (tall), *low-cost* (cheap) flats. Some housing estates have a bad reputation for unemployment, drugs and crime. If you're going to visit someone on a housing estate, find out what the best time to go is (probably not late at night), and which areas to avoid. But remember that the UK has a low crime rate compared with many other countries in the developed world.

Words to Know

flat	semi-detached house or 'semi'	
detached house	terraced house	garden
fence	driveway	rubbish bins
housing estate	suburbs	suburbia
the commuter belt		

The words *house* and *home* mean more or less the same thing – 'the place where I live' – but you use them a little differently. Americans use the word *home* a lot more than the British, who tend to use the word *house*. This means you may talk about 'my house' rather than 'my home' – even if you live in a flat. You hear people use the word *home* more commonly in certain expressions, such as 'Welcome home', or in idioms such as 'Home is where the heart is'.

English speakers often use the word *place* to refer to their own home. So an English-speaking friend might invite you to visit by saying 'Why don't you come round to my place', or 'Let's meet at my place'. One of the most stereotyped expressions you can use to invite someone you're romantically interested in to come to your house or flat is 'My place or yours?'. Don't use this expression unless you're using it ironically or as a joke!

Postal addresses

Whether you're staying in a flat, a semi or a hotel, you have an address. Here are some common abbreviations for different names for streets:

> ✔ Road: Rd.
>
> ✔ Street: St.
>
> ✔ Avenue: Ave.
>
> ✔ Circle: Circ.
>
> ✔ Court: Ct.
>
> ✔ Gardens: Gdns.
>
> ✔ Junction: Jct.
>
> ✔ Place: Pl.
>
> ✔ Square: Sq.
>
> ✔ Station: Sta.

In English, you say the number of the house or flat first and then the name of the road or street, so '53 Eastern Road', not 'Eastern Road 53'. Each area in the UK has a postcode, which you put on letters, and you also need to fill out forms with your address, so it's worth remembering it if you're going to stay in the UK for more than a few weeks. A UK postcode usually has a group of two or three numbers or letters, followed by another group of three numbers or letters. For example, a London postcode could be W2 3FL, a Manchester postcode M1 9SN and an Exeter postcode EX2 7NA.

Email and web addresses

These days many people have a virtual address – their email address and maybe even a website. It's important to know how to say your email address, so that you can give it to friends or over the phone when asking for information. The @ sign is 'at' and the [.] is 'dot'. So you say the email address `john smith@yahoo.co.uk` as follows: 'john smith at yahoo dot co dot uk'. You may need to spell parts of your email address, so you need to be sure you know the necessary letters of the alphabet to do this.

The *A–Z*

The London *A–Z* is one of Britain's best-known street directories, and almost every house in London has one on its bookshelves – and almost every cab driver has one in his taxi! The *A–Z* (pronounced 'ay to zed') is a street directory to London with a detailed index to help you find a street. The index uses street abbreviations, so 'Oxford Street' appears as 'Oxford St.' in the *A–Z*. The *A–Z* also has Underground stations marked on it. Anyone who spends any time in London usually buys one, and you can buy them in all sorts of sizes, from small pocket size *A–Z* to larger versions, in book stores and in many London newsagents'.

When saying or listening to a web address, you may need to know other signs as well:

Words to Know

@	(at)
.	(dot)
/	(forward slash, or slash)
\	(back slash)
-	(hyphen)
_	(underscore)

all *one word*

all lower case (lower-case letters, such as n, f, g)

all *caps* or all capital letters (caps are capital letters, like N, F, G)

Straight Talking

 Pierre calls *UK Sports* magazine to take out a subscription.

Magazine employee:	Hello, *UK Sports* magazine. Can I help you?
Pierre:	Hello, yes, I'd like to take out a subscription to your magazine, for six months.
Magazine employee:	Certainly, sir, I'll need to take your personal details for that first. Your full name, please?
Pierre:	Yes, it's Pierre Delacroix. That's D-E-L-A-C-R-O-I-X.

Magazine employee:	Thanks. And your postal address, please?
Pierre:	Seventy-three B, Parkway Terrace, Inverness.
Magazine employee:	Right, do you have the postcode for that?
Pierre:	Yes, it's IV1 4PL.
Magazine employee:	Thanks. And can we have your email address please, sir? That way we can contact you more easily.
Pierre:	Sure. It's pierre underscore delacroix – all lower case – at yahoo dot co dot uk.
Magazine employee:	Okay, that's great. You may want to take a look at our website; we have some great offers this month on sporting equipment. If you'd just like to write it down . . .
Pierre:	Okay, go ahead.
Magazine employee:	The web address is www dot uksports – all one word, all lower case – dot co dot uk.

Neighbourhood Watch

In large cities in the UK, many people don't have much contact with their neighbours. In large blocks of flats, for example, you may not even know your neighbours' names. In the UK, neighbours have a lot less contact, even in smaller towns, than in many other cultures – in fact, people often criticise British society for being very individualistic.

However, a sign you may see in your area is for 'Neighbourhood Watch'. This is an association between neighbours, the police and community groups within a neighbourhood to prevent crime, and to make an area safer. The UK imported the idea from the USA in the early 1980s, after the success of similar schemes there. As many as ten million people are currently part of neighbourhood watch schemes across the UK.

Typical British houses

A house may have one or more storeys, so you talk about a 'two-storey house', for example. You also talk about a 'one-bedroom', 'two-bedroom' or 'three-bedroom' house or flat. The main rooms in the house are the bedroom (where you sleep), the bathroom (with the toilet, bath or shower), the kitchen (where you cook), the living room (where you usually have a sofa and watch TV) and the dining room (where you eat meals). People in the UK often spend a lot of time in the kitchen, if the room is large enough and has a central table, when they aren't watching TV in the living room. Many families eat all their meals, and even entertain guests, in the kitchen, which is in many ways considered the heart of the house.

Because of the cold weather, most flats and houses in the UK have central heating these days, with radiators to warm the house. Radiators carry hot water that a gas- or oil-fired boiler heats. Some people still use electric fires or heaters. Many people use gas for central heating in the UK and cooking. Many older houses and flats have fireplaces, but most large cities in the UK have restrictions on lighting fires, and you need to use special smokeless fuels for fires, not wood, to reduce pollution from chimneys.

Air conditioning isn't very common in the UK in private homes. Because of the British climate, people in the UK protect their houses more against the cold than the heat. Many offices do have air conditioning for the hotter summer months, although the London Underground *doesn't* have air conditioning, and is famous for being very, very hot in the middle of summer.

Words to Know

a two-storey house	a one-bedroom flat	
bedroom	bathroom	living room
dining room	kitchen	central heating
radiators	fireplace	chimney
air conditioning		

Finding Somewhere to Live

If you want to rent a flat during your stay in the UK, you can look in several places. The local newspaper usually has *small ads* (see Chapter 10) – small advertisement for flat rentals. Another option is to look in the window of local newsagents', where people sometimes leave hand-written small ads on card, for flats to rent in the immediate area. You can also try rental agencies, or *estate agents*, who have lists of flats to rent; estate agents usually charge a commission for their services. You can usually see the flats for rent listed in the window of an estate agent's, as well as flats to buy.

Here's a small ad from a local newspaper:

> FOR RENT. 3-bedroom flat Sharpe St. Spacious kitchen, living & dining room. No garden. Non-smoker pref. £950 p.month excl bills. Call Richard 01482 779 385.

Written out in full, this ad says: *For rent, a three-bedroom flat in Sharpe Street, with a spacious kitchen, a living room and a dining room. There's no garden. Non-smokers are preferred. £950 rent per month, excluding bills. Call Richard on phone number 01482 779 385.*

When you rent a flat or a room in a shared flat, you probably want to know about any extra costs such as bills, or a deposit, and also about any special house rules (such as no smoking) or duties (such as looking after a garden or house plants). You also want to know how long the rental period is for, and about local transport. You can ask if the flat has facilities such as a TV, washing machine and central heating, and furniture, or if you can safely leave a bicycle somewhere. Finally, if the flat sounds okay, you probably want to go and see it before you make a final decision about renting it.

Straight Talking

Akira calls Richard about renting a flat.

Richard: Hello?

Akira: Oh, hello, I'm ringing about the flat advertisement I saw in the newspaper last week. Is that Richard?

Richard: Yes, speaking. Hi. Right, it's 950 pounds per month, but the bills for gas and electricity are extra.

Akira:	Yes. I saw in the ad that you also prefer non-smokers. That's fine, I'm a non-smoker, and I'm glad there's no garden as I'm not very good with plants! But I'm only here in Hull for six months. How long is the rental for?
Richard:	Well, I'd prefer to rent it for at least a year, but you're the only person who's rung so far, so I'd be happy to rent it just for six months at the moment.
Akira:	Okay. What about public transport? Are there any bus stops nearby?
Richard:	Yes, there are two buses that go into the centre of town from the end of the road.
Akira:	Okay, and what about facilities like a washing machine . . .
Richard:	The flat is fully equipped. There's a washing machine, fridge and cooker, all the furniture, a TV and a DVD player. And central heating, of course. It's gas.
Akira:	Sounds great. One last question – is there somewhere I can leave my bicycle?
Richard:	Yes, there's a large entrance hall; it's a two-storey semi. The downstairs neighbour leaves his bike in there already. No problem to put two bikes there.
Akira:	I'd love to come and see the flat, if that's all right?
Richard:	Yes, of course . . .

Sharing a flat

If you're in the UK to study at a university, student housing is sometimes on the university campus. If you're studying at a language school, or a smaller college, then you may stay with a host family or share a flat with other students. Foreign workers who are in Britain for longer periods of time also frequently share flats, because this is more economical than renting a flat by yourself.

Sharing a flat with others isn't always easy, especially if your flatmates are strangers or come from a different culture to yours. Although people sometimes say that it's harder to share a flat with friends!

Flatmates often share the work that you need to do around the flat – the housework or *household chores* (small jobs). Many household chores use the words *do* or *make*. As a general rule, when you talk about housework you use *do* for general activities or jobs and *make* for things that you create or construct.

Words to Know

make the beds	make breakfast / lunch / dinner
make a cup of tea / coffee	make a cake
make a mess	make an overseas phone call
do housework	do the washing (for clothes)
do the washing up (for dishes and cutlery)	
do the dishes	do the ironing
do the cleaning	

Housework and homework are two very different things. *Housework* consists of the small jobs that you do around the house, such as making the beds or doing the dishes. *Homework* is extra school work that children do after school, at home.

You may need to do other things around the house, and here's a list of useful phrases with verbs:

Words to Know

invite a friend over	hang a picture
move furniture	turn on the heating / TV / lights
turn off the heating / TV / lights	watch TV / a DVD
pay the rent / the bills	get the paper / milk delivered

Can you . . . ? Asking for help from flatmates

You may want to ask your flatmates for help with the housework. Here are some phrases you can use:

- Can / Could you give me hand?
- Could you do me a favour?
- Could you help me with this?
- Would you mind helping me for a minute?

English speakers use shortened forms of sentences to ask for help from friends they know well. So you could hear 'Do me a favour?' or 'Give me a hand?' or even 'Do something for me?'. Remember that this is very direct and informal, and if you use it yourself, you must know the person you're asking for help very well! You probably won't use these forms in a business or work context, for example.

Can I . . . ? Asking permission

To ask someone whether it's all right to do something, you can use these phrases:

- Can I [borrow your newspaper]?
- Could I [borrow your newspaper]?
- Do you mind if I [use the phone]?
- Would you mind if I [use your computer for a minute]?
- Do you think I could [use your computer for a minute]?

Could you not . . . ? Asking someone not to do something

Sharing a flat can create tension with flatmates, and sometimes you may need to ask your flatmates *not* to do something! Here are some polite ways of asking this:

- Can you please not [smoke in the house]?
- Could you please not [smoke in the house]?
- Do you mind not [eating my food in the fridge without asking]?
- Would you mind not [using my computer without asking]?
- Do you think you could not [use my mobile phone without asking]?

In the preceding phrases for asking permission and asking someone not to do something, 'could' is more polite than 'can', and 'would you?' is more polite than 'do you?'. Most polite of all is 'Do you think I / you could . . .'. In English, the more indirect you make the request, the more polite it is! You only use direct forms with very good friends in informal situations – so you might hear someone say 'Lend me your phone?' to a good friend. You can make a direct request a little more polite by adding a question tag, so 'Lend me your phone, *could you*?'.

Straight Talking

Helena and Miriam share a flat. Miriam hasn't been helping in the flat much.

Helena:	Miriam, could we have a chat? There are a few things about the flat that we need to talk about. Is now a good time?
Miriam:	Sure.
Helena:	Okay, the first thing is the housework. In the last flat I shared, my flatmate and I did the cooking and washing up on alternate days. How about if we do that here?
Miriam:	That sounds fine. Sorry if I haven't been doing much washing up lately. I promise to do my share from now on.
Helena:	That would be great. Do you mind if I cook on Monday, Wednesdays and Fridays then? I have my yoga class on Tuesday and Thursday evenings, so those days it would be difficult for me to cook.
Miriam:	I can do Tuesdays and Thursdays and Sundays, and on Saturdays we can do our own thing, because we usually go out.
Helena:	That's great, thanks. There's just one more thing.
Miriam:	Yes?
Helena:	Do you think you could not smoke in the house?
Miriam:	Hmmm. Well, how about if I don't smoke in the living room and kitchen, but I smoke in my own bedroom?
Helena:	Well, okay. Thanks. We also need to pay the bills on time. I'm worried that the phone is going to be cut off.
Miriam:	Yes, you're right. I'll take the phone bill and get it paid on Monday, okay? I made a lot of overseas calls to my family last month.
Helena:	Thanks.

Inviting guests and staying with other people

You may invite visitors to your flat, for example for a meal. These visitors are your *guests*, and you are the *host*. If you invite friends to stay for more than a day, and to stay overnight, they are your *house guests*. If your flat is big enough, you may have a spare bedroom or a guest bedroom for your friends to stay in.

You yourself may stay as a guest in a house during your stay in the UK. Many foreign visitors come to the UK every year to study English, and to stay with a 'host family'. It's a good idea to find out as much as you can about your host family before arriving in the UK, such as whether they have any children or pets, and any unusual house rules they may have. You also want to know if they have any experience of overseas guests living in their house before! Agencies organise these home stays both abroad and in the UK.

Straight Talking

 Gina is going to the UK to stay with a host family. She calls the agency to get more information.

Agency:	Host Families UK, can I help you?
Gina:	Hello, yes, this is Gina Li. I received your email confirming my host family in Cardiff for next month. I'd like some more information, please.
Agency:	One second Ms Li, I'll call up your file. [Pause] Yes, that's right, we've placed you with the Redcliff family in Cardiff, Wales, as you requested.
Gina:	Thanks. I have some extra questions about the family, if that's okay? The first is: do they have any children? I prefer to stay in a family with no young children, as I said in my application form.
Agency:	No, no children living in the house. They have a son at university, but he'll be in student housing while you're there.

Gina:	Okay, thanks. Could I also just check that there are no dogs or cats? I'm allergic to cats.
Agency:	Not to worry, Ms Li, we were very careful to make sure there are no pets in this family. We realise that an allergy can be a serious thing.
Gina:	Good. And of course I wanted a non-smoking house.
Agency:	There's no smoking allowed in the house.
Gina:	Okay, just one last question. Have the Redcliffs had people from other countries staying with them before? Or am I the first overseas visitor for them?
Agency:	We've had the Redcliffs on our books for five years now, Ms Li, so they're very experienced with overseas visitors. I'm sure you'll be very happy with your stay.
Gina:	Well, thank you for your help.
Agency:	You're welcome. Please ring again if you have any other questions, and we'll send you your travel details in a week or so. Goodbye.
Gina:	Bye.

Au pairs

Another very common way of living as a guest with a host family is to work as an *au pair* (a French term) or live-in nanny. Most au pairs aren't from English-speaking countries, and they want to live in the UK to learn and practise English. Working as an au pair is a cost-effective way of improving your English, and an especially attractive job for young women from abroad. An au pair is often a woman, and she often looks after the children in a house and helps with the housework and cooking, in return for board and lodging (food and accommodation) and possibly a small salary. There are very clear guidelines about what an au pair in Britain can expect to do as part of her job, and how many hours a week she should work. Au pairs should get at least one day off work a week. If you want to work as an au pair in the UK, find out about these minimum conditions *before* you agree to a job. The UK has several au pair or nanny agencies and you can find them by searching on the Internet.

Words to Know

guest	house guest	host
host family	spare bedroom / room	
guest bedroom / room	au pair / live-in nanny	
board and lodging		

If you stay with a host family in the UK, you're most likely to spend time with them at breakfast and at dinner in the evening (refer to Chapter 5 for more information on meals in Britain). One of the most important things to remember about speaking to your host family is that you always need to be very polite, and to use the words 'please' and 'thank you' (or 'thanks') frequently.

Straight Talking

Gina is staying with a host family, the Redcliffs, in Cardiff. This is her first morning there.

Ms Redcliff: Good morning, Gina. Did you sleep well? Would you like some breakfast?

Gina: Good morning. Yes, please, that would be lovely.

Ms Redcliff: What would you like? A full English breakfast with bacon and eggs, or a continental breakfast?

Gina: The full English breakfast will be too much for me, I think. What's the continental breakfast?

Mrs Redcliff: I've got some croissants from the baker's for you, or there's toast with jam, marmalade or honey. And fresh orange juice, and of course tea or coffee.

Gina: The continental breakfast sounds perfect. I'll have some toast with jam, please. And some coffee. Thanks, I can see that I'm going to enjoy Wales!

Fun & Games

1. Name the rooms of the house in Figure 9-1:

A   B

Figure 9-1:
The rooms
of a house.

C   D   E

Key:

A. Bathroom   B. Bedroom   C. Dining room   D. Kitchen   E. Living room

2. These pieces of furniture and objects are shown in Figure 9-1. Unjumble the letters in each word, and say which room each piece of furniture or object belongs to.

erwsho	plam	bleat	crkooe	gru
thab	teprac	carih	gedfir	carihram
oitelt	ebd	aplet	nsik	soaf

Key:

   A. bathroom: Toilet, bath, shower

   B. bedroom: Bed, carpet, lamp,

(continued)

C. dining room: Plate, chair, table

D. kitchen: Sink, fridge, cooker

E. living room: Sofa, armchair, rug

3. Say these emails and web addresses:

a) marta.sanchez@spainexports.com

b) costas_nikiforou@yahoo.co.uk

c) paulwilson@marketing.ukexports.com

d) www.uksports.co.uk

e) www.flats-rental.com

f) www.nanniesuk.com/conditions

Key:

a) marta dot sanchez at spainexports (all one word) dot com

b) costas underscore nikiforou at yahoo dot co dot uk

c) paulwilson (all one word, all lower case) at marketing dot ukexports dot com

d) www dot uksports (all one word) dot co dot uk

e) www dot flats dash rental dot com

f) www dot nanniesuk (all one word) dot com forward slash conditions

Chapter 10

Written English

. . . .

In This Chapter

▶ Reading English-language newspapers and magazines

▶ Understanding signs

▶ Completing forms

▶ Composing letters

▶ Writing emails in English

▶ Looking at the difference between written and spoken English

. . . .

For many people in many different situations, learning a language is often more about learning how to communicate with other people orally than learning how to write it. Listening and speaking are usually the most urgent parts of a language to improve on when you really want to communicate with people – and reading often comes next, with writing arriving much later.

If you're living and working in England then you need to be able to read and write English well, but most people's primary objective is to be able to speak to others. In this chapter we take a look at written English – both as something you need to be able to write, but also as something you need to be able to produce, whether you're filling in a form or writing to a local newspaper to complain about something!

Looking at Newspapers and Magazines

Newspapers and magazines are a popular part of most people's lives. In the UK you see lots of people reading a newspaper on the way to work, or having a long breakfast on Sunday, perhaps in a pub or cafe, with a huge pile of Sunday newspapers. *Sunday papers* are made up of many different sections, such as news, culture, style, gardening, motoring and finance, and a glossy magazine – and they can take a whole day to read.

Apart from the traditional newspapers (which we talk about in the sidebar 'British newspapers'), you find many dozens of different magazines in a typical newsagent's – magazines on anything from popular music to computing, gardening, photography, knitting, politics and society. In fact, you can probably find a magazine for pretty much any area of interest. Some people subscribe to their favourite magazine (subscriptions are usually cheaper than buying each issue separately) and have it delivered. Some people prefer to read their favourite publications on the Internet – though we recommend you don't do this in the bath!

Words to Know

tabloid	broadsheet	freesheet
home (UK) news	international	world
business	technology	science
health	sports	weather
obituaries	puzzles	cartoons
horoscopes	personals	TV guide

Straight Talking

Klaus is reading the newspaper on the way to work and chatting with his colleague Karen.

Klaus: Don't you ever read a newspaper on the way to work, Karen?

Karen: Not really. I watch the news on telly before I leave for work, and then I usually just listen to music on the train. Do you always read the paper?

Klaus: Not all of it. I read the news, you know national, international – those sections. And then I have a quick look through the other parts.

Karen: I think they're pretty boring – all those political features and loads of pages of sport and business.

Klaus: Well, you don't have to read those parts. I like the football section and I often read the obituaries and the TV guide, to see if there's anything on tonight.

Karen: Obituaries? Usually, I have no idea who they're writing about.

Klaus: No, but it's interesting to read about other people's lives.

Karen: If you say so!

[They arrive. Klaus gets up and leaves his newspaper on the seat.]

Karen: Are you leaving the paper here?

Klaus: Yes, I'm just taking the second section to read on the way home.

Karen: Do you mind if I take the main part?

Klaus: But I thought you didn't like papers!

Karen: Well, there's the horoscopes. Oh, and the cartoons. And I usually read through the personals. And . . .

British newspapers

British newspapers are generally divided into two different types: broadsheets and tabloids. Broadsheets traditionally have been much bigger than tabloids, which often have bright red titles (like the *Sun*). In traditional terms, people consider broadsheets to be of better quality (featuring sections such as home news, international news, business and so on) and tabloids are more famous for their stories about celebrities, football players, television and sex!

This difference is not as clear as it used to be, especially because broadsheets have changed size and adopted tabloid sizes (probably because they're much easier to read on the train and the bus). Now you'll find *The Times* is the same size as the *Daily Mirror*, which can be very confusing when you buy a newspaper. To confuse things even more, there's a third size called the 'Berliner', which the *Guardian* uses.

Most of the national and regional commercial newspapers traditionally take a certain political stance, although sometimes this isn't obvious – so many readers expect the *Daily Telegraph* to be more sympathetic to the Conservative Party and the *Guardian* to be more suitable for Labour Party voters.

These days, most cities and towns distribute free newspapers on public transport, in shops and on the streets. These are generally called *freesheets*, papers such as *Metro* and *The London Paper*. Mostly, though, freesheets tend to get their news from the Internet, and you won't find any long stories or deep political analysis – these are papers that you read on the way to work. Plus you can do the Sudoku puzzles!

Understanding newspaper headlines

Newspapers and magazines have a structure and a language all of their own, and speakers of other languages often have problems understanding the *headlines* (or titles) of the stories. This is because newspapers usually leave out a lot of words in headlines. Here are some funny example headlines – can you see where the joke is in each of them?

- **Drunk Gets Nine Months in Violin Case** [a drunk person has been given nine months in prison after his prosecution for a crime involving a violin]. The joke is that it seems to say that the drunk will be spending nine months inside a violin case.

- **Eye Drops off Shelf** [eye drops, a type of medicine for eyes, have been removed from supermarket shelves for some reason]. Here the joke is in visualising an eye rolling off a shelf somewhere!

- **Eastern Head Seeks Arms** [the leader of an 'Eastern' country is looking for guns and other weapons]. The joke here is the wordplay between 'head' and 'arms', as though the head is looking for a pair of arms.

- **Squad Helps Dog Bite Victim** [a group of people – a *squad* – helped someone who was bitten by a dog]. Here, of course, it seems as though the people helped the dog bite the victim.

- **Stolen Painting Found by Tree** [a stolen painting has been found next to a tree]. The tree didn't find the stolen painting!

- **Miners Refuse to Work after Death** [Miners are refusing to work since someone, probably another miner, died at work]. They aren't refusing to work after they've died!

Getting personal

Certain sections of newspapers are more personal than others – they include obituaries (stories about famous people who have recently died), announcements (often about weddings or official engagements by politicians or royalty) and personals (small adverts for people who are looking for partners). Each of these has its own vocabulary, but perhaps you'd like to take a look at the personals?

Straight Talking

 Pascale is looking through the personals column of the local newspaper during a coffee break at work.

Pascale:	I don't understand half of these messages; it's like some kind of secret code.
Melanie:	What do you mean? The paper?
Pascale:	The personal ads – I thought it might be fun to meet some new people.
Melanie:	So what's the problem?
Pascale:	Well, what does GSOH mean?
Melanie:	Easy: good sense of humour.
Pascale:	Oh! So all English men have a good sense of humour, do they?
Melanie:	They do in personals!
Pascale:	What about WLTM?
Melanie:	Would like to meet!
Pascale:	Why does it have to be so complicated?
Melanie:	Because you pay per word in the personal adverts. Any others?
Pascale:	Loads! N/S, LTR, ISO . . .
Melanie:	Let's see: non-smoker, long-term relationship, in search of!
Pascale:	You seem to know a lot about all this . . .
Melanie:	Oh, I read them all the time – you never know!
Pascale:	It's all too complicated for me. I think I'll join a gym or something.

Reading your horoscope

And what of the other great personal section of the newspapers – the horoscopes? Here you find plenty of adjectives to describe people. Here's a look at some common ones:

Words to Know

Positive adjectives	Negative adjectives
generous	stingy
placid	fiery
selfless	selfish
optimistic	pessimistic
funny	serious
sceptical	gullible
sociable	unsociable
reliable	unreliable
modest	boastful

Horoscopes often use future tenses, lots of definitive phrases (because everything has been arranged by the stars and the planets!) and plenty of possibility for alternative actions (because we're all a bit different!). You find examples of the following language in horoscopes.

Modal verbs

Plenty of verb structures like *will, may, might* and *could* talk about possibility or probability:

- ✔ You will meet a tall, dark stranger. (Definite.)

- ✔ You may / might meet a tall, dark stranger. (Possible.)

- ✔ You could meet a tall, dark stranger. (Not very likely.)

- ✔ You won't meet a tall, dark stranger. (Impossible.)

Star signs

The twelve star signs are:

Aries	The Ram	Libra	The Scales
Taurus	The Bull	Scorpio	The Scorpion
Gemini	The Twins	Sagittarius	The Archer
Cancer	The Crab	Capricorn	The Goat
Leo	The Lion	Aquarius	The Water Carrier
Virgo	The Virgin	Pisces	The Fish

You usually say 'I'm Aries' or 'I'm an Aries'.

Conditionals

In the context of horoscopes you use conditionals to talk about things that may happen if something else also happens:

- ✔ If you work hard, you will surely be promoted today.
- ✔ If you continue to be generous, true love will find you.

Imperatives

In horoscopes, you use imperatives (the infinitive form of the verb) to direct advice:

- ✔ Don't try to do too much today.
- ✔ Stay away from temptation at the pub!

Straight Talking

 Juan and Peter are sitting in the pub after work. Peter is looking depressed.

Peter: I knew it was going to be a bad day when I read my horoscope!

Juan: Your what?

Peter: Horoscope.

Juan: You don't believe them, do you?

Peter:	It was exactly right today. Listen: 'Your fiery nature will get you into trouble today at work with a sceptical superior who will think you are unreliable. Keep your mouth closed, don't boast about your achievements and you may survive the day!'
Juan:	What does 'fiery' mean?
Peter:	Umm . . . unpredictable, maybe a little bad-tempered.
Juan:	Right! What about 'sceptical'?
Peter:	That's like when someone doesn't believe everything you tell them.
Juan:	Well, that makes sense – you're certainly fiery!
Peter:	I'm not! But you know what Mike's like – he never believes a word I tell him.
Juan:	Well, I hope you kept your mouth shut for the day?
Peter:	I wish! Anyway, let's have a look at yours!
Juan:	You really believe in these things?
Peter:	Of course! Let's see. 'Your generous and sociable nature will shine today–'
Juan:	Oh yes, that sounds exactly like me!

Deciphering Signs

Signs are often a problematic source of information. Sometimes they involve unfamiliar pictures and images, and other times they have complicated instructions or phrases that can be difficult to understand. In this section we take a look at some of the more common signs around town.

One of the most important areas to understand is road signs. Look out for common features in these:

- ✔ Signs with a red triangle, as Figure 10-1a shows, usually give warnings about potential dangers.
- ✔ Signs with a red circle, as Figure 10-1b shows, usually give instructions.

> ✔ A sign with a blue or green background (Figure 10-1c) usually gives directions; green for major roads, and blue for motorways.

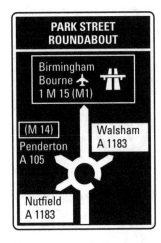

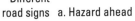

Figure 10-1:
Different
road signs
in Britain.

 a. Hazard ahead

 b. No right turn

c. Motorways are shown on a blue background; other major roads on a green background

For more on signs in driving, see www.driving-test-success.com/uk-road-signs.htm.

Signs often use imperatives – look out for them because they usually tell you what you are and are not allowed to do. Some official signs also tell you what happens to you if you ignore them – sometimes this can be a fine (money you have to pay) or prosecution (when you're arrested by the police and have to go to court later). Here are some frequent British signs and where you may find them:

> ✔ **No Smoking:** Plenty of places – pubs, restaurants, public transport, public venues such as libraries and so on.

✔ **No Trespassing:** On private property; this sign tells you that you aren't allowed to enter the property.

✔ **No Parking:** Also very common; watch for fines!

✔ **No Waiting:** On high streets and other busy roads; it means you aren't allowed to park your car there.

✔ **No Swimming:** At lakes, rivers and beaches that are considered to be dangerous; you won't find this sign at the swimming pool, but you may find lots of other signs about diving, eating and so on.

No Junk Mail

✔ **No Commercial/Junk Mail:** On letter boxes; if you're delivering commercial mail such as brochures and similar products then please be kind and respect the wishes of the owner.

No Fly Posting

> ✔ **No Fly Posting:** On walls, shop windows and so on; it means you can't put posters there.

As you can see, signs are usually quite clear – if you see 'no' on a sign then you're not supposed to do something. If you don't recognise the words on the sign, take a good look at the picture as it often helps. And if you see a sign saying 'Beware of the Dog', it's a good idea not to open the gate or the door!

Filling in Forms

At some point during your stay in Britain you'll probably have to fill in some forms. As in most countries, Britain has forms for everything: if you want a new passport or a visa, if you want to open a bank account or get an Internet connection at home, to join a gym or a library or a DVD rental shop . . .

Most forms have plenty of elements in common, but you do need to get them right. Official people are very particular about their forms, and they like you to complete them properly.

You usually need to fill in forms in black (or blue) ink, and in BLOCK CAPITALS – and make sure you write clearly in the spaces provided! Sometimes you won't have to write anything, but someone asks you the questions and fills the form in for you, often on a computer.

Straight Talking

Goran is applying for a visa to visit Vietnam for a holiday.

Official:	Right, I need to ask you a few questions for the application form.
Goran:	Sure, no problem!
Official:	Surname?
Goran:	I'm sorry?
Official:	Your surname . . . um . . . family name?
Goran:	Oh yes, I see. It's Simic: S-I-M-I-C.

Official:	First names?
Goran:	Goran: G-O-R-A-N.
Official:	Date and place of birth?
Goran:	Fourth of May, nineteen eighty-two, Zagreb, Croatia.
Official:	Nationality – Croatian, I suppose?
Goran:	Yes, that's right.
Official:	Passport number?
Goran:	Seven-two-seven-one-three-eight-two-four-nine.
Official:	Date and place of issue?
Goran:	I'm sorry, I don't understand.
Official:	When and where did you get your passport?
Goran:	Oh, okay – twenty-seventh of July, two thousand and seven, here in London.
Official:	Purpose of your visit?
Goran:	It's for a holiday, actually.
Official:	Single entry visa?
Goran:	Sorry?
Official:	How many times will you be visiting Vietnam?
Goran:	Oh, just once.
Official:	Good, thanks – I'll just print this and then you can sign it.

A type of form that you may need to complete is a job application form. If you fill in this kind of form, be prepared to write about the following things:

✔ **Your education and qualifications:** British people usually put the type of education and the place in reverse order, like this:

University of Barcelona (UAB), 1989–93 – BA in English Philology, First Class

If you have a degree or anything higher then it's not usually necessary to put all the schooling you took (primary, secondary and so on), just your higher education.

- **Your work experience:** Put the name of the company or institution, the dates and your role:

  ACME Industries, 1993–97, Head of Marketing

  In some cases it's a good idea to expand on this, explaining exactly what your role was:

  My job involved overall responsibility for corporate marketing as well as managing the marketing team of 20 people across our 4 international offices

- **Your hobbies and interests:** Keep it simple and put down things you enjoy. For more on hobbies, see Chapter 7.

- **Your skills:** Here you usually put languages, driving licences and any awards or certificates for relevant skills. Don't say you speak a language if you don't – but if you do want to mention your language skills, try this:

  Fluent spoken and written Spanish (mother tongue)

  Fluent spoken English

  Intermediate Portuguese

  Good working knowledge of Catalan

Writing Letters

These days the informal letter has almost disappeared in English, with people preferring to send emails, use social networks such as Facebook or send a quick SMS. However, at times you need to write a more formal letter, so you need to know a little bit about the structure of writing letters in English.

Here are some simple rules:

1. **Start by putting your address at the top on the right.**

2. **Add the address of the person you're writing to on the left, below your own. Add the date too.**

3. **Start your message with 'Dear'.**

   If you know the person you're writing too, you can use their first name – Dear Michael – or, if the relationship is more formal, Dear Mr Jones. If you don't know the name of the person you're writing to, you can use 'Dear Sir' or 'Dear Madam'. And if you don't know the name or the sex of the person you're writing to, write 'Dear Sir or Madam'.

4. **Write your letter in clear paragraphs, remembering to be careful to avoid slang words, abbreviations and bad spelling.**

5. **Finish your letter with 'Yours sincerely', if you started with a name, or 'Yours faithfully' if you started the letter with no name.**

Here's an example of a letter applying for a job:

John Dunn & Sons Ltd., 17 The Square Luton Bedfordshire LU12 9TR	13 Greenbrooke Terrace, London SW16 8ED

Monday 12th January, 2010

Dear Sir or Madam,

I'm writing with reference to your advertisement in *The Times* of today in which you advertise for a marketing executive for an immediate start in your Luton branch.

As you will see from my CV (enclosed), I have 20 years' experience in the field and am currently actively seeking work after a short break working for the VSO in Mongolia.

I would be grateful if you would give my CV your consideration and am available for interview at your convenience should you be interested in my particular skills and experience.

I look forward to hearing from you.

Yours faithfully,

Juan Serra

Communicating Electronically

We talk about writing and sending text messages in Chapter 8. The other major form of electronic written English is email. Most jobs these days require you to make some use of email, so knowing the conventions is a good idea.

You don't usually need to start emails with the same sort of greetings you might use for other written correspondence such as letters. Formal letters start with Dear Sir or Dear Madam, or Dear Mr Johnson, but emails often omit the salutation and start with the first name, or Mr plus name.

Ending an email is usually less formal too. A formal letter often ends with 'Yours sincerely' (for letters starting with Dear plus name) or 'Yours faithfully' (for letters starting with Dear Sir or Madam). Emails often end with phrases such as 'Best wishes', or simply 'Best'.

However, you write some emails in formal language when they relate to work or official matters. With friends and family you can be as informal as you'd normally be when speaking to them.

Differentiating between Spoken and Written English

The main difference between spoken and written English is probably a question of formality – with written English tending to be more formal – but it's not quite as simple as that.

The level of formality depends on the context of your communication. Written English can also be quite informal (as with text messages, email and so on), and equally spoken English can be quite formal (think of a news broadcast on the television, for example).

 As with most languages, context is king. Try to think about where you are and who you're speaking or writing to. An email to your boss is different to an email to your partner – in the first you may write 'I was wondering if you'd like to get together for dinner tonight to discuss . . .', and in the second perhaps 'Hey, honey! Dinner later? XXX'. So, written language can be formal or informal – it depends who you're writing for.

Abbreviations are common in text messaging, but many professional people write complete sentences in texts and write emails as if writing a traditional letter. If you reply to someone then copy their style as much as possible – at least in a professional setting.

If you do a presentation at work, it may be inappropriate to use a lot of slang and colloquial expressions. You need to know your audience! Assessing who you're writing or talking to is a valuable skill. Watch out for examples of spoken and written English as you move around during the day, and make a mental note of the situation and the people involved. After a while these things come more naturally.

Unlike a lot of languages, English doesn't have a more polite or formal mode of address or verb structure, so formality comes from your choice of words and your intonation – or the structure of your written texts that indicates formality.

One of the big errors people often make when speaking a new language is using too many slang terms and swear words because they think this makes them sound more native. Be particularly careful with swearing in English. Swear words that aren't strong in your own language may be very offensive when translated into English – and many embarrassing situations arise.

Swearing from non-native speakers of languages can often sound a little forced and unnatural. Again, the trick is to wait and listen – find out who swears around you and when, and then if you feel comfortable and swearing is something that you'd naturally do, you can start to experiment. Remember, though, that people listening to you may find it a little strange.

Swearing in written English (apart from in novels and other literature) is quite rare, and you should do so with caution.

Fun & Games

● ●

1. Match the adjective with the description.

How would you describe someone who:

   1) Buys gifts and drinks for people regularly?....................

   2) Always helps other people?   ....

   3) Jokes about everything? ....

   4) Likes going to parties and social gatherings?   ....

   5) Always expects the worst to happen?   ....

   6) Has a high opinion of herself?   ....

   7) Doesn't believe everything she's told?   ....

   8) Lets people down a lot? ....

   9) Has a very calm nature?....................

   10) Believes everything she's told?   ....

sociable	generous	pessimistic	gullible	unreliable
sceptical	selfless	placid	funny	boastful

Key:

   1) Generous

   2) Selfless

   3) Funny

   4) Sociable

   5) Pessimistic

   6) Boastful

   7) Sceptical

   8) Unreliable

   9) Placid

   10) Gullible

(continued)

2. Are these examples of spoken or written English?

1) Choose one of the options below. ....

2) CU@8 in the pub X ....

3) What're you up to, mate? ....

4) I am looking forward to hearing from you. ....

5) Hi, John, it's Gary – how's it going? ....

6) Smoking is prohibited in the building. ....

7) Have you got a second? ....

8) That's the end of my presentation. Any questions? ....

9) Flyposters will be prosecuted. ....

10) And in today's headlines, the prime minister's under pressure. ....

Key:

1) Written

2) Written

3) Spoken

4) Written

5) Spoken

6) Written

7) Spoken

8) Spoken

9) Written

10) Spoken

Part III
English on the Go

"There are several appropriate English curses you could scream at this point, let's review..."

In this part . . .

We hope that you get the opportunity to visit the UK, and to practise your English while you are there. The first thing you need to pack is this book! In this part, we give you lots of phrases related to travel and moving around that you can use. We help you to deal with banks and credit cards, and show you where and how to change money. We also help you with travel arrangements such as booking into a hotel, or asking for directions and using public transport in a new city. We include a chapter on how to handle emergencies, and how to describe health problems, as well as legal issues.

We hope you won't need to use the emergencies chapter, and that you'll spend most of your time referring to the travel sections. Enjoy your trip to the UK!

Chapter 11

Money, Money, Money

● ●

In This Chapter

▶ Using cash machines and credit cards in the UK

▶ Visiting the bank

▶ Changing money

▶ Sending and receiving money to and from another country

● ●

*R*egardless of the amount of money you have to spend while you're in Britain, whether on holiday or working, this chapter is a good place to find out the ins and outs of spending it.

Like a lot of countries, Britain relies more on 'plastic' (credit and debit cards) than it does on cash these days, and it's more normal to pay by card than any other way. You can still pay in cash, of course, and use cash machines at most major banks and building societies as well as in large shopping centres.

Splashing the Cash: Coins and Notes

Unlike most of continental Europe, Britain hasn't joined the euro currency yet and still retains its own currency made up of 'pounds' and 'pence'.

The coins in Britain are the following:

▶ 1p (one pence, or one 'p')

▶ 2p

▶ 5p

▶ 10p

▶ 20p

▶ 50p

▶ £1 (one pound)

▶ £2

And the notes are:

- £5 (five pounds)
- £10
- £20
- £50

Banknotes are different colours so they're easy to distinguish from each other. You find a picture of the Queen on each of them. Besides the Queen, you also find pictures of famous people on the banknotes. These change, but currently they are: Elizabeth Fry, social reformer (£5); Charles Darwin, naturalist (£10); Sir Edward Elgar, composer (£20); Adam Smith, moral philosopher (£20); and Sir John Houblon, former governor of the Bank of England (£50).

Here are some useful words for talking about money:

Words to Know

pay (in) cash	pay by cheque	pay by card
'Do you take cards?'		
pay in a cheque	cash a cheque	take money out
pay money in	cashier	safety deposit box
coins	notes	

Getting Your Money from a Cash Machine

Some people like machines that talk (not us – we hate getting into lifts and being talked to: doors closing . . . going up . . .), and you need to get used to a certain type of language when dealing with them. If you use a cash card from your home country, you may get offered a menu in your own language, but more often than not you have to get your cash out in English. Here's what you need to know:

1. **Insert your card, enter your PIN (*Personal Identification Number*, which is your four-digit number) and push the green confirm button.**

2. **Select a service, such as withdrawing cash.**

   You can also check how much money you have (your balance), and other things.

3. **Select the amount you want to withdraw or enter a particular amount.**

4. **Decide whether you want a receipt.**

   You're usually given a choice of viewing the receipt on the screen, printing it out or not having a receipt at all.

5. **Take your card, then take your cash and receipt.**

   Many cash machines make a noise at this point to remind you that your cash is waiting. If you don't take your cash pretty quickly you may find the machine taking it back!

Sometimes something may go wrong and the machine may 'swallow' your card (keep it). A telephone number to call is generally displayed on the machine in case of emergencies.

Make a note in your diary of the telephone numbers on the back of your credit and debit cards – if you lose your cards or somebody steals them, you can phone and cancel them before someone spends all your money!

Funny money

Here are some useful phrases connected with money:

✔ Pay through the nose for something (pay too much money for something): 'He paid through the nose for that car.'

✔ Cost an arm and a leg (cost a lot of money): 'That meal cost an arm and a leg.'

✔ Be worth a pretty penny (have a high value): 'That new house of theirs must be worth a pretty penny.'

✔ Not have two pennies to rub together (be very poor): 'Since he lost his job they haven't had two pennies to rub together.'

✔ Go Dutch (share the costs between people): 'Shall we go Dutch on dinner?'

✔ Be hard up (not have a lot of money): 'I'm really hard up this month since I paid all the bills.'

✔ Be on the house (free, paid by the owner): 'It's my birthday,' said the owner, 'drinks are on the house.'

✔ Laugh all the way to the bank (make a lot of money). 'Since they published their book they've been laughing all the way to the bank.'

✔ Have more money than sense (spend too much money carelessly). 'He's bought another sports car – he's got more money than sense.'

✔ Set you back (cost): 'A house like that will probably set you back about £300,000.'

Using Your Credit Card

We probably don't need to give you a lesson in banking or looking after your money – but just make sure that you keep track of what you're spending when you're in another country.

Most shops, restaurants, pubs, petrol stations and other places in the UK accept credit cards and you should have no problem paying with them. Some smaller shops may have a minimum charge for credit cards because it costs them money to accept payment by credit card, so it's good to ask before you start shopping.

Paying by card

Britain operates on a system called 'chip and pin', which means that all cards have a little computer chip inside them that operates by using a 'pin code' (Personal Identification Number or PIN). When you pay the shop assistant asks you to 'punch in your PIN' or 'enter your PIN'. This means that you have no paper to sign. It's said to be a much more secure system than the old one.

If you have an older credit card with no chip and pin, you should still be able to use the card almost everywhere (though we have had some problems with vending machines such as those used on the London Underground).

Straight Talking

Piotr is at his local *gastropub* (a pub that serves good food as well as drinks). He's having dinner with Michael, a colleague.

Piotr:	Hi, I'd like to order some food and drinks, please.
Bartender:	No problem. What number table are you at?
Piotr:	Oh, I don't know.
Bartender:	The numbers are on the table top – a small round metal tag. I need the number so we can bring you your food.
Piotr	Okay, one second. [He goes to look for the number.] Okay, it's table fourteen.
Bartender:	Great! What can I get you?

Piotr:	One fish and chips and one steak and ale pie, please. And a bottle of the Chilean red wine you recommend.
Bartender:	Okay, that's twenty-four sixty-five please. [Piotr hands over a credit card.] Do you want me to keep this here in case you want more food or drink?
Piotr:	Sure, thanks very much.
Bartender:	Okay – we'll bring everything over when it's ready.

[At the end of the evening, Piotr goes to pay.]

Bartender:	That's thirty-nine seventy-four in total, please. I'll just put that through for you.
Piotr:	It's a foreign card, not chip and pin.
Bartender:	No problem. Here's your receipt – and if you could just sign this for me, please?
Piotr:	Sure. And thanks for everything.
Bartender:	You're welcome, sir. Have a good evening.

Many pubs keep your credit card behind the bar, enabling you to buy drinks and food all evening and pay one bill when you leave, instead of paying each time. This is more convenient for you and cheaper for them. Try asking at the bar if you're planning an evening out.

Losing your card

It happens! If you lose your credit cards or someone steals your wallet, you need to act quickly. If you happen to simply lose your wallet then all you need to do is phone the emergency numbers on the back of your cards (you did write them down, right?), cancel them and order replacements. If someone steals your wallet, on the other hand, it's best to cancel your cards but also report the theft to the police – this makes sure that your bank knows you've done everything possible to minimise problems (head to Chapter 14 for advice on reporting a crime).

Straight Talking

 Someone has stolen Gina's purse and she is phoning the credit card company to cancel her cards.

Card company:	Credit International, Stephen speaking, how can I help you?
Gina:	Yes, hello. I've had my purse stolen and I'd like to cancel my cards, please.
Card company:	I'm sorry to hear that, madam. I just need to get some basic information from you, if that's okay?
Gina:	Of course, no problem.
Card company:	Okay, could I have your full name please?
Gina:	Sure, it's Gina Li.
Card company:	Is that L-I?
Gina:	That's right.
Card company:	Great, and can you confirm which of our cards you have, please?
Gina:	Yes, I had a CI Shopping and a CI Classic.
Card company:	Okay. Now I need to ask you a couple of security questions. First, your date of birth, please?
Gina:	It's the third of April, nineteen seventy-two.
Card company:	And your mother's maiden name?
Gina:	Wang.
Card company:	Thank you, Ms Li. I'll just cancel those cards for you now and order some new ones for you.
Gina:	That's very kind, thank you.
Card company:	Can you confirm the address for the new cards, please?

Gina:	Yes, it's thirteen Wood Drive, London, NW1.
Card company:	No problem. The cards should be with you in three or four days. Is there anything else I can do for you today?
Gina:	No, thank you – you've been very helpful.

Using a Bank

Banks are usually open in the morning and afternoon up until somewhere between 3.30 and 5 p.m. with bigger branches often staying open all day. As with most other countries, you'll probably end up queuing for some time, and – if you're as lucky as we are – you'll always find yourself queuing behind the guy who wants to change his lifetime collection of one-pence coins into banknotes.

The most common things people do in banks in Britain are the following:

✔ Pay money into their account

✔ Take money out of their account

✔ Cash a cheque

✔ Change money

✔ Arrange a bank loan

✔ Pay bills

A bank may often have a separate counter for foreign transactions like changing money and different desks for different operations – arranging loans, and so on. Make sure you're in the right queue from the beginning. You usually find a sign on desks or above counters. If you just want to do basic operations such as cashing a cheque, then you should be fine in any queue that says 'Cashier'.

Straight Talking

Chrysanthi is at the bank, trying to get some change.

Cashier: Next, please.

Chrysanthi: Hi, I'd like to change some notes into coins, please.

Cashier:	No problem, what do you need?
Chrysanthi:	Could I have ten pounds of ten-pence coins, ten pounds of twenty-pence coins and twenty pounds of fifty-pence coins, please?
Cashier:	Okay, there we go – that's forty pounds, please.
Chrysanthi:	Oh, sorry, I haven't quite finished yet. Could I also have fifty pounds of one pound coins, five of two-pence coins and five of one-pence coins?
Cashier:	Right, that makes a total of one hundred pounds, please.
Chrysanthi:	Great, thanks. I'd also like to cash this cheque, please.
Cashier:	I'm afraid we can't cash that cheque – you need to pay it into an account. Do you have an account with us?
Chrysanthi:	Yes, I do – I'll pay it in then, thanks.

If you plan to open a bank account in Britain, do some research to find out which one offers you the services you need, and how much they charge for those services. A large number of online banks exist these days and they're often cheaper to use and offer better rates. With an *online bank* you can do most of your banking from home or an internet cafe, and use cash machines for the rest.

Opening an account can take a lot of time and a lot of patience. You need to be able to prove that you're legally resident in Britain and have somewhere to live. Banks often ask for *utility bills* – things like gas, electricity or phone bills that have your address on them. The British bank may want to do a credit check on you, and all these things can take time. Allow at least three weeks for opening an account and make sure you have enough money with you to cover that period.

Changing Money

You can change money in Britain in various ways – you can do it at a bank or a change bureau (these are usually marked with a multilingual sign that says 'Change, Cambio, Wechsel' and so on) or in various shops and even with people on the street in major cities.

You should be able to change most currencies at a dedicated exchange office, but if you're coming from a smaller country or one where the currency is a little volatile then you may have problems. Banks can order foreign currencies and may be able to help you with any problems you may encounter at a change office.

Don't forget that there are two rates for currency exchange – the rate that the office or bank buys your currency for and the rate at which they sell you currencies. The only thing to know here is that the currency exchanger always wins, so don't spend too much time looking around for the best deals! Find somewhere that doesn't charge you commission and change your money there. Airports often offer worse rates than offices in cities, so wait until you're in town before changing.

Banks and money exchange offices (or exchange bureau, bureau de change) are the most reliable ways of changing money. Smaller, unofficial change operations in shops or on street corners can often seem attractive (no commission, a better rate of exchange) but you put yourself at risk for disaster if you change money with somebody who may be dishonest. If you do try to change money with one of these operations, keep an eye out for false banknotes and potential danger. We really can't recommend this option.

Straight Talking

Goran is at a bureau de change in London.

Goran:	Hi, I'd like to change some Euros into pounds, please.
Cashier:	No problem. How much do you want to change?
Goran:	Two hundred and seventy Euros, please.
Cashier:	Sure. That works out at one hundred and sixty pounds and fifty-nine pence.
Goran:	That's fine, thanks.
Cashier:	How would you like that?
Goran:	I'm sorry?
Cashier:	Big notes, smaller ones?

Goran:	Oh, I see. Could I have twenties, please?
Cashier:	Sure – here you go. That's twenty, forty, sixty, eighty, one hundred, and twenty, forty, sixty and fifty-nine pence.
Goran:	Thanks very much.
Cashier:	You're welcome – and here's your receipt. If you could just sign one copy for me.
Goran:	Sure – here you are.
Cashier:	Thank you. Enjoy your stay in London.
Goran:	I'm sure I will, thanks very much.

Britain has a lot of mythology about money, especially in London. If you believe TV programmes set in London then you'll think that everyone speaks 'cockney' and talks in riddles. You may see references to a *pony* (twenty-five pounds) or a *monkey* (five hundred pounds) or to *sky divers* (that's *fivers* or five-pound notes, also known as *taxi drivers* and *McGyvers*!) – but these words are only really common on TV and in books, so it's best not to use any of them.

Like most languages, English has a variety of ways of referring to money and it's not often you hear anyone say 'five pounds and sixty-nine pence, please'. If you're out shopping, you're more likely to hear 'that's five sixty-nine, please' and if you're watching TV adverts then you'll probably quickly get used to hearing things like 'only five six nine'.

There's a catch here, of course: 'five sixty-nine' means five pounds and sixty-nine pence, whereas 'five six nine' means five hundred and sixty-nine pounds. So be careful when you're buying – that new sofa may seem like a good bargain, but it may be a lot more than you think!

To really sound like a financial native, you'll need the following words:

- **A fiver** (five pounds): 'Can I borrow a fiver, please?'
- **A tenner** (ten pounds): Note that you can't have a 'twentier' or a 'fiftier'.
- **Just under a tenner:** This usually means £9.99.
- **A grand** (one thousand pounds): 'He sold his flat for four hundred grand'.
- **Quid** (a pound): 'Could you lend me ten quid, please?'
- **Dosh** (money in general): 'I'm out of dosh, again!'

Sending and Receiving Money to and from Another Country

Many people who visit Britain to work want to send money back to their home country or, perhaps, have money sent to them if times are hard. This would have been quite complicated a few years ago, but any big town or city now offers you a variety of ways of doing this.

You can, of course, use traditional methods such as bank transfers, but often the fees are high and the transaction can take a long time. The person receiving the money also needs to have a bank account for you to transfer the money to. Although this should be an easy way to do things, the differences between banking methods in many countries can complicate things considerably. Another way to send or receive money is via a money transfer company.

You can find money transfer services (via a reputable company such as Western Union) in newsagents, hair salons, cafes and more. Because of the variety and availability of these services, check that the company is well known before using it. Note that some larger companies allow you to send money online, by phone or by visiting one of their agents.

When you send money you pay a commission (as you do when you change money) – be sure to check how much it's going to cost you before agreeing to anything. Note that for large amounts (usually over six hundred pounds) you usually need to present at least one form of identification such as a passport or driving licence.

Generally, you need to fill out a money transfer form, hand over the cash and the fee and show some identification, and then the cashier gives you a receipt and a tracking number. You can share this tracking number with the person you're sending the money for when they go to a local venue to collect the money. Watch out for restrictions on how much you can send with each visit; rules may vary.

Straight Talking

Gina is at a money transfer office in Manchester.

Gina: Hi, I'd like to send some money to my family in Shenzhen, please.

Cashier: Okay, how much are you thinking of sending?

Gina: Two thousand five hundred pounds, please.

Cashier:	Right, I'm going to need to see two forms of identification for that, as it's over two thousand pounds.
Gina:	Sure! What kind of ID do you need?
Cashier:	I need one document that proves you are who you say you are, something like a passport or driving licence, and one with your name and current address on it, something like a utilities bill – gas, phone, you know.
Gina:	No problem. Here's my passport and a letter from my bank. Is that okay?
Cashier:	Absolutely! Now, you'll need to fill out this money transfer form and then bring it to me along with the money plus the transfer fee of sixty pounds.
Gina:	Oh, I see. I didn't realise it would cost so much.
Cashier:	Well, the fee covers our time plus any exchange services, and of course your money does arrive within a couple of hours or so, which is much quicker than using a bank.
Gina:	Yes, of course.
Cashier:	You could try our website – it's usually cheaper online, but you won't be able to send as much each time.
Gina:	No, it's fine, thanks. I'll just fill in the form.

Fun & Games

1. Rearrange the letters to make the money words.

UEHQCE   A paper document used to pay for something
_____

SHAIREC   Person who works in a bank
_____

RCYNRUCE   The money of a country (such as pounds, roubles)
_____

TOCNUAC   Where your money is kept at the bank
_____

GHEXNACE   You can change money at a currency
_____

RNENTE   A slang word for ten pounds
_____

CIPERTE   Paper given to you when you pay for something
_____

GANHCE   Money returned to you when you pay for something
_____

POIETDS   Pay money into your bank account
_____

DWHTIRWA   Take money out of your bank account
_____

Key:

Cheque, cashier, currency, account, exchange, tenner, receipt, change, deposit, withdraw

2. Put the cash machine instructions in the most logical order.

Select the amount you want to withdraw or key in a different amount.

Insert your card.

Select a service (withdraw cash).

Take your card.

Choose a language.

Confirm you would like a receipt.

Enter your PIN number.

Take your cash and receipt.

Key (other answers are possible):

1. Insert your card.

2. Enter your PIN number.

3. Choose a language.

4. Select a service (withdraw cash).

5. Select the amount to withdraw or key in a different amount.

6. Confirm you would like a receipt.

7. Take your card.

8. Take your cash and receipt.

Chapter 12

Finding a Place to Stay

. . . .

In This Chapter

▶ Choosing where to stay

▶ Booking a hotel room

▶ Checking in and out

▶ Expressing complaints

. . . .

*I*f you travel to the UK on holiday, you may want to stay in a hotel. Many different categories of hotel exist, and as in most countries, how much you're prepared to pay determines the kind of hotel you can stay in. You have many options, from cheaper hostels and B&Bs to more expensive hotels. But as any traveller knows, a cheap hotel doesn't necessarily mean bad quality, and you can find inexpensive, high-quality accommodation all over the UK, especially outside of the major cities and tourist areas.

Finding Accommodation

Britain has accommodation to suit everyone and all budgets. Apart from the usual hostels, B&Bs and hotels, you can find other types of accommodation in the UK such as farmhouses, inns, cottages, self-catering apartments (where you have your own cooking facilities), country house hotels and even castles.

You can use the Internet to search for accommodation, and the British Tourist Board website (www.visitbritain.com/en/accommodation) is a good place to start. Travel websites such as www.expedia.co.uk and www.lastminute.com are often good places to find hotels at bargain rates.

Youth hostels

If keeping your costs down is important for you, you can find a wide range of budget accommodation available in the UK. At the cheapest end of the scale are youth hostels, also called backpackers' hostels. You find these in most major cities, not only in the UK but in many other countries as well.

You usually sleep in a shared dormitory (or 'dorm'), often in bunk beds, with separate dormitories for men and women. Some youth hostels also have a small number of single and double rooms, so you don't always have to stay in a dormitory. Youth hostels often have kitchen facilities, so that you can prepare your own meals.

Although they're called 'youth' hostels (for young people), there's no age limit, but you normally need a youth hostel membership card to be able to stay there. Some youth hostels may have a limit on the number of nights you can stay. You can find information about youth hostels in the UK at www.yha.org.uk.

Guesthouses and B&Bs

If sharing a dormitory with a group of strangers isn't your idea of fun, the next most inexpensive option is to find a cheap guesthouse or B&B. B&B stands for 'bed and breakfast', but people usually refer to them simply as B&Bs (pronounced 'bee and bees'). Many B&Bs are run by families, and you rent a room in their private house. In smaller B&Bs, you may be lucky enough to have your own bathroom but you may have to share a bathroom with other guests. The B&B usually has a shared lounge, often with a TV, and a breakfast room. Family B&Bs don't usually offer services such as room service or laundry. Other B&Bs are simply small hotels, in which rooms may have private bathrooms. You may also have other facilities such as room service and laundry.

People often choose to stay in B&Bs rather than in small hotels because they're less impersonal than hotels, and you often get to meet your hosts. In very busy towns, such as Brighton, York and Edinburgh, B&Bs display a sign in the window that says 'Vacancies' or 'No Vacancies'. This way you can easily see whether the B&B has a room available (a *vacancy*) or not. Breakfast in a B&B is usually available on demand – that is, your host may ask you what you'd like for breakfast, and cook it for you on the spot. You can usually choose between a full English breakfast and a continental breakfast.

Hotels

Hotels range from those with fewer facilities, and rated with no or one star, to luxury five-star hotels with all the facilities you could imagine! Basically, with hotels you pay for what you get – you pay less for fewer services, and you pay more for more services.

Living in a hotel

Several famous people have lived in hotels. One famous resident of the Savoy Hotel in London was the actor Richard Harris (1930–2002). They say that shortly before he died he was taken out of the hotel on a stretcher to an ambulance, and as he passed through the dining room he raised his hand and said in good humour to guests having dinner 'It was the food'!

Straight Talking

 Maria is on holiday in Scotland. She visits the tourist office in Edinburgh to find out about accommodation in Glasgow.

Tourist office employee: Good morning. Can I help you?

Maria: Yes, please. I'd like to spend a few days in Glasgow. Can you give me some information about accommodation, please?

Tourist office employee: Certainly. What sort of hotel would you like to stay in? Glasgow has a wide range of inexpensive hotels, and of course plenty of middle range and more expensive hotels.

Maria: Something not too expensive, please.

Tourist office employee: Here's the list of middle range hotels, of two or three stars. Take a look at this, and see if there's anything that suits you.

Maria: Thank you. [She looks at the list.] These all look a little out of my price range. What about outside Glasgow? Are there any hotels a bit further from the centre of the city?

Tourist office employee: We do have information about cottages and country hotels in the area around Glasgow, but these are quite far out of town, and without your own transport it will be difficult to get into town. The cheapest place to stay would be the youth hostel, which is in Glasgow itself, in the West End.

Maria: Okay, thanks. The youth hostel sounds like the best option.

Tourist office employee: Here's the phone number. You can call them and see if they have a bed available. I think it's dormitory accommodation in the youth hostel, with bunk beds, but you can check when you phone them.

Words to Know

accommodation	tourist office
one-star/two-star/three-star hotel	farmhouse
inn	cottage
self-catering apartment	country house hotel
youth hostel / backpackers' hostel	dormitorybunk beds

Expensive hotels have lots of services and luxurious facilities. Middle range hotels have an average number of services and facilities. What are the differences between services and facilities? A hotel *service* is something the hotel does for you, such as *room service* (bringing your food to your room). A hotel *facility* is something that the hotel has, such as a gym or a swimming pool. However, many hotels use these two words interchangeably.

Some of the services you can expect in the average UK hotel include laundry service, room service and newspaper delivery. Depending on the type of hotel you stay in, the hotel may have facilities such as a swimming pool, a sauna, a gym, free parking and air conditioning. In the larger, more expensive hotels you may find a gift shop, or even a hairdresser's or a beauty salon!

The average hotel offers some of the following facilities in your room: an Internet connection, satellite TV, coffee- and tea-making facilities, a safe to keep your valuables and a minibar.

Most hotels in the UK are non-smoking. It's against the law in the UK to smoke in common areas such as the hotel lobby, lifts, the dining room or restaurant and in the hotel bar. In some hotels it may be possible to book a *smoking room* (a room in which you're allowed to smoke) but this is increasingly uncommon. If you want to smoke in a hotel, you usually have to stand outside on the pavement.

Words to Know

swimming pool	beauty salon	snack bar
tennis court	air conditioning	gift shop
room service		

Remember that with compound nouns (nouns with two words) you usually put the stress, or emphasis, on the first word. So you say *swimming* pool, not swimming *pool*, or *air* conditioning, not air *conditioning*. Hotels seem to have a lot of services and facilities that use compound nouns.

Booking Your Accommodation

Reserving (or *booking*) a hotel room before you travel is always a good idea. Hotels in large cities or popular tourist destinations often fill up in advance, especially in the tourist season. You can usually find somewhere to stay, even at the last minute, but your choice of accommodation is limited if you leave booking until the last minute. Also, when you book in advance, you may be able to pay slightly less, and some hotels offer special discounts for stays during the week or for weekend stays. You can usually find out about discounts and special offers via a hotel's website, or via a local tourist office.

The quickest and easiest way to book a hotel room is over the phone. But if you're booking your accommodation from outside the UK, you may want to do it via the Internet.

Booking on the Internet

Most Internet hotel booking forms look very similar (see Figure 12-1).

Typically, they ask you to fill in the following information:

- ✔ Your arrival and departure dates
- ✔ The number of nights you'll be staying
- ✔ The type of room(s) you want
- ✔ The number of occupants for your room(s)

> **Heather View Hotel, Newcastle-upon-Tyne**
>
> Welcome to our hotel booking form. Please fill in the information below to reserve a room. When you have completed the form, please click 'Check Availability'.
>
> Date of arrival:
>
> Date of departure:
>
> Number of nights:
>
> Type of room: standard single room
>
>   standard double room
>
>   standard twin room
>
>   suite
>
> Number of occupants:
>
> **Check Availability.**
>
> To view details of our rooms follow this link: <u>Room descriptions</u>
>
> Check-in after 12.00
>
> Check-out by 11.00
>
> If you need assistance with your reservation please call us on +44 (0)191 98554, or email enquiries@heatherview.com.

Figure 12-1:
An example
of an online
booking
form.

If a room is available for the dates that you need, the website usually takes you to a page where you add your personal details, such as your name and address. Many hotels also ask for your credit card details to reserve your room, and some hotels charge your credit card in advance. Make sure you read the conditions (the *small print*) on the website before you book your room with a credit card. If you cancel your reservation, for example, you may have to pay some or all of the room fee.

Booking over the phone

If you're already in the UK, it may be easier to book a hotel room by phone. It may also be quicker to book by phone, because you can check availability of rooms immediately and either change your dates or look for another hotel if a room isn't available. When you book a hotel room by phone, you can expect the receptionist to ask for the same kind of information you need for an online hotel reservation. You need to give the date of your arrival and how many nights you'd like to stay, and say what kind of room you'd like. You may also want to ask about prices and any other facilities or services you need.

Straight Talking

 Maria and a friend are visiting Newcastle upon Tyne, and the tourist office has recommended the Heather View Hotel. Maria calls the hotel to book a room.

Receptionist: Heather View Hotel, how may I help you?

Maria: I'd like to book a room for this weekend, for Friday and Saturday night. Do you have any vacancies?

Receptionist: Just one moment, I'll check. Yes, we do have some rooms for this weekend. What kind of room would you like?

Maria: A twin room, please, with two single beds. There are two of us.

Receptionist: Would you like a twin room with an ensuite bathroom, or a room with a shared bathroom?

Maria: Ensuite please. How much is that per night?

Receptionist: It's seventy pounds a night, without VAT. It includes breakfast.

Maria: Okay, could I book the room, please?

Receptionist: Certainly, madam. Your name please?

Maria: It's Maria Sanchez.

Receptionist: Thank you, can you spell your surname, please?

Maria: It's S-A-N-C-H-E-Z.

Receptionist: Thank you. Your reservation is made then, in the name of Maria Sanchez, for two nights, this Friday and Saturday, one twin room with ensuite bathroom. That will be a total of one hundred and forty pounds, not including VAT.

Maria:	Thank you. Just a few more questions. What time is check-out on Saturday? And is there an Internet connection?
Receptionist:	Check-out is at eleven. Yes, all the rooms have WiFi Internet connections, which you need to pay for separately.
Maria:	Okay, thank you for your help. See you on Friday.
Receptionist:	You're welcome, Ms Sanchez.

Useful phrases include:

- ✔ Do you have any [rooms / vacancies]?
- ✔ How much is it per night?
- ✔ Can I see the room?
- ✔ I'd like a room facing the street.
- ✔ I'd like a room [in the back / on the ground floor].
- ✔ What time is [check-in / check-out]?
- ✔ Is breakfast included?
- ✔ Is there a [gym / laundry service / Internet connection / swimming pool]?
- ✔ Does the hotel have WiFi?
- ✔ I'd like to book a [single / double/ twin room] with an ensuite bathroom.
- ✔ Does that include VAT [value added tax]?

Be careful of the difference between a twin room and a double room. A double room usually has one double bed, and a twin room has two separate single beds. But sometimes twin rooms have one double bed instead of separate single beds. So it's best to check when you book your hotel room whether it's going to be a twin room with one bed, or a twin room with two separate beds!

Plugs in the UK are different from the plugs used in the rest of Europe and in North America. A UK plug has three square prongs, so it's a good idea to buy an adapter for your plugs before you come to the UK, or to buy one in a large town when you're in the UK. The best place to buy a plug adapter is usually in the airport. Electrical currents and voltages are universal in the UK and Europe, but may be different to North American appliances. Bring any plugs, transformers or laptop computer cables that you may need with you when you visit the UK.

Checking In

When you arrive at a hotel, you first need to check in at reception. If you have a reservation, you can give the receptionist your name and surname. Most hotels ask you to fill out a form with your personal details such as your name, home address and passport number. They may also ask for some form of identification, such as a passport or driving licence.

Straight Talking

Maria arrives at the Heather View Hotel, and checks in at reception.

Receptionist: Good afternoon, can I help you?

Maria: Yes, please. I have a reservation – my name is Maria Sanchez.

Receptionist: Yes, here it is. A twin room with ensuite bathroom, for two nights. Could you please fill in the registration form, and add your passport details here, at the bottom of the form? Please also add your signature here.

Maria: Yes, of course. The room includes breakfast, right? What time is breakfast?

Receptionist: From seven to ten on Saturdays and Sundays. You'll find the dining room on the first floor. Here's your key card.

Maria: Thanks very much.

Receptionist: Not at all, and I hope you enjoy your stay with us.

In the UK, the floor of a hotel at ground level is called the ground floor. This is different to the USA, where the floor at ground level is called the first floor! In some more expensive hotels in Britain you may find a floor called the *mezzanine floor*, which is usually between the ground floor and first floor. The mezzanine floor may have the dining room or conference rooms, and you usually access it from the ground floor.

Complaining about the Accommodation

Sometimes a hotel looks a lot better in the hotel brochure or on the website than in real life. If you find that services offered when you booked your room aren't available, or things in your room don't work properly, then you can complain to reception.

Straight Talking

Maria is having a few problems with her room in the Heather View Hotel. She goes down to reception to complain.

Maria: Excuse me, I'm afraid I need some help – I'm having a few problems with my room.

Receptionist: Oh, I'm sorry. What seems to be the problem?

Maria: The central heating in my room isn't working, so the room is too cold. Also, there's something wrong with the shower; there's very little water coming out. Could you send someone to look at it?

Receptionist: I'm terribly sorry. I'll send somebody from Maintenance up to your room right away.

Maria: That's not all. I'm having problems connecting to the Internet from the room. I wonder if you could check it for me?

Receptionist: Right, to connect to the Internet you need an access code, and you pay for that separately.

Maria: Okay, please could you give me a code and charge my room.

Receptionist: Certainly, madam. And I'm sorry about the other problems. We'll have somebody look into them right away.

Maria: Thank you. Also, I wonder if I could have some more towels and another pillow, please?

Receptionist: Yes, of course. We'll bring them to your room.

Useful phrases include:

- The room is too [hot / cold / noisy / small].
- The room isn't [warm / big] enough.
- The [shower / central heating / kettle] isn't working.
- There's something wrong with the [shower / central heating / kettle / light / phone].
- I'm having problems with . . .
- I wonder if [you / I] could . . .
- Could you get someone to take a look at it?
- Could you please send someone up?

Even if you're unhappy with the service or facilities in a hotel, always complain politely. You can use certain phrases to sound more polite when you're complaining or asking reception for help. Say 'I'm afraid I've got a complaint' or 'I'm sorry, but I've got a bit of a problem with . . . ' rather than 'I want to complain'. Ask the receptionist for help by using phrases like 'Would you mind sending someone to fix it?' or 'Do you think you could take a look at it?'. It's also important to use the right intonation with these phrases. If your voice is flat, you can sound rude or impatient.

Checking Out

Most hotels have a check-out time, which is the latest time you can leave your room. If you stay longer, you may be charged for an extra day, so find out what time check-out is when you arrive. Check-out time is usually in the morning, for example between 10 a.m. and midday. In some hotels you can arrange to stay an extra few hours, and to pay a reduced rate for this instead of paying for a full day. It's important to discuss this with reception in advance, not after check-out time.

Straight Talking

Maria is checking out of the Heather View Hotel.

Maria: I'd like to check out, please.

Receptionist: Yes, madam. What is your room number?

Maria: Room one hundred and twelve.

Receptionist: Right, that was for two nights. Did you have anything from the minibar?

Maria: No.

Receptionist: Okay, I see that you have a charge for an Internet connection. Is that correct?

Maria: Yes, that's right. I'd like to pay by credit card, please.

Receptionist: Certainly. Here's your bill, madam. I hope you've enjoyed your stay with us?

Maria: Well, I had some problems with the room when I arrived, but Maintenance came and sorted it all out very quickly; thank you for that.

Receptionist: Our pleasure. We certainly hope that it didn't affect your stay.

Maria: Not at all. Thank you for your help. Could you call me a taxi, please?

Receptionist: Yes, of course.

Fun & Games

1. What facilities and services does the City Gate Hotel offer?

Key:

1) room service

2) air conditioning

3) Internet access

4) laundry service

5) swimming pool

6) conference rooms

2. Match the words on the left with the correct definition on the right.

youth hostel	a large room with several beds
self-catering apartment	a hotel room for two people, with one double bed
budget accommodation	cheap accommodation, mainly for young people; you normally need a membership card to stay here
dormitory	inexpensive hostels and hotels
bunk beds	a hotel room for two people, with two single beds
check-in time	you need to leave your hotel room by this time
check-out time	you can occupy your hotel room from this time
twin room	one bed on top of another
double room	a private bathroom attached to a hotel room
ensuite bathroom	a place to stay with cooking / kitchen facilities

Key:

youth hostel – cheap accommodation, mainly for young people; you normally need a membership card to stay here

self-catering apartment – a place to stay with cooking / kitchen facilities

budget accommodation – inexpensive hostels and hotels

dormitory – a large room with several beds

bunk beds – one bed on top of another

check-in time – you can occupy your hotel room from this time

check-out time – you need to leave your hotel room by this time

twin room – a hotel room for two people, with two single beds

double room – a hotel room for two people, with one double bed

ensuite bathroom – a private bathroom attached to a hotel room

Chapter 13

On the Move

. . . .

In This Chapter

▶ Planning a trip

▶ Booking flights

▶ Using public transport

▶ Renting a car

▶ Finding your way around

▶ Describing places on your travels

. . . .

*I*magine it's your first time in a new city. You're keen to get around and see the sights, but you've left your guidebook at home. Not to worry – if you have enough useful phrases, you can ask your way around. You can find out not only where things are, but the best way to get there – by bus, train, Underground or on foot. In this chapter we also help you with your pre-travel arrangements, such as booking a flight, and sorting out paperwork such as visa, passport and driving licence.

Making Travel Plans

Some people say that the best part of a trip is the planning. Looking at guide-books, reading about the country, working out the best route and how to travel . . . if you have enough time to do this properly, preparing for a trip can be fun. Your trip to the UK may be for a variety of reasons. Perhaps you're coming to work or to study, or you're visiting family or friends. Perhaps you're on a holiday or a short weekend break, or on a business trip. Whatever the reason for your trip, you probably want to prepare for it as best you can.

The Chunnel

The Channel Tunnel, or 'Chunnel', is a tunnel that runs under the English Channel – the sea between England and France. The high-speed Eurostar passenger train uses the Channel Tunnel, and so do Eurotunnel roll on/roll off transport trains – these carry your car through the tunnel. Freight trains (trains carrying goods) also use the Chunnel. The idea for a tunnel between England and France goes back to 1802. But it took a long time for the idea to become reality, so the tunnel didn't open until 1994. It took six years to build and cost 80 per cent more than originally planned.

Travelling to the UK

If you decide to visit the UK, the first thing you need to arrange is how to get there. Although the UK is a collection of islands, it's still very easy to access with a combination of bus or private car and ferry, or by rail. And, of course, you can always fly in by aeroplane.

Staying legal: Visa and passport requirements

Most European Union passport holders don't need a visa, but if you're from a country outside the European Union, you must check well in advance whether you need a visa. To get a visa, your passport must be valid and not about to expire. Depending on the type of trip you're planning, you may need a different type of visa. For example, longer-term study visas are different from short-term visitor visas.

The quickest and easiest way to find out about the visa requirements for your country of origin is to check on the Internet. Try this page to get you started: www.ukvisas.gov.uk/en.

Deciding what to pack

After you decide how to travel to the UK, and what places you're going to visit, you need to decide what to pack. The weather in the UK is one of its most famous features, and you need to check what sort of clothing is appropriate for the time of year you're planning to visit. It's always a good idea to pack an umbrella in your luggage, and winters can be very cold, especially in the north. Summer, on the other hand, can be quite hot. Many public places in the UK are prepared for cold weather, and buildings and transport usually have good central heating. Public transport and public buildings usually don't have air conditioning though, so in the hot summer weather they can be extremely hot. Just ask anyone who's taken the London Underground on a hot day in August.

Apart from taking clothing that's suitable for the weather, what you pack in your suitcase depends on the type of trip you're planning. For a summer holiday or a camping trip or a backpacking holiday staying in youth hostels, you can take things such as a sleeping bag, a torch (or flashlight), a swimsuit (for women), swimming trunks (for men), sun cream, sunglasses and walking boots. For a trip in winter, or if you're expecting cold weather, you need to take a heavy coat or jacket, a scarf, gloves and a possibly a hat. For a business trip you take more formal clothing in a suitcase, such as a suit, jacket and tie. You probably take a briefcase as well, to carry meeting papers and perhaps a laptop computer.

Words to Know

suitcase	briefcase	backpack / rucksack
luggage	backpacking holiday	camping trip
business trip	sleeping bag	torch / flashlight
swimsuit	swimming trunks	sun cream
sunglasses	walking boots	coat / jacket
scarf	gloves	suit tie

When in Rome . . .

The English expression 'When in Rome, do as the Romans do' means that following the customs of the country you visit and trying to adapt as far as possible is a good idea.

Your home country may have very different traditions and customs than the UK. We suggest you find out about some of the typical behaviours and customs of your hosts before you travel. One of the most attractive things about the UK is that many of the larger cities have a wide range of cultures, nationalities and groups living in the same place – although you find big differences in attitudes and behaviours between a large cosmopolitan city such as London and a small village in rural Wales. Nowadays the UK is such a multicultural country that it's quite difficult to say what 'British' behaviour is or isn't.

What is Britishness? Certain stereotypes about British behaviour exist, but be aware that characteristics such as being cold and formal or the famous British 'stiff upper lip' are often no more than that – stereotypes. The *stiff upper lip* refers to an attitude of taking stress and adversity without showing any emotion.

The best way to prepare for the differences in customs that you find in the UK is to find out something about who you're going to stay with, or who you're going to meet, in advance. For example, if you're going to a business meeting to the UK and will meet with business people from different countries around the world, it's best to find out something about all these countries and customs.

The following British customs may be different from the customs in your own country:

- ✔ **Body language:** Hugging and kissing or touching other people is reserved for close family members only. It's not a good idea to put your arm around somebody's shoulders, for example, unless you know the person extremely well. Personal space (the distance between you and the person you're talking to) varies a lot between cultures. If you notice that somebody you're talking to slowly moves a little way back, it probably means that you're standing too close.

- ✔ **Eating out:** To call the waiter's attention, say 'Excuse me' politely. You should *never* snap your fingers to call a waiter, because this is very rude. In a pub, it's common to take turns to buy a *round* of drinks (a drink for everyone). If you eat dinner at someone's house, try not to leave any food on your plate. We talk more about eating out in Chapter 5.

- ✔ **Gifts:** If you stay in somebody's house, take a small gift for your host. You can also take a small gift such as flowers, a box of chocolates or a bottle of wine if someone invites you to dinner at their house. People usually open a gift as soon as you give it to them if it's wrapped in paper.

- ✔ **Greetings:** In the UK you usually shake hands when you first meet people, and say 'Nice to meet you'. Kissing people on the cheek is for close friends only and is very unlikely in a business context.

- ✔ **In the home:** When you visit somebody's house, the person may offer to show you around the house, although people can be very private and even close the doors to other rooms. If someone shows you around their house, it's polite to admire the furniture and decor. You never smoke in a house without permission. It's common for people to smoke outside the house, either in the street or in the garden.

Recommending places to visit

If you visit the UK on holiday but aren't sure where to go, take a look at some tourist information on the Internet or read a guidebook. Tourist board websites are a good place to start, and you could take a look at the official UK tourist board website www.visitbritain.com, which gives you information about Britain in a wide variety of languages. Different parts of Britain, such as Scotland, Yorkshire, or South-east England also have regional tourist board websites, and these can help you find interesting places to visit in areas that you already plan to go to. Simply type 'Yorkshire tourist board' (or the region of your choice) into a search engine (such as www.google.co.uk), and you can find links to the region's tourist board website.

Many people like to ask friends or family for advice, especially if they've already visited the country. You may want to ask friends in the UK itself for advice on places to visit. If you're planning to visit England, you could also pick up a copy of *England For Dummies* (Wiley)!

Many people confuse the words *trip*, *journey* and *travel*. *Trip* and *journey* are nouns, so you talk about 'a trip' and 'a journey'. A journey is generally longer and more complicated than a trip, so we suggest using the word *trip* if you aren't sure. For example, you can say 'I'm going on a trip to the UK' or 'I'm going on a business trip'. *Travel* is an abstract noun or a verb, so you talk about 'travelling to the UK' or say 'I like travel' – but never say 'I'm going on a travel'.

Straight Talking

Oscar visits the UK for the first time and asks his friend Roger for suggestions about where to go and what to see.

Oscar:	I'd like to visit the north of England, but only have two days free. Where do you suggest I go?
Roger:	You should definitely visit the Lake District. It's very beautiful and is really worth seeing.
Oscar:	Yes, I read something about it in my guidebook. It's on the way to Scotland, right?
Roger:	Well, it's south of the border with Scotland. I'd recommend Lake Windermere – it's famous for its beautiful scenery. You must see Stagshaw Garden.
Oscar:	What about places to stay? Are there a lot of hotels to choose from?

Roger:	I wouldn't recommend staying in a hotel. It would be much nicer to stay in a B&B, which is smaller and has more of a home feeling.
Oscar:	So how long should I stay at Lake Windermere? Are there other things to see nearby?
Roger:	Personally, I'd stay in one place and then you can get a bus to see other areas of interest nearby, or rent a car.
Oscar:	Okay, that sounds like a good idea. Thanks for your recommendation!

Here are some useful phrases to ask about and recommend places to visit:

- I'd like to visit . . .
- Where do you suggest I go?
- How long should I stay?
- Are there other things to see nearby?
- You should definitely visit . . .
- I'd recommend . . . / I wouldn't recommend . . .
- Personally, I'd . . . / Personally, I wouldn't . . .
- You must see . . .
- . . . is really worth seeing.

Booking a Flight

While you're in the UK, you may need to book a flight to another part of the UK or to another country. With many airlines you can do this online, but you may want to telephone a travel agency to find out about different flight options.

Straight Talking

Oscar needs to book a flight from London to Belfast for a business meeting and two days of tourism. He telephones a travel agent.

Travel agent:	Hello, Express Travel. May I help you?
Oscar:	Hello. I'd like some information about flights from London to Belfast, please.
Travel agent:	Certainly, sir. When would you like to travel?
Oscar:	I need to fly on Monday the sixteenth, in the morning, around eight a.m.
Travel agent:	And when are you coming back?
Oscar:	I'd like to come back on Thursday the nineteenth, late afternoon. My times are flexible for coming back.
Travel agent:	Right, just let me have a look . . . hmmm, the direct flights on the morning of the sixteenth are already full. There's a large international trade fair on in Belfast for that week, so it's going to be difficult to find a cheap direct flight. Are you happy to fly business or first class?
Oscar:	Well, are there any other options? For example, what about a flight via another UK airport?
Travel agent:	Just let me check availability. You could get a flight to Manchester, and then a connecting flight from there to Belfast, which would get you into Belfast around eleven a.m.
Oscar:	Hmmm – I get into Belfast very late.
Travel agent:	There's no problem with a direct flight back to London on the nineteenth. There's one leaving Belfast at five p.m.
Oscar:	That sounds fine, but the flight to Belfast sounds complicated.
Travel agent:	The only direct flights available on Monday morning to Belfast are first class or business class, I'm afraid.
Oscar:	Okay, can you hold the return flight for me and I'll check with the company whether they'll cover the expenses of business class. Otherwise I may need to fly the night before.

| Travel agent: | Certainly, sir. I can hold the return flight for you for twenty-four hours. You will need to make payment for the flight within twenty-four hours, or you may lose it. |
| Oscar: | Thanks, I'll get back to you as soon as I can. |

Words to Know

| direct flight | return flight | connecting flight |
| stopover | business class | first-class |

Here are some phrases to help you book a flight:

- ✔ I'd like some information about flights to . . .
- ✔ I need to fly [on Monday / on the fourth / in June].
- ✔ My times are flexible for coming back.
- ✔ Let me check availability.
- ✔ I can hold the return flight for you for [24 hours / one day].
- ✔ You will need to make payment for the flight within [24 hours / immediately].
- ✔ I'll get back to you as soon as I can.

Checking in and going through security

Catching a plane in the UK is very much like catching a plane anywhere in the world. When you arrive at the airport, you first need to check in, by showing your tickets and your passport at the check-in desk, and leaving any bags and suitcases that will travel in the hold of the plane. You can take hand luggage on a flight, but you need to check that your bag is small enough and that it doesn't weigh too much. Most airlines only allow one piece of hand luggage and many have a weight limit. Some budget airlines charge you extra for every bag that you check-in, and people travelling on budget airline flights often take only hand luggage with them. This is fine if your trip is short, but if you're going to be away for more than a few days, you probably want to check in a larger suitcase. The flight attendant at the check-in desk gives you a boarding pass with your name, the flight number, the boarding time and the gate you need to go to.

Straight Talking

 Oscar is checking in for a flight to Belfast.

Flight attendant: Good morning, sir. May I see your passport, please?

Oscar: Yes, here you are. I'm on the eight a.m. flight to Belfast. Business class.

Flight attendant: Right. Do you have any bags to check in?

Oscar: Yes, I have this suitcase to check in and this briefcase as hand luggage.

Flight attendant: Did you pack your suitcase yourself?

Oscar: Yes

Flight attendant: Are you carrying any sharp items in your hand luggage? Please look at this card of security instructions and make sure that you aren't carrying any of these items in your luggage.

Oscar: No, that's all fine.

Flight attendant: Okay. Would you like an aisle or a window seat?

Oscar: An aisle seat, please. How long is the flight?

Flight attendant: It's fifty minutes.

Oscar: Is breakfast served on board?

Flight attendant: Yes, sir, it is. Here's your boarding card. Boarding time is seven thirty-five at gate fifteen. You have seat number thirty-three C. Please go directly to the boarding gate now, as it may take you a while to get through security.

Oscar: Thank you.

Flight attendant: You're welcome. Enjoy your flight.

After check-in, you need to go through security and passport control. These days many airports have very strict security controls, and you're not allowed to take liquids through the controls. The European Union has rules for what you can and can't take through security, and it's a good idea to check what these are with your travel agent, or online, before you fly. Even things like a small bottle of deodorant may not be allowed through security, so put toiletries into your checked-in luggage rather than carrying them in your hand luggage. In large, busy airports such as London Heathrow you need to allow yourself plenty of time to get through security and passport control to get to the departures hall and your departure gate. At busy times it may take you quite a while just to get through security, and you don't want to miss your flight!

At the departure gate, you need to wait until staff announce your flight departure. Then you hand your boarding card to the flight attendant and board the plane. You need to find your seat and put your hand luggage in one of the overhead lockers. Then you can sit down, fasten your seatbelt and wait for take-off!

Words to Know

check-in desk	boarding card	hand luggage
luggage	baggage	bags
suitcase	phone number	sharp items
passengers	departure gate	departures hall
security	liquids	passport control
window / middle / aisle (pronounced I'll) seat		
overhead locker	flight attendant	
seatbelt	take-off	

London airports

London has four major airports: Heathrow, Gatwick, Stansted and Luton. The best known of these, and the biggest, is Heathrow, with Terminals 1–5. Many international flights arrive at Heathrow, and it handles the most international air traffic in the world – but it's only the world's third busiest airport after Atlanta and Beijing! Many of the budget airlines flying from cities in Europe arrive at Stansted and Luton, which are much smaller airports. Gatwick is also a large airport that currently has two terminals (North Terminal and South Terminal).

Eating and shopping on board

Your flight may include a meal or drinks, although some budget airlines charge quite high prices for these. International flights often have duty-free goods for sale. This means that you can buy perfume, gifts, souvenirs and other goods at lower prices than you pay in shops. You can buy duty-free alcohol and cigarettes in the airport shops.

Straight Talking

Oscar is on a morning flight to Belfast. The flight attendant is serving breakfast.

Flight attendant:	What would you like to drink, sir?
Oscar:	Orange juice, please.
Flight attendant:	With ice?
Oscar:	No, thanks. And a cup of coffee, please.
Flight attendant:	Certainly, sir. Would you like cream and sugar with that?
Oscar:	Just sugar, please.
Flight attendant:	Here you go. Breakfast will be served in a minute.
Oscar:	Thank you.

[The flight attendant serves breakfast.]

Flight attendant:	We have a choice of a cheese sandwich or scrambled eggs today. Which would you like?
Oscar:	Scrambled eggs, please.
Flight attendant:	Here you are, sir.
Oscar:	Thank you.

Landing and leaving the airport

If you fly into the UK from another country and do not hold a European Union passport, you usually have to fill in a landing card with information such as your name, date of birth, place of birth, passport number and your address in the UK. You don't have to fill in a landing card for internal flights within the UK.

When you land, you get off the plane and go to the baggage reclaim area where you can pick up your suitcase. It's unlikely that you will be stopped at customs, especially if you're taking an internal flight in the UK or within the European Union. You usually find two or three exit doors from the baggage reclaim area. One is marked in green and says 'Nothing to declare'. Another is marked in red and says 'Goods to declare'. You need to take this exit and show any restricted goods that you may be carrying to a customs official. Depending on the airport, you may see a third exit marked 'Arrivals from the European Union'. After you pass through one of these exits, you're in the arrivals hall where you can take a taxi, bus or train into town, or where your friends may be waiting for you.

When somebody meets you at the airport, he may ask you 'How was your flight?'. If you came by car or bus or train, he may ask 'How was your trip?'. It's useful to know how to describe a journey in different ways so that you can answer this question with more than just the word 'Fine'!

Straight Talking

Oscar's flight has arrived at Belfast Airport. His work colleague Brian meets him at the airport.

Brian:	Hello, Oscar, nice to see you again!
Oscar:	Hi, Brian, how are you?
Brian:	Fine, fine.

Oscar:	I'm sorry I'm late – our flight was delayed at Heathrow. We sat on the runway for an hour before take-off.
Brian:	Yes, I saw it was announced on the arrivals board. Anyway, you're here now. How was your flight?
Oscar:	Okay. It was extremely bumpy when we were coming in to land, but at least it was short!
Brian:	Good, did they give you something to eat?
Oscar:	Yes, I had breakfast on the flight.
Brian:	Okay, that's good because we need to go straight into the centre of town for our meeting. Let's go!

When you describe a journey, try using intensifying adjectives such as *extremely*, *horrendously* or *totally* instead of *very*. For example, you may say 'The flight was extremely bumpy' or 'The flight was horrendously bumpy' (*horrendously* stronger than *extremely*). But you don't say 'The flight was totally bumpy', because you use 'totally' only with certain adjectives; for example 'I was totally exhausted after the flight'. If you're not sure which intensifying adjective to use, stick to *extremely* for emphasis and it will usually be correct.

Words to Know

duty-free goods	duty-free shops	
budget airline	international flight	
internal flight	landing card	to be delayed
runway	to take off	to land
arrivals board	departures board	baggage reclaim
bumpy	customs	customs official
nothing to declare	goods to declare	arrivals hall

Getting Around

The public transport system in most UK cities is very good. UK residents and visitors to the UK often complain that public transport is expensive compared with other European cities. All major British cities have extensive bus and train networks, and some cities have underground trains or metro systems.

Using the Underground

The most famous underground train in the UK is the London Underground, or 'the Tube'.

Some UK cities have special tickets or passes that you can use on public transport. London, for example, has an Oyster card, which looks like a credit card, and you can use this on the Underground and on buses. You add credit to an Oyster card and the fare for the journey is automatically subtracted from the credit on your card when you pass through the Tube barriers or when you get on a bus. You need to pass your Oyster card over a special yellow rounded disc for the fare to be subtracted. It works out slightly cheaper to use these kinds of cards than to pay the full fare for individual journeys, and buses are generally speaking cheaper than the Underground. Most Londoners use the Oyster card system to get to and from work, but if you're in London for a short period of time (such as a day or weekend) and are planning to make more than two journeys a day, you can get other types of ticket. For example, you can get a one-day travel card that allows you an unlimited number of journeys on the same day after 9.30 a.m. Adults travelling with children can also get special tickets. The best thing to do is to ask at the Underground ticket office about what kinds of tickets are available.

Straight Talking

Oscar is buying a ticket for the London Underground. He goes to the ticket office to ask about the different kinds of tickets he can buy.

Oscar: Good morning, I'd like to know what kind of ticket I can buy for the London Underground for just a few days.

Employee: Well, that depends. You can buy a one-day travel pass if you're going to make several journeys. That means for under ten pounds you can make as many journeys as you want in one day, on the Tube and also by bus.

Oscar:	Actually, I have two free days in London and wanted to do some sightseeing. What about an Oyster card?
Employee:	An Oyster card works best for people who live in London and make two journeys a day to and from work. Then each journey works out a bit cheaper.
Oscar:	So do you think it's a good idea to get a one-day travel card for today and then another one for tomorrow?
Employee:	Like I said, if you want to make more than two journeys a day that's probably best. But you can only use a travel card after nine-thirty.
Oscar:	And I can travel anywhere on the Tube with the card?
Employee:	You have to buy it for certain zones. We're in Manor House Tube station, which is zone four. If you want to go to the West End, that's zone one. So you need a card for zones one to four.
Oscar:	Okay, can I have one travel card for zones one to four, please? And can I pay by credit card?
Employee:	Yes, certainly. Here you go. Please sign here.
Oscar:	Thank you. Do you have an Underground map?
Employee:	Yes, you can take one from the rack just here.
Oscar:	Thanks.

The London Underground

The London Underground is the oldest metro system in the world – the first section opened in 1863. It currently has 270 stations and about 400 kilometres (about 250 miles) of tracks, so it's also the biggest underground system in the world. To add to those superlatives, it's also one of the most expensive public transport systems per kilometre, and many people say that it's the hottest place to be on a sunny day in August. The London Underground is also known as 'the Tube' because of its tube-shaped tunnels, which are narrow and cylindrical like a tube. People consider the London Underground map to be a classic design, and many underground train networks around the world have copied the colour coding and non-geographical layout. The Tube map dates from 1933 and, along with red double-decker buses, is one of the classic images of London.

Travelling by train

Not many British cities have underground trains. Much more common are overground trains. You're most likely to use a train to get from one city or town to another. Rail fares in the UK are often expensive. If you book in advance, fares can often be a lot cheaper – in some cases you may save up to 50 per cent on your booking. So it's definitely worth trying to book longer distance trains, such as those between major cities, well in advance. You can book tickets in advance in person at the railway station, or from abroad by Internet or by telephone. British trains have first-class and second-class seats, and a complex system of discounted fares, such as one-day returns. If you buy a one-day return or *day return*, which means going to a place and coming back on the same day, it's often almost the same price as a single fare, and not much more. It's also usually cheaper to buy a return fare even when the journey out is on one day and you're coming back on another day than it is to buy two single fares.

You can also find discounts on rail fares for children, students and pensioners, although you need a pensioner's or student card to prove that you're eligible for a discount. If you want to buy a first-class seat, you need to ask for it – most people travel second class and the ticket office employee will give you a second-class ticket unless you say otherwise.

Straight Talking

 Oscar is buying a train ticket from London to Brighton.

Oscar: Good morning, a ticket to Brighton, please.

Employee: Is that single or return?

Oscar: Return, please.

Employee: Are you coming back today?

Oscar: Yes.

Employee: In that case you want a day return.

Oscar: Yes, please.

Employee: That's twenty-five pounds please.

Oscar: Which platform does the train leave from? And what time is the next train?

Employee:	The next express train leaves at 11.06. The platform will be announced on the departure board, but it usually leaves from platform twelve.
Oscar:	Thank you very much.
Employee:	You're welcome.

Words to Know

a single / one-way / return / day return ticket (rail)

an Oyster card (London Underground)

a travel pass   zones   a fare

discount   first class / second class

platform   departures board

express train / slow train

Going by bus

Public buses are often a good way to see a town. If you aren't using a travel pass and you want to pay individual fares for individual journeys, try to make sure that you have the exact amount of money for your bus tickets with you, because many bus drivers don't accept bank notes (such as a five-pound or ten-pound note) and don't carry much change.

CULTURAL WISDOM

Queuing

The British are famous for many things and one of these is queuing (pronounced 'kyu-ing'). *Queuing* means standing in an orderly line while you wait for something. Queuing is especially important at the bus stop. When you arrive at the bus stop make sure you stand behind the last person in the line and not right at the front. The British consider it good manners to wait for the people in front of you in the queue to get on the bus. Don't push your way to the front when the bus arrives. You also need to queue to buy things such as bus or train tickets. They say that if one person stands alone on the pavement looking at nothing for long enough in the UK, an orderly queue (pronounced 'kyu') will form behind him.

You can find bus routes printed on the bus stop, although sometimes figuring out in which direction the bus is going can be a little difficult. Don't be afraid to ask someone for help.

Straight Talking

Oscar wants to get a bus from St Paul's Cathedral to Piccadilly Circus in London. He asks a man at the bus stop for help.

Oscar: Excuse me, I want to go to Piccadilly Circus from here. Should I get the number sixteen bus?

Man: No, mate, you need the number nineteen.

Oscar: Oh, okay.

Man: Anyway, you're on the wrong side of the road. This bus goes east. You want to go west. Cross the road and get the bus at the bus stop there on the other side.

Oscar: Okay, thanks. Do you know how often they come?

Man: They're fairly frequent at this time of day – about every five or ten minutes. But you know what they say: buses only ever come in threes . . . [This well-known phrase means that you can spend hours waiting for a bus and then three of the same number bus come along at the same time.]

Oscar: Right, thanks. Thanks for your help.

Man: No problem, mate.

Black cabs

Another popular image of London is that of the London taxi, or 'black cab'. These days you see 'black' cabs of many different colours and some of them have advertising along the sides. Black cab drivers take a special examination to test their knowledge of the streets of London, which is a huge city. The examination is called 'the Knowledge' (the full name is 'The Knowledge of London Examination System'), and it came into existence in the 1860s. The test is said to be one of the most difficult taxi examinations in the world, and drivers need to take the test an average of 12 times to be able to pass.

You hear the word *get* a lot when talking about transport. You 'get in' and 'get out of' a car or taxi. You 'get on' and 'get off' a plane, a bus or a train. As a general rule, you use 'get in' and 'get out of' for smaller forms of transport such as cars and taxis. For larger forms of transport where you can stand upright, you use 'get on' and 'get off'.

Taking a taxi

Sometimes you may want to get a taxi (or cab) to get from one place to another. Most cities have licensed taxis and these often have the name and telephone number of the company on the door. You can also find minicabs in many cities in the UK. Minicabs tend to be cheaper than licensed taxis. You find minicab offices in many high streets and near underground and over-ground train stations and bus stations. You usually book your minicab ride in the office and sometimes you pay for the journey in advance.

Tipping your taxi driver is optional in the UK. Some people simply round up the fare to the nearest pound. So if your fare is £8.65, you could give the driver £9.

To talk about how to get from A to B, you use the verb *go*. So you can go by car, by train, by Tube, by taxi and by bicycle. But when you walk, you go *on* foot, never *by* foot.

Renting a Car

If you want to get 'off the beaten track' (or visit places where there are few tourists), you may want to rent a car. All major cities in the UK have car rental (or hire) offices, including international companies such as Avis and Hertz. Booking your car rental before you come to the UK, either via a travel agent or a car rental company website, may be cheaper than renting a car in the UK. You often get special discounts, for example for weekend or seven-day rentals.

You may need to have an international driving licence to rent a car in the UK and you need to get this from your own country. If you're from a European Union country, you can drive with your licence in the UK for a period of time, depending on the type of vehicle you want to rent. It's best to check whether your licence is valid in the UK directly with the rental company before you visit the UK. You can also find out about driving in the UK on a non-UK licence at the website www.direct.gov.uk/en/Motoring/DriverLicensing/DrivingInGbOnAForeignLicence/DG_4022556.

On the whole the UK has fewer tolls than in many other European countries. Very few British motorways have tolls, although you pay tolls on the Forth

Bridge and the Tay Bridge in Scotland, the Severn Bridge that connects England and Wales, and the Tyne Tunnel and Mersey Tunnel in the north of England. Most famous of all is the controversial London *congestion charge*, for which cars in central London pay a daily fee, currently five pounds a day.

An extremely important thing to remember in the UK is to drive on the left-hand side. This may be a little confusing when you get to a roundabout for the first time.

Straight Talking

Oscar arrives in Belfast and he rents a car to visit some of the surrounding countryside.

Oscar:	Good morning, I have a reservation for a car under the name of 'Suarez'. I made a reservation via your website.
Employee:	Yes, just one moment. Can you spell the name, please?
Oscar:	Yes, it's S-U-A-R-E-Z. First name Oscar.
Employee:	Yes, here it is. Just for two days, is it?
Oscar:	Yes, that's right. I believe you have a special weekend rate?
Employee:	Yes, you've booked a car at the weekend rate, unlimited mileage. Let's do the paperwork first. Do you have an international driving licence?
Oscar:	I come from a European Union country, and have my Spanish driving licence.
Employee:	Okay, that's fine. Can I see it, please? I need to make a copy for our records. What about car insurance? Would you like me to include insurance with the rental?
Oscar:	That's already covered by my Spanish car insurance, thank you.
Employee:	Right, you've booked an economy model and we have this one available. Its diesel, so you need to put diesel into it, not normal petrol.

Oscar:	Okay.
Employee:	We'll give you the car with a full tank of diesel. If you bring it back full there will be no charge, but if we need to add more diesel, we'll need to charge you for that per litre.
Oscar:	Okay, I understand.
Employee:	Please could you fill out these papers for me, and we'll proceed with your reservation . . .

Petrol stations in the UK are also known as 'service stations'. Many petrol stations are self-service, but some aren't. If you need to put petrol or diesel into your car, or use a petrol station for another service, you may find these expressions useful:

✔ Where is the nearest petrol station?

✔ Is there a petrol station near here?

✔ Fill it up, please.

✔ Thirty pounds of [super / regular / unleaded / diesel], please.

✔ Where are the bathrooms, please?

✔ Where can I put air in the tyres?

✔ Do you have something I can clean the windshield with, please?

✔ Where can I find a mechanic?

✔ I've got a flat tyre.

Asking for Directions

A good way to get around a small city and to see the sights is on foot. Cities with historical centres, such as Oxford and Cambridge, have lots of small winding roads and it may be difficult to find your way around. But if you have the right expressions at your fingertips, you don't need to worry about getting lost – you can simply ask someone the way. You need to know the expressions to ask somebody for directions, but you also need to be able to understand the response. Here are some of the prepositions you can use to describe where places are:

✔ Opposite

✔ Next to

✔ Near

✔ Not far from

✔ Between

✔ Behind

✔ Across the road from

✔ On the corner of

✔ In the middle of

You may also need to understand how to get to a place. Here is a typical set of directions:

> *Turn left over there, then go straight ahead and take the third right. Go past the bus station to the end of the road and it's the first street on the left.*

Sometimes directions are difficult to understand in a foreign language. Don't be afraid to ask for clarification or to ask the person to repeat a direction. If you have a map, ask them to show you the route on the map. Here are some phrases to help you find your way around:

✔ Excuse me, where is the station?

✔ Could you tell me the way to the station, please?

✔ How do I get to the station, please?

✔ Turn [left / right].

✔ Go straight ahead.

✔ Go along this street.

✔ Take the [first / second / third] left.

✔ Go to the end of the road.

✔ Go [over / under] the bridge.

✔ Go past the [station / post office].

✔ It's the second on the right.

✔ It's on [your / the] [left / right].

✔ I'm sorry, was that left or right?

✔ So it's on the left or the right?

✔ How far is it?

✔ Is it far from here?

✔ Can you show me on the map, please?

In some parts of UK, it's common to use the word *right?* to check that someone is listening to you. So don't be surprised if you ask for directions in London and someone says to you, 'Okay, you turn right, right? And then you take the first left, right? Then go straight ahead, right, and keep going . . .'. The word *right* in these sentences simply means 'okay'.

Straight Talking

Oscar is in Belfast and is walking around the city centre. He wants to visit the Grand Opera House. He asks a man in the street for directions.

Oscar:	Excuse me. Can you tell me the way to the Grand Opera House, please? Is it far from here?
Man:	Not far at all; it's about a five-minute walk. Go to the end of the street and turn left at the corner. Go on for about fifty metres, past the post office, then turn left again. Then you'll see it down on your right.
Oscar:	Okay, so first I go to the end of the street and turn right . . .
Man:	No, no. You turn left at the end of the street.
Oscar:	So I turn left, then left again?
Man:	Yes, and straight along that street and it will be on your right. You can't miss it.
Oscar:	Okay, thanks a lot.

To ask the distance to somewhere, you can use the word *far*. For example: 'How far is the cathedral from here?' The reply to this might be 'Not far; it's a five-minute walk'. British people tend to use the word *far* more often in questions and negative sentences. In positive sentences they tend to use the phrase 'a long way', so 'It's a long way; about a 45-minute walk'. If you use *far* in a positive sentence, you often add *quite* – 'It's quite far; about a 45-minute walk'.

Words to Know

castle	stadium	art gallery
shopping centre	cathedral	church
clock tower	opera house	bus station
train station	underground / Tube station	
bridge	docks	river
beach	waterfront	harbour

Describing Towns and Cities

The UK has a lot of towns and cities to visit, from historical towns and villages to large industrial centres. Before you visit a place, you might want to ask friends for a recommendation, or you yourself might want to recommend a place for others to visit.

Here are some useful phrases for describing towns and cities:

- ✔ It's an industrial area.
- ✔ It's quite [crowded / noisy / cosmopolitan / touristy].
- ✔ It's [bigger / smaller / noisier / more beautiful] than . . .
- ✔ It's a popular tourist destination.
- ✔ It's near the border with Scotland/Wales.
- ✔ It's famous for the medieval cathedral.
- ✔ It has a beautiful historical centre.
- ✔ It has spectacular views.
- ✔ It has beautiful scenery.

Straight Talking

Oscar is telling his friend Roger about his trip to Belfast.

Roger: How was your trip to Belfast? What did you think of the city?

Oscar: I liked it a lot. It's smaller than I had expected, and not as crowded as other big cities.

Roger: What did you visit in the city?

Oscar: Oh, you know, the typical tourist places. The Grand Opera House, Belfast Castle, the Albert Memorial Clock Tower . . .

Roger: What's the nightlife like? I hear Belfast is a very lively city.

Oscar: Yes, the streets were full of people at night in the centre, but maybe that's because it's summer!

Roger: Did you visit the countryside at all?

Oscar: Yes, I rented a car for two days and drove around a bit. There are some spectacular places in Ireland!

Roger: Well, it's famous for its beautiful scenery, and they say that people are much friendlier than in other parts of the UK.

Oscar: That's certainly true! I got lost a few times in the centre of Belfast and people were very friendly and helpful.

Notice you use the expression 'What is / are . . . like?' to ask for someone's opinion of something or a place. So you may say 'What is Belfast like?' or 'What are the people like?' but not 'How is Belfast?' or 'How are the people?'. However, you can say 'How was [your trip to] Belfast?'. The answer to 'What is Belfast like?' could be 'It's great / interesting / quite cosmopolitan . . .' or such. Remember that this question means something different to 'Do you like Belfast?'. The answer to *this* question is 'Yes, I do' or 'No, I don't'!

Fun & Games

1 Match these questions with the correct answer.

a) What do you suggest I visit in town?	The platform will be announced on the departure board.
b) Are there any seats available for the Tuesday flight?	I don't mind; any seat is fine.
c) Would you like an aisle, middle or window seat?	No, you need the number 19.
d) Would you like cream and sugar with that?	Yes, I loved it. It's very cosmopolitan.
e) Do you need a landing card?	Just black coffee, thank you.
f) How was your flight?	Just a one-way ticket, please.
g) Do you want a single or return ticket?	No, thanks, I have an EU passport.
h) Which platform does the train leave from?	It's a lot less industrial than I expected.
i) Should I get the number 16 bus?	I'm afraid it's fully booked, unless you fly first class.
j) What's the city like?	A little bumpy, to be honest.
k) Did you like the city?	You should definitely see the cathedral.

Key:

a) What do you suggest I visit in town? You should definitely see the cathedral.

b) Are there any seats available for the Tuesday flight? I'm afraid it's fully booked, unless you fly first class.

c) Would you like an aisle, middle or window seat? I don't mind; any seat is fine.

d) Would you like cream and sugar with that? Just black coffee, thank you.

e) Do you need a landing card? No, thanks, I have an EU passport.

f) How was your flight? A little bumpy, to be honest.

g) Do you want a single or return ticket? Just a one-way ticket, please.

h) Which platform does the train leave from? The platform will be announced on the departure board.

i) Should I get the number 16 bus? No, you need the number 19.

j) What's the city like? It's a lot less industrial than I expected.

k) Did you like the city? Yes, I loved it. It's very cosmopolitan.

   2. Now decide *where* each of these questions is asked:

at the bus stop   on the aeroplane in the tourist office   at the airport
at a friend's house   after a trip   at the train station   at the travel
agent

Key:

in the tourist office – a

at the travel agent – b

at the airport – c, f

on the aeroplane – d, e

at the train station – g, h

at the bus stop – i

at a friend's house after a trip – j, k, (f)

   3. Put these words in the right group.

boarding card   clock tower   backpack   check-in desk   castle
bus   departures hall Tube   town hall   underground briefcase   overground train suitcase cathedral   baggage reclaim rucksack

Types of Luggage	At the Airport	Types of Transport	Tourist Attractions

Key:

Types of luggage: suitcase, briefcase, backpack, rucksack

At the airport: check-in desk, baggage reclaim, departures hall, boarding card

Types of transport: Tube, underground, overground train, bus

Tourist attractions: cathedral, town hall, clock tower, castle

4. Put these sentences in the correct order. The first and last ones are done for you.

<u>1)</u> Book your flight.

__ Put your hand luggage in the overhead locker.

__ Arrive at the airport.

__ Check in your luggage and get your boarding card.

__ Fasten your seatbelt.

__ Go to your boarding gate.

__ Board the plane and find your seat.

__ Go to the check-in desk.

__ Go through security and passport control.

<u>10)</u> Order your drink from the flight attendant

Key:

1) Book your flight.

2) Arrive at the airport.

3) Go to the check-in desk.

4) Check in your luggage and get your boarding card.

5) Go through security and passport control.

6) Go to your boarding gate.

7) Board the plane and find your seat.

8) Put your hand luggage in the overhead locker.

9) Fasten your seatbelt.

10) Order your drink from the flight attendant.

Chapter 14

Handling Emergencies

· ·

· ·

At some point during your time in Britain something could go wrong – though we hope it won't be anything serious. At such times you need to know how to get help with your problems, from general situations to more specific things such as health problems, visiting the dentist and dealing with the police. In this chapter we guide you through these steps to ensuring a trouble-free stay.

Being able to get help quickly and efficiently is the important thing – you don't want to be searching for a dictionary or a phrasebook at inopportune moments.

Getting Help Quickly

When you have a problem you need to know how to get help as quickly as possible. Here are a few phrases to get you started:

✔ Can somebody help me, please?

✔ Please, I need help, over here!

✔ Can you get help, please?

✔ Somebody call [an ambulance / the police].

You can always just shout 'Help!' or 'Fire!' and usually somebody will come running if you shout loud enough.

Dealing with Health Problems

When you arrive in a new town or city, make sure you register with a doctor and a dentist. If you're covered by the British National Health System (which has agreements with EEA members and other countries) under one of its provisions (check at `www.adviceguide.org.uk/index/family_parent/health/nhs_charges_for_people_from_abroad.htm`) you can usually register with a doctor and a dentist free of charge, although if you aren't staying long you may have to pay for private treatment.

The National Health System is excellent in Britain. To find your local doctor (*GP* or *general practitioner*) visit `www.nhs.uk/servicedirectories/Pages/serviceSearch.aspx`. If you have an accident or are dangerously ill, you can go to the Accident and Emergency (A&E) department of your local hospital, but for smaller health problems try your doctor first and he or she will recommend you to an expert if necessary.

The chemist only gives out most medicines with prescriptions, so you'll probably need to see a doctor if you have anything worse than a cold or flu. You almost always need to pay for medicines.

If your residence status doesn't give you access to NHS services or your country doesn't have a reciprocal agreement with Britain (this applies to most countries outside of the European Community) then you need to pay for private treatment.

Describing your symptoms

Whenever you visit a doctor, a hospital or a dentist it's important to know how to describe how you feel, and be able to explain which part of your body hurts or where the pain is. In this section we take a look at visits to the doctor and the dentist and explore talking about your body.

The first thing to be able to do is to describe where it hurts. Figure 14-1 shows the different body parts.

I'm fine!

When someone you know asks you how you are, it's customary to say something like 'Fine, thanks!' or 'Not too bad!' or 'Can't complain!', even if you're not feeling very well. The question is an everyday question between people in Britain, but nobody expects to hear about your medical problems when you answer it. It's not that people don't care, it's just one of those things! You need to get used to asking people how they are, but don't expect any gory details in return.

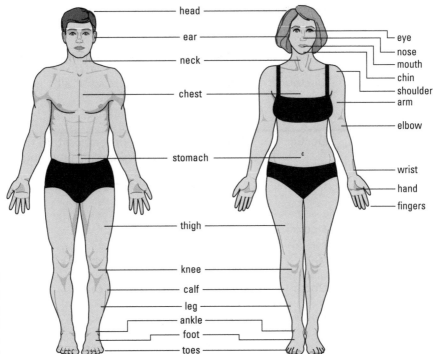

Figure 14-1:
The different
parts of
the body.

Try using the following phrases to explain how the part hurts or bothers you:

- My [neck / back / chest / leg] hurts. [describes pain]
- I've got a terrible pain in my [chest / leg / stomach]. [describes pain]
- My throat is sore. [describes inflammation]
- I've got a [fever / temperature / pain in my . . . / sore . . .].
- I can't sleep.
- I'm having trouble [walking / sitting / breathing].
- I'm feeling a bit tired and haven't got any energy.

Straight Talking

 Gina has gone to see the doctor.

Doctor: Hello, how are you today?

Gina: Hello. Not too good actually.

Doctor:	Oh dear, what seems to be the problem?
Gina:	I've got a sore throat and a bit of a cough, and I don't seem to have very much energy at the moment.
Doctor:	Right. Have you had a fever at all?
Gina:	I don't think so, not really.
Doctor:	Well let's just take your temperature to make sure. What about aches and pains – anything?
Gina:	Actually, yes – I've been aching all over since yesterday.
Doctor:	And are you eating okay?
Gina:	Yes, absolutely – as much as usual.
Doctor:	Sneezing, coughing, sore eyes?
Gina:	Yes.
Doctor:	It sounds like that flu that's going around at the moment. I'll give you a prescription for some medicine. Stay at home for a couple of days, drink lots of liquids and get some rest. I'm sure you'll be fine in two or three days.
Gina:	Thanks very much. I thought it might be the flu, and I didn't want to bother you, but it didn't seem to be getting any better.
Doctor:	No problem. Come back and see me in four days if you don't feel any better, okay?

If you have more serious health problems, then head to a hospital and get checked out. It's always better to be safe than sorry. If you have a real emergency you can call 999 and ask for an ambulance (see the 'Reporting trouble' section later in this chapter); otherwise, make your way to your nearest Accident and Emergency department at the hospital.

In Britain *everyone* has a right to emergency medical treatment, but you may have to pay if you're kept in hospital for treatment. If you can, take someone with you to take care of all these details.

Ensure that you have proper medical insurance when you travel. Along with proper documentation like a passport and visa, make sure all these papers are valid and available for this kind of emergency.

Straight Talking

Joan has gone to Accident and Emergency at the local hospital. After a short wait he is seen by a doctor.

Doctor: So, Mr Castells, what seems to be the problem?

Joan: It's my foot, Doctor. I fell down the stairs and I can't stand on it any more – it really hurts.

Doctor: I see. Let's have a look at it then. Does it hurt here?

Joan: Ow! Yes, it does.

Doctor: It is a bit swollen. Could be a small fracture, or maybe you've just twisted your ankle in the fall. I think you should have an x-ray.

[A while later, after the x-ray.]

Doctor: I'm afraid you've broken your ankle, Mr Castells.

Joan: Oh dear. So what happens now?

Doctor: Well, we'll give you some painkillers for the next day or two, and we're going to have to put your ankle in a plaster cast for a while.

Joan: What about my work?

Doctor: What do you do?

Joan: I'm a postman.

Doctor: Well, I'm afraid you'll have to have a few days off!

Visiting a dentist

Going to the dentist is usually a little less difficult – when speaking about what ails you at least – than seeing a doctor, because you only need to talk about your mouth. Most of the time using the simple sentence 'I have tooth-ache' and pointing at the painful area is enough for the dentist to get going.

If you're covered by NHS healthcare in Britain you have an automatic right to a NHS dentist in your area (for more information, enter your postcode at www.nhs.uk/Pages/HomePage.aspx). NHS dentists are cheaper than private dentists and charge agreed rates for treatments.

Private dentistry can be very expensive but you can find your nearest private dentist at www.privatehealth.co.uk/private-dentistry/find-a-dentist.

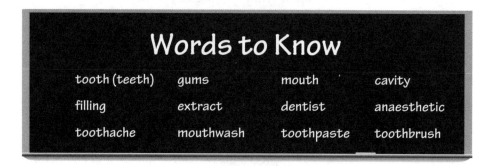

Words to Know

tooth (teeth)	gums	mouth	cavity
filling	extract	dentist	anaesthetic
toothache	mouthwash	toothpaste	toothbrush

Coping with Crime and Legal Problems

Luckily, most people go through life without experiencing any sort of crime. But sometimes you can have a bit of bad luck and find yourself in a difficult or upsetting situation. In this section we look at what to do if that happens to you, how to contact the police and what to do when you speak to them.

Getting into trouble

Mistakes can happen and at some point you may find yourself on the wrong side of the law – perhaps you parked in the wrong place or you had a car accident. The first thing to do is to make sure you stay calm. Police in Britain are trained to deal with people politely but firmly, and you should show them the same courtesy.

If the matter is minor, such as a parking offence, you may be able to deal with the issue yourself. Sometimes you may have a good reason and you can argue your case calmly and respectfully – though you'll probably still have to pay the fine. For more serious problems, first make sure you have some representation: ask to call your consulate and get some help. And remember, in Britain you're innocent until proven guilty.

CULTURAL WISDOM

The forces of law and order

In Britain, police officers are often known as 'Bobbies', though historically they were also called 'Peelers'. Both of these names come from the name of the man who established the first regular police force in 1829, Sir Robert Peel (Bob is a diminutive form of Robert).

You find police officers all around the streets of Britain, in cars, on foot and sometimes on horses. You also find *special constables*, who are volunteer officers with limited powers, and other uniformed people such as *traffic wardens*, who watch where you park and put a ticket on your car if you've parked in the wrong place.

The British police not only help with solving crimes and crime prevention, but they're also happy to help you out with directions or advice – they really are a friendly bunch, unless you get yourself into trouble . . .

Start with the real emergency phrases:

- I'd like to call my consulate, please.
- Could I speak to a lawyer who speaks [Spanish / Russian / Japanese], please?

Straight Talking

Rudi has been stopped by the police for running a red light.

Policeman: Good afternoon, sir.

Rudi: Good afternoon, Officer. Is there a problem?

Policeman: I'm afraid there is, sir. You just drove through a red light.

Rudi: Really? I thought it was on amber when I went through.

Policeman: I'm afraid the camera flashed, which indicates the light was red when you drove through it, sir.

Rudi: Oh dear. This has never happened to me before. I'm really terribly sorry. What happens now?

Policeman: Is this your car, sir?

Rudi: Yes, Officer, it is.

Policeman:	Could I see your driving licence and documentation, please?
Rudi:	Yes, of course. Here you are.
Policeman:	Thank you, sir.
Rudi:	Do I need to call a lawyer or my consulate?
Policeman:	No, sir. I'm going to issue with a fixed penalty notice – that's an automatic fine of sixty pounds that you'll be able to pay later.
Rudi:	Oh, I see.
Policeman:	You'll also have three penalty points put on your licence. Oh, wait a minute, this isn't a British driving licence, is it?
Rudi:	No, Officer, sorry.
Policeman:	In that case, Sir, I'm afraid you'll be issued with a court summons and will have to go to court to argue your case.
Rudi:	Oh dear, this is all very upsetting, Officer.
Policeman:	Here are your documents. You'll be hearing from us soon. Please drive carefully for the rest of your trip.
Rudi:	I certainly will, Officer. I'm sorry for the trouble.

Reporting trouble

We hope that you never need to report a crime, but if ever you're a victim or witness of a crime, this section can help.

In a *real* emergency (such as witnessing a fire, or someone being attacked) phone 999. The Emergency Telephone Operator will ask you which service you require: police, ambulance, fire service or (in some areas) coastguard. Try to keep calm and answer the simple questions the operator asks such as:

- What's happened?
- What's your name?
- What's the number of the telephone you're calling from?

✔ Where is the incident?

✔ Is anybody hurt?

The operator may also ask other questions depending on your answers.

If your situation is less urgent, visit your local police station. Find out where your nearest station is when you move to a new area. You may also find police or *police community support officers* (normal citizens who are trained to support the work done by the police) patrolling the streets in your town. To find out more details of your local police station, visit `www.police.uk/ forces.htm`.

When you visit a police station explain why you're there and what's happened to you. If you've lost something or had something stolen you'll need to fill out some forms and perhaps answer a few questions. If the crime is more serious, however, a police officer will interview you in private with the support of other people from the police services.

Stay calm, speak clearly and give as much information as possible. In large cities the police may be able to use the services of interpreters. Don't forget, as a last resort you can always call the embassy or consulate of your country for help.

In general you say that you rob banks, burgle offices and homes, and steal things:

✔ The gang **robbed** a bank (and stole lots of money).

✔ Help! I've been robbed! They **stole** my wallet!

✔ My house has been **burgled**; they stole the TV and the DVD player.

More crime verbs:

✔ **Attack** someone (a man attacked him with a knife).

✔ **Shoplift** clothes from a shop.

✔ **Kidnap** someone (they kidnapped the child and demanded a ransom).

✔ **Mug** someone (they mugged him and stole his wallet)

Straight Talking

Someone has stolen Monica's bag from a cafe.

Monica: Excuse me, Officer. I've had my bag stolen.

Officer: I see, miss. When did this happen?

Monica:	Just a couple of minutes ago.
Officer:	Here in the street?
Monica:	No, from the cafe over there. I was just paying for my coffee and when I looked I saw a man running away with my bag. I tried to catch him, but he was too quick, I'm afraid.
Officer:	I see. What did he look like?
Monica:	Oh, umm . . . let's see . . . he was quite tall, with short black hair and black sunglasses.
Officer:	And did you see what he was wearing?
Monica:	Yes, a pair of jeans, white trainers and a short black jacket. Oh, and a hat – one of those woollen ones.
Officer:	Right – I'll radio in and see if we can find him. Did you see which way he went?
Monica:	Yes, towards the market.
Officer:	Just let me radio in and we can sit down and you can give me all your details, okay?
Monica:	Okay. Thank you.

Words to Know

mugger	murderer	robber
shoplifter	terrorist	burglar
thief	vandal	rapist

Most of the time all you have to do is describe what happened (remember your past tenses) and who did it (physical appearance, clothes). The police should be able to do the rest. Don't try to be a hero and stop anyone committing a crime – leave it to the experts. You'll be enough of a hero if you can report it properly!

Visa and Residency Problems

Ensure that you have your paperwork in order before you travel, and make a note of any key dates when you're in Britain. You need to apply for visa extensions (or a change of status) well in advance. In these days of heightened security the authorities have less sympathy for people who simply forget, so do help yourself by ensuring you're legal during your stay.

If you're already in Britain and need to make changes to your visa or other paperwork, look at the UK Border Agency website for some answers to common questions: www.ukvisas.gov.uk/en/alreadyintheUK.

Make sure your visa or residence status is current and that you're legally allowed to live and work in Britain. Like most countries the rules are quite complicated and vary according to where you come from, so the best advice is to check, and then check again.

Above all, don't panic! If you have a good reason to be in Britain there's a good chance that the authorities will listen to you with a sympathetic ear. However, like the medical problems we talk about earlier in this chapter, prevention is better than cure!

Fun & Games

• •

1. Write the parts of the body on the figure below.

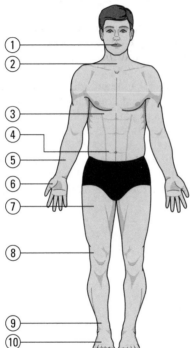

Figure 14-2:
Identify the
parts of the
body.

Key:

1) Mouth

2) Neck

3) Chest

4) Stomach

5) Arm

6) Hand

7) Thigh

8) Knee

9) Ankle

10) Foot

2. Complete the following sentences with one of these words:

attacked / burgled / vandal / lawyer / terrorist / robbed / shoplifter / stole / raped / arrested

1) They _____ his house and stole his TV.

2) Did you see the news? Two men _____ a bank in town this morning.

3) Someone just _____ my phone from my bag.

4) He was _____ by a man with a knife.

5) A _____ broke windows and covered the walls in graffiti.

6) They arrested a _____ as she left the shop with four CDs in her bag.

7) I saw on the TV that they caught that man who _____ and killed four women in Birmingham.

8) They arrested four men on _____ charges. One of them had bomb plans in his bag.

9) He was _____ by the police for driving too fast in town.

10) Can I call my _____, please?

Key:

1) burgled

2) robbed

3) stole

4) attacked

5) vandal

6) shoplifter

7) raped

8) terrorist

9) arrested

10) lawyer

• •

Part IV
The Part of Tens

"Euphemisms are kinder words used in place of harsher, unpleasant words. I use them all the time to describe my daughter's wardrobe."

In this part . . .

We share our top ten tips to help you improve your English – fast! We suggest ten ways to learn to speak English quickly. You can do some of these things in your own country, before you visit the UK. Now that the Internet is everywhere, you have all sorts of opportunities to practise your English without even setting foot in the UK! We also give you a list of ten common expressions that you may hear native English speakers use, and another ten expressions that you can use to sound especially fluent in English.

We also give you some insider information about ten holidays in the UK that you may not know about. Depending on what dates you visit the UK, you could find yourself taking part in some of these holidays and festivals.

Chapter 15

Ten Ways to Learn English Quickly

*Y*ou can find plenty of ways to improve your English in daily life, from joining clubs and associations, to watching films and listening to English radio. You can even take advantage of the latest technologies to learn new words and chat to people. Finally, you can make English fun by using it with your own games and tests.

Spending Time in the UK

Most big towns in Britain have plenty of places to go where you have an opportunity to practise your English. You can choose from social places, locations where you can study and public venues. Try the pub as a good first option: you can generally find someone to talk to there. You may also be able to join a pub sports team or a pool team or take part in regular events such as pub quizzes or other games.

Joining a gym, sports or other club is also a good idea, as is taking an evening course in something light or social – think photography rather than accountancy!

If you want to practise your English on a more consistent basis, organise an exchange with someone who wants to learn something from you. Most newsagents, small shops and supermarkets have a board where you can post notices. Post a note saying what you're looking for and what you can offer. Here's an example:

Italian Man Seeks English Conversation Classes

Can offer Italian language or cooking classes in return

Call Antonio on: 123 978 456

Be careful when responding to advertisements in newspapers, magazines or shops, or meeting people who respond to yours. Never give out too much personal information and make sure you meet people in public places, at least for the first time.

Travelling to English-Speaking Countries

You don't need to confine yourself to Britain. Over 80 countries around the world have English as an official language, from Antigua to New Zealand, so you have plenty of places to choose between.

That's a lot of places and a lot of people to talk to. You'll not only improve your English, but you'll see new places, meet new friends and find out about a lot of different cultures. You'll also hear a lot of rich and varied types of English too, because (thankfully) not everyone sounds like a newsreader for the BBC. These variations, accents and dialects are what make English an interesting language to speak.

Don't forget to send us a postcard!

Tuning In to Radio and TV

Radio and TV are great ways to improve your English. Television programmes generally divide up into different subjects – for example movies, documentaries, the news, soap operas, comedy and so on. Choose a type of programme that you really like and watch it as regularly as possible. Watching something like the news, for example, is a great way to learn the vocabulary of current affairs, and if you watch the news regularly you'll soon find your vocabulary expanding.

Before you watch the news, make a list of the big stories of the day. Then add some key words that you think you might hear in the stories: for example, a political story on the news might feature words such as *government*, *prime minister*, *cabinet*, *Downing Street*, *minister*, *Conservative*, *Labour*, *Liberal*

Democrat, opposition. Don't forget to practise what you listen to or watch the next day by reading the newspaper and chatting to friends and colleagues.

Watch quiz shows – these often give you more clues about a society and how it works, and what the people think and are interested in. If it's not too painful, watch the talent shows and soap operas – you'll find a lot of people talking about those the next day.

Making lists of related vocabulary like we suggest here can help to consolidate the vocabulary you know in a particular area. Doing this with different types of programmes helps with your listening comprehension and also enriches your vocabulary.

Listening to Music and Podcasts

Music is another great way of learning some English, although you do have to be careful with some of the lyrics. Remember that pop and rock music has a lot of slang in it, and you need to be careful where you use this kind of language. Ballads and easy listening music have more everyday English in them – but don't go telling everyone you meet that you'll love them for ever after listening to too much Lionel Richie!

On CDs you often find the lyrics of the songs on the album. Read along to them as you listen to the music. You'll be surprised how much you understand, and before long you'll be singing along in English to all your favourite songs.

It's cheaper these days to buy music online from a store such as the Apple Store in iTunes (`www.apple.com/itunes/download`), but of course then you don't get the cover art or the lyrics. If you like to download music you can still find the lyrics on a website such as SongLyrics.com (`www.song lyrics.com`) and more information about the singer or group on a website such as Wikipedia (`www.wikipedia.org`).

Podcasts are also good for improving your listening – and the great advantage of them is you can take them anywhere: on the bus, in the car, walking around town or when you're out doing the gardening or shopping. Many large companies produce regular podcasts in plain English.

The BBC website is full of audio and video podcasts on all sorts of subjects, from daily news to politics, science to technology, comedy, music and learning. Start here: `www.bbc.co.uk/podcasts`.

The BBC produce so many podcasts that they'll probably keep you busy for quite some time. But if you're looking for something special, then you can try the UK Podcasts Directory (`www.ukpodcasts.info`) or simply use a search engine like Google (`www.google.co.uk`) and search for 'UK podcasts'.

You can download and listen to podcasts on your computer by using free software such as Apple's iTunes (www.apple.com/itunes/download). When you add a podcast to iTunes it automatically downloads the latest version every day. When you've downloaded podcasts, you can then transfer them to your MP3 player or your mobile phone (if it plays mp3 files) and take advantage of all the spare time you have each day to improve your listening skills.

The great advantage of things like podcasts is that they're usually divided into genres (or specific subjects) so they're a great way to develop your English in particular fields. If you listen to a news podcast every day you'll soon have a much wider vocabulary connected with the news, you'll find it easier to listen to and to understand every day and you'll also have something to talk about with colleagues at work!

If you have a special interest, find an English language podcast on that subject and listen to it regularly; if it's work related it will help you when talking to colleagues, but it's also useful to find podcasts on your favourite hobbies too. Try starting at the Podcast Directory (www.podcastdirectory.com) and see what you can find.

Watching Movies and DVDs

You have plenty of opportunities for watching movies in English, both at the cinema or by joining a DVD rental club or perhaps borrowing them from your local library. DVDs are probably the best option because nowadays most of them come with various options for the language and the subtitles. You can start off by watching the film in your own language if the audio track is available, then watch it again in English this time, and turn on the subtitles in your language. Finally, watch it in English only with no subtitles.

One of the great advantages of watching films on DVD is that you can pause and rewind and watch the same scene over and over again until you're happy that you understand everything. It's probably best to watch the film through once without stopping otherwise you might find that you're not enjoying the film at all!

You can also turn watching a DVD into a kind of game – watch a scene in the film with the subtitles turned off and write down some of the keywords from the scene. Then watch the scene again this time with the subtitles turned on, and check to see whether the keywords you heard come up in the scene itself.

If you really want the full effect then go to the cinema. In most cinemas you won't find subtitled films (you'll need to go to smaller independent cinemas or art cinemas to see this kind of film) so you really need to concentrate if you visit the cinema. However, choosing films you're really interested in helps you concentrate and understand more.

Before going to the cinema, read some reviews of the film you're going to see – find out the important information and names of characters and perhaps watch a trailer on the Internet to give you a good idea of the story. If a book version of the film exists, read it before going (or afterwards, if you don't want to ruin the surprise) and compare it with the film. You can also find out a lot of information about films at the Internet Movie Database at www.imdb.com. There you'll find trailers, a synopsis of the film (though be careful not to read the *spoilers*, information that can tell you too much about the movie and spoil any surprises) and information about the actors and actresses.

Surfing the Web

Using the Internet for any research into your hobbies and interests is a great idea. A large part of the content of the web is in English for you to enjoy and benefit from. You can start by looking at news sources such as the BBC (http://news.bbc.co.uk) and CNN (www.cnn.com), but it doesn't stop there. You can get all sorts of hints and tips about living in the UK, improving your English and making friends around the world in other English-speaking countries.

Find blogs about the area you live in – these are great ways to improve your English and find out a little bit about what goes on around you. Try the UK Blog Directory at www.ukblogdirectory.co.uk or simply use a search engine to look for local blogs (try a search like 'London blogs').

Try keeping a blog of your experiences in English. This helps you to think about your written English but also gives you a chance to express how you feel about your new home and explain some of the humorous or puzzling things that happen to you every day. Writing on a regular basis like this really helps.

Explore social networking sites like Facebook (www.facebook.com) or MySpace (www.myspace.com) or (if you're in the mood) dating and singles sites where people advertise to meet other people.

Chatting with a Keypal

When we were young and learning French at school it was typical to have a *penpal*, a person the same age in another country with whom we would exchange letters during the school year. Having penpals is a great way to practise your English, and of course it's much easier and quicker these days with the Internet.

A *keypal* is an electronic penpal, so instead of exchanging letters you exchange emails. A penpal might just be a social friend, but can also be someone who works in the same area as you, a professional contact with whom you talk about work.

Whoever you find to write to, try to dedicate some time each day or so to sit down and write an email. It takes a bit of effort and dedication to keep this kind of thing going, so it's important to find the right person and to stick at it.

If writing emails doesn't appeal to you, why not try something more lively and in real time? Consider one of the following:

- ✔ **Live Messenger (`http://download.live.com/?sku=messenger`):** Use this application to chat to friends and colleagues using text.

- ✔ **Skype (`www.skype.com`):** Keep in touch with family, friends and colleagues using Skype. You can make free calls to friends in your Skype network and cheap calls to phones around the world. This is great for keeping in touch with family back home too – much cheaper than any other phone network.

- ✔ **Twitter (`www.twitter.com`):** Sign up to find and follow people who have the same interests as you. You can only send messages shorter than 140 characters, so this is for people who don't want to write too much!

Getting a Second Life

If you work a lot with technology, or you enjoy using the Internet at home, you can do much more besides looking at websites and listening to podcasts. Why not try a virtual world such as Second Life where you can meet people from all around the world and chat in English?

In Second Life you create a character and wander around the virtual world talking to people from all sorts of different countries and backgrounds. You can practise your written English by using the text chat, or plug in a microphone and speakers to talk to people. The great thing about Second Life is that people are always online and most of them are happy to talk.

You can register for a free account and download the software you need at `www.secondlife.com`. After you've registered and installed the software, try visiting some of these places:

- ✔ Virtual Dublin: `http://slurl.com/secondlife/dublin/80/75/24`
- ✔ Virtual Liverpool: `http://slurl.com/secondlife/mathew%20 street/140/86/32`

✔ Virtual London: `http://slurl.com/secondlife/Knightsbridge/197/166/22`

You may also have the chance to visit places from your home country if you're feeling a little homesick occasionally. Take a look at this website for more suggestions on real world places in Second Life: `www.avatarlanguages.com/freepractice.php`.

You can also get real English lessons in Second Life through language schools such as LanguageLab (`www.languagelab.com`). Taking lessons online is a very flexible way of improving your English because you can usually study at times that suit you – perhaps in the evenings or at the weekends.

Reading Books

Britain has a good network of libraries so you don't have to spend your hard-earned money on buying books all the time. Most libraries also stock videos, DVDs and music CDs, and in some you'll find computers with access to the Internet as well as helpful people to show you how to use everything.

Start by finding out about your local area – you can find books on the geography and history as well as local information on events and festivals, and all manner of reference information. This is a great way of building your local knowledge.

Find an author you've read in your own language and re-read the book in English. If you know the story it's easier to follow. Don't spend too much time looking up all the words but just try to get an idea of the language and the sounds. Learn a few words if you like, but don't let a dictionary spoil your enjoyment of a good book. Don't forget, you don't have to understand everything to enjoy reading.

Don't forget to take anything you borrow from the library back before the time is up – it's polite and it might stop you having to pay a fine for keeping the item too long!

Playing Games

A practical game that really helps widen your vocabulary is to use those little sticky notes you can buy in any newsagent's or stationer's and stick them around your flat or house. On one side put an English word you need to know, and on the other side put an explanation or a picture or even a translation.

As you move around the house, keep an eye out for the stickers and see how much you remember each day. Change the stickers regularly as you remember the words.

Buy a set of fridge magnets with English words on them. Stick up important words or short sentences on the fridge door and take a look at them every time you open the fridge. Again, vary the words and phrases when you think you've learnt the ones on the door.

Try easy crosswords in local free newspapers. In the UK most papers have two types of crosswords: cryptic and normal. The cryptic ones usually have complicated clues with lots of word tricks in them, but the normal ones usually just use synonyms and these help to expand your vocabulary. You'll probably find this difficult at first, but with the help of a good dictionary or thesaurus you'll quickly learn a lot of new words by doing these puzzles.

You can also find a lot of games and language quizzes on the Internet. Try a few each day – perhaps 15 minutes of practice. You can find word games here: www.manythings.org.

Chapter 16

Ten Favourite English Expressions

*E*very language has phrases that people commonly use, and English is no exception. Popular expressions people use in Britain are different from those people use in other English-speaking countries, such as New Zealand or India or the USA. In this chapter we take a look at ten common British expressions.

You may already know some of these phrases, or perhaps you've heard them if you've already visited the UK.

A Bit Much

You use this expression to describe something that is annoying or excessive. You can use the phrase to describe either a situation or a person. For example, imagine that you need to go to three separate offices to get an official piece of paper for something – in this case you can express your annoyance with the bureaucracy by saying 'It's a bit much'.

Here's a look at how Jacques and Gil use the expression in the context of office work:

Jacques:	I rang the Belgian office yesterday about that order that still hasn't arrived.
Gil:	What did they say?
Jacques:	They kept me waiting on the line for twenty minutes while they looked for the paperwork.
Gil:	That's a bit much!

Jacques: Yes, I was furious. Especially as it was their fault that the order didn't arrive.

You can also express your annoyance with a person you find too friendly or overbearing or rude by saying 'She's a bit much'.

Jacques: What do you think of Helen? Do you get on well with her?

Gil: Yes, she's really friendly and outgoing. She came up to me on my first day at work and invited me out for a coffee.

Jacques: Yes, she is friendly, but she can be a bit much.

Gil: Do you think so? I quite like her.

At the End of the Day

This expression means the same as 'in conclusion'. You use this expression to make a final point or to summarise what you've been saying.

Jacques: The Belgian office kept me waiting on the line for twenty minutes. Then they told me that they couldn't find the paperwork for the missing order.

Gil: How annoying! What are they going to do now?

Jacques: I'm not sure. They said they'll send me an email as soon as they find out what has happened. At the end of the day, it's their responsibility to sort this out.

Gil: Right, I hope they can get the paperwork to you soon.

Fancy a Drink?

People use this expression a lot to invite someone to have a drink, for example in a pub. The full form of the question is 'Do you fancy a drink?' and it means 'Would you like (to go for or have) a drink?'. You don't use the phrase only to offer alcoholic drinks: you may hear somebody say 'Fancy a cup of tea?' or 'Fancy a coffee?'. A friend may use this expression to invite you to go to a pub, or to go to a cafe for a coffee – people often use the expression as a way of inviting you out, which we talk about in Chapter 6. You may also hear expressions such as 'Fancy a movie?' or 'Fancy a meal?'.

You can answer this question many different ways. If you'd like to accept the offer, you can say 'Sure, that sounds great' or simply 'Yes please!'. If you want to refuse the offer, you can say 'No thanks, I'm busy' or 'Sorry, I can't because . . .' and give an excuse. *Note:* If you refuse an invitation in English, it's polite to give a reason.

Jacques: We've got half an hour before the movie starts – fancy a coffee?

Gil: Sure, good idea. There's a place over the road that looks quite nice. Shall we go there?

Jacques: Okay, but the coffee is on me!

'It's on me' means 'I will pay for it'. This is a very common expression in the UK.

Fingers Crossed

To cross your fingers while talking is to symbolise good luck, or to show that you hope a wish will come true. This is a custom that comes from when people believed that by crossing their fingers they could keep away bad luck and witches. Nowadays you say the phrase 'fingers crossed', or 'cross fingers', to show that you wish for a happy outcome for a situation.

Jacques: So the Belgian office told me they would send me an email as soon as they found the missing paperwork. Guess what? This morning I had another phone call.

Gil: And what did they say?

Jacques: It turns out that the London office had the paperwork all along. I rang Pete in London and asked him to get this order sorted out as soon as possible.

Gil: Well, fingers crossed. The client is already unhappy with the delay.

In this case Gil is expressing his hope that the situation will end well, by saying 'fingers crossed'. He could also say 'Fingers crossed that this gets sorted out quickly', but by simply using 'fingers crossed' it's clear that he's hoping for a happy ending to the situation they're discussing.

Good Weekend?

In informal situations, friends often use short forms of questions. If you'd like to ask a friend if he or she had a good weekend, you can simply say 'Good weekend?'. The full form of the question is 'Did you have a good weekend?', but it's very common in informal situations to cut a question down to the simplest elements. You may also hear questions like 'Good holiday?' instead of the full form 'Did you have a good holiday?'.

To answer this question you could say 'Yes, thanks, it was great' or 'Not bad' or 'Not that great – we couldn't get tickets for the concert'. If you give a negative answer to a question like this (for example, 'Not that great') you should also give a (brief!) reason for why your weekend wasn't that good.

Jacques: Good weekend?

Gil: Not that great – I forgot that it was Simone's birthday, so she was furious!

How's It Going?

This is an informal way of asking people how they are. The question 'How are you?' is also used a lot, and is more neutral, so is more appropriate for more formal situations such as a business meeting, or for when you meet someone you don't know. You use 'How's it going?' between friends, so make sure you use this in the right situation. A good answer to this question is 'Fine thanks, and you?', which you can also use to answer the question 'How are you?'. Here's an example of two friends using the expression:

Jacques: Hi, Gil, I haven't seen you for ages! How's it going?

Gil: Jacques! Great to see you! I'm fine, and you?

Jacques: Fine, fine, can't complain!

See You Later

You can use this very common expression in informal situations to say goodbye to friends. You can also say 'Goodbye' or 'Bye', but 'See you later' is friendlier and more informal. When you use the expression it doesn't literally mean that you'll see the person a little later – weeks may go past before you see each other again.

Jacques: Okay, time for me to go. Thanks for the coffee. See you later.

Gil: Sure, you're welcome. See you.

You can use the phrase 'See you' on its own, as Gil does in this example – he simply replies 'See you' to Jacques. You can also combine 'See you' with other time words, so you can say 'See you tomorrow' or 'See you next week' or 'See you next Tuesday'.

Tell Me About It!

When you use this expression you're expressing sympathy and telling some-body that you already know what it's like to be in the same situation. Imagine a friend tells you that at rush hour it took him an hour and a half to get home instead of the normal 45 minutes. You can respond by saying 'Tell me about it', meaning that you know very well that rush hour traffic can be terrible. The conversation may look like this:

Jacques: It took me an hour and a half to get home last night. The traffic was terrible!

Gill: Tell me about it! I stopped taking the car and now I use public transport – it's much quicker.

The phrase isn't an invitation for Jacques to tell Gil the details about the rush hour traffic. The expression 'Tell me about it' does *not* require an answer – it's simply a way of expressing sympathetic agreement. You pronounce this expression in a flat, world-weary sort of voice – it's best to listen to other people using this expression, and the intonation that they use, before you try it yourself.

Text Me

In 2009, 85 per cent of the adult population in Britain had a mobile phone, and that number is increasing. Along with keys and money, a mobile phone is one thing people always take with them when they leave home. Not surpris-ingly, mobile phone language has become a natural part of English. Now tex-ting language exists, so, for example, when you send a mobile text message you often type 'CU' instead of the full version 'See you' (check out Chapter 8 for more about texting).

In a land of so many mobile phones, text messaging has become a very popular form of communication. It's much cheaper to *text people* (to send a text message) than to call them. Because of this, the phrase 'text me' has become as common as 'call me'. 'Text me' simply means 'send me a text message', and you can use this expression when making arrangements. Here's how you can use the phrase in conversation. Jacques and Gil are on the bus together on their way home from work:

Jacques:	What time does the film start?
Gil:	I'm not sure. I'll need to check when I get home.
Jacques:	Okay, text me and I'll meet you there fifteen minutes before it starts.
Gil:	Okay, I'll text you as soon as I get home then.

You can ask a person to send you a text message by saying 'Text me', and you can also promise to send a text message to somebody by saying 'I'll text you' as this conversation shows.

You Must Be Joking!

People use this expression to express disbelief, especially if someone tells them something unusual or unexpected. Imagine that a friend tells you that he had to pay £20 for a pint of beer in a pub – this is an enormous amount of money for a drink, so to express disbelief or shock, you can say 'You must be joking!'.

Remember that you use this expression only as a response to unusual or shocking pieces of information, and you need to pronounce it in a slightly exaggerated manner, not in a flat or a dull tone of voice.

Jacques:	My landlord has increased our rent by a hundred and fifty pounds a month.
Gil:	You must be joking! That's far too much! Are you going to look for another flat?
Jacques:	I'll have to – I can't afford the rent any more.

Chapter 17

Ten (Actually 11) Holidays to Remember

In This Chapter

▶ Meeting some of Britain's multicultural holidays

▶ Knowing when and where to celebrate special British events

▶ Having a day off work for a public holiday

*E*verybody loves a holiday – a time to escape from your normal routine, to put your feet up and relax or to explore new places. Many people in Britain have at least one long holiday a year, of a week or several weeks – this kind of holiday is known as a *vacation* in the USA. On this sort of holiday, you might go camping or to the seaside or to visit another country.

But during the course of a normal year, people in Britain also celebrate religious and non-religious festivals – these are also known as *holidays*, even if they only last one day. Some religious holidays, such as Christmas or Easter Monday, are very important in the UK, and people get these days off work or school to celebrate. Of course, even on special religious holidays such as these some people still do need to work, such as hospital and public transport workers who need to provide minimum services. But be aware that on a day like Christmas Day, no public transport runs in even large cities such as London. Don't try to use buses, trains or the Underground on Christmas Day!

The word *holiday* comes from putting *holy* and *day* together. Originally, holidays were only for special religious days, but in modern times holidays – days off work and school and when shops and services close – are to celebrate both religious and non-religious events.

As an increasingly multicultural society, different communities in Britain celebrate a large number of holidays and festivals. In some cases, religious and popular holidays mean that people don't need to go to work on that day.

But in other cases, work continues as normal. Valentine's Day, for example, is known as a holiday, but people work on this day.

You probably already know about Christmas and Easter, which are an important part of the Christian calendar all over the world, so in this chapter we look at holidays and festivals that you may know less about, but that are an integral part of life in many parts of the UK.

Multicultural Celebrations

Britain has a few public holidays for Christian religious holidays. In many schools and workplaces, people also celebrate religious holidays for other faiths. In some primary schools, for example, teachers encourage children to create greeting cards for holidays celebrated by people of faiths other than Christianity.

Britain has a large community of people from the Indian subcontinent, which means that some people celebrate Indian festivals in the UK. One of the best-known Hindu, Buddhist and Sikh festivals is called Diwali, or the Festival of Lights. This is a particularly beautiful festival in which people light small oil-burning lamps or candles that symbolise the triumph of good over evil. Diwali takes place on the new moon between 13 October and 14 November each year.

In Britain, Hindu and Sikh communities celebrate Diwali. People give each other gifts and sweets, and clean and decorate their houses with candles and oil lamps. The city of Leicester in England holds large Diwali celebrations every year. In the East End of London, people often combine Diwali and the English holiday of Guy Fawkes Night (or Bonfire Night – see the later section) into a joint event with fireworks and bonfires.

Other religious festivals celebrated in Britain include the Muslim festival of Eid and the Jewish festival of Hannukah. Eid falls on the same day every year in the Islamic calendar, but in the Gregorian or Western calendar it occurs approximately 11 days earlier each year. Hannukah is also known as the Festival of Lights, and it occurs between late November and late December in the Gregorian calendar.

Diwali, Eid and Hannukah aren't public holidays in the UK – work continues as normal in Britain on these days.

Public (or Bank) Holidays

People in the UK usually call public holidays *bank holidays* – because banks close on these days. If a public holiday falls on a weekend day (on a Saturday or a Sunday), the holiday usually moves to the following Monday. This is so that people don't lose the holiday if it falls on a weekend, which is usually a day off for many people.

Bank holidays celebrated all over the UK include Christmas Day (25 December), Boxing Day or St Stephen's Day (26 December), New Year's Day (1 January), Easter Monday and Good Friday (the dates for these two days vary every year, but they usually occur in March or April). In addition to these mainly religious holidays are the May Day bank holiday (the first Monday in May), the spring bank holiday (the last Monday in May) and the summer bank holiday (the last Monday in August).

The May Day bank holiday occurs on 1 May, or on the next Monday after 1 May. In many countries 1 May is International Workers' Day, although in the UK the May Day bank holiday isn't always associated with this and is celebrated more as a spring festival. Some towns, such as Whitstable in Kent and Hastings in Sussex, hold festivals with traditional music and dancing for May Day.

New Year (1 January)

In the Gregorian calendar, New Year starts on 1 January, and that day is always a public holiday in the UK. The night of 31 December – New Year's Eve – is a time of celebration, and parties (both public and private) take place everywhere. In some cities people like to go to the central square of the town to listen to the clocks strike midnight and to bring in the new year. Particularly large public gatherings for New Year in Britain take place around the London Eye in London and in Cardiff, Birmingham, Leeds, Manchester, Glasgow and Edinburgh. A canon is fired from Edinburgh Castle at midnight. Television channels broadcast many of these celebrations live.

New Year in Scotland is called Hogmanay, and it has its own unique traditions. One of the best-known Hogmanay traditions is called *first footing*, which involves visiting friends or neighbours and being the first person to set your foot over the doorstep, which brings good luck to the house for the rest of the year. Traditionally, first footers carried symbolic gifts such as salt, coal or whiskey. Nowadays it's more common to simply visit friends and neighbours during the night of 31 December – and this can continue into the early hours of 1 January and even continue until 2 January, which is also a public holiday in Scotland (but not in the rest of the UK).

Chinese New Year (January or February)

Chinese New Year is the most important event in the Chinese lunar calendar. In the UK people celebrate this holiday in cities that have large Chinese communities. London claims to have one of the biggest Chinese New Year parades outside of Asia.

In Soho, the heart of the Chinese community in London, also known as Chinatown, people put up red paper lanterns up in the streets two weeks before the Chinese New Year celebrations begin, and take them down two weeks later. During the celebrations themselves, groups of dancers carrying paper and cloth dragons dance through the streets to music and singing. Chinatown is a very small part of London, so it can get very crowded with tourists and visitors at this time of year.

Chinese New Year is usually celebrated with the family, with people exchanging small gifts of food and sweets, and red envelopes of money. It is also the time to give the house a thorough clean. The most important part of Chinese New Year is a large dinner with the family. In China, Chinese New Year lasts 15 days, although in the West Chinese communities may celebrate a slightly shorter version of the holiday.

Valentine's Day (14 February)

People celebrate Valentine's Day, or Saint Valentine's Day, on the same day – 14 February – all over the world. It is the day on which lovers express their feelings for each other, and give each other cards and gifts such as flowers or chocolates. St Valentine was an early Christian saint, and his name became associated with romantic love in the early Middle Ages in Western Europe. In the early 19th century it became popular for lovers to exchange hand-written love letters or notes on Valentine's Day, and nowadays lovers exchange commercially produced greeting cards.

Valentine's Day is an extremely commercial celebration in the UK, and it's almost obligatory to buy chocolate and cards for your partner on the day. For this reason some people are critical of Valentine's Day.

St Patrick's Day (17 March)

St Patrick is the patron saint of Ireland, but people celebrate St Patrick's Day all over the world, not only in Ireland. The most famous (and the largest)

St Patrick's Day's parade takes place in New York City with up to 2 million spectators! People also celebrate St Patrick's Day in the UK, Australia, New Zealand and Canada – in fact, anywhere where a sizeable Irish community exists. The holiday is a Christian festival but it also celebrates everything Irish, and the dominant colour of St Patrick's Day is green. Large St Patrick's Day parades in the UK take place in Birmingham, Liverpool, Manchester and in London around Trafalgar Square – in 2008 people dyed the water of the fountain in Trafalgar Square green for St Patrick's Day.

One of the best-known alcoholic drinks from Ireland is Guinness, a dark beer, and before St Patrick's Day you see many pubs in the UK announcing special deals on Guinness and other beers to celebrate St Patrick's Day. On St Patrick's Day, you find pubs around the UK full of people celebrating, even if they aren't Irish.

Mother's Day (March) and Father's Day (June)

If you happen to be in the UK on Mother's Day or on Father's Day, you'll probably first find out about this event by looking at shop windows. Many people complain that Mother's Day and Father's Day are purely commercial and that shops promote these occasions just to make money. Where does Mother's Day come from? One explanation is that Mother's Day comes from the USA and was invented by a woman called Anna Jarvis in 1912. But at the end of her life she was so disappointed at how commercial the day had become that she protested publicly against it, was arrested by police for disturbing the peace and said that she wished she had never thought of creating Mother's Day in the first place.

Mother's Day is held on different dates in different parts of the world. In the UK Mother's Day falls on the fourth Sunday of Lent (a period in the Christian calendar) and is celebrated usually in March. Typically, on Mother's Day children buy their mothers flowers or a small gift of chocolates or jewellery, and a greeting card.

Father's Day is similar in many ways to Mother's Day. It's held on different dates in different parts of the world and just as Mother's Day celebrates motherhood, Father's Day celebrates fatherhood. Children typically buy small gifts for their fathers. The idea behind Father's Day also comes originally from the United States in the early 1900s, and the US passed a law in 1966 which made it an official day in that country. In the UK, people celebrate Father's Day on the third Sunday in June.

Notting Hill Carnival (London, August)

Carnival is a festival associated with the Christian calendar, and is mainly celebrated in Catholic countries. Carnival usually takes place between late January and late February every year. Probably the most famous Carnival celebrations in the world are those held in Rio de Janeiro in Brazil, in New Orleans in the USA (also called Mardi Gras) and in Venice in Italy.

Britain isn't an obvious venue for Carnival, as it's mainly a Protestant Christian country. In the UK, immigrants from the West Indies brought with them the Caribbean Carnival, and in London every year the famous Notting Hill Carnival is held in the summer. This Carnival is no longer connected to religion in any way, and it's even held at a completely different time of year to Carnival in other countries, but the roots of this Carnival come from the Christian tradition. The Notting Hill Carnival is led by the Caribbean community in the area, many of whom have lived there since the 1950s. It has become a huge annual event in the UK, and can attract more than 2 million visitors during the two days that it's held every August. This makes it the second biggest street carnival in the world after Rio!

The Notting Hill Carnival was first held in 1959 as a reaction against racist attacks against the Caribbean community in London, and since then it has become a celebration of the multicultural nature of London. People from all over the world attend this event.

Apart from the Notting Hill Carnival, some other towns and cities in Britain hold an annual carnival. This kind of carnival isn't connected to the Christian calendar either, and can mean a street parade or a festival.

Halloween (31 October)

Americans celebrate Halloween more than the British, but in recent years it has become increasingly popular in Britain and in certain parts of Europe. The word *Halloween* originally comes from All Hallows Eve, and it is also known as All Saints Day. All Hallows Eve (the night of 31 October) involves honouring the dead and in some countries, such as Spain and Mexico, families visit graveyards on 1 November in order to honour and remember dead members of the family. The family may say prayers, offer flowers and clean and tidy the grave.

From this celebration of 'the day of the dead' come many of the commercial images we associate today with Halloween – skulls, skeletons and children dressing up as supernatural figures.

Traditions for Halloween today include *trick or treating*, in which children dress up as ghosts or witches or in other costumes and visit neighbouring houses to ask for sweets.

Other typical images of Halloween include carved pumpkins with candles inside. The main impetus for importing Halloween from the USA into Britain and Europe has come from commerce – companies hope to make money from selling Halloween goods. For this reason British and other European people often see the holiday with sceptical eyes.

Bonfire Night (5 November)

People celebrate this festival, also called Guy Fawkes Night, in the UK and in some other countries of the Commonwealth such as New Zealand and South Africa. The day marks an event from 5 November 1605 in which a group of men, including Guy Fawkes, were caught planning to blow up the Houses of Parliament in London. There's some controversy over the celebration of this date – some people claim that there was no plot to blow up the Houses of Parliament and that these men were framed because they were all Catholics.

Whatever the historical truth behind the incident, people still celebrate Bonfire Night in many parts of the UK, with fireworks and large bonfires. It's common to put an effigy or figure of a man on the fire – this figure originally represented Guy Fawkes, but in modern times people like to burn effigies of unpopular politicians. One of the biggest celebrations of Bonfire Night takes place in Lewes, near Brighton in southern England – this small town usually has up to six large bonfires on Bonfire Night.

Armistice Day (11 November)

Armistice Day celebrates the end of the First World War on 11 November 1918. The war formally ended at 11 o'clock in the morning on 11 November – 'the 11th hour of the 11th day of the 11th month'. Armistice Day is a day on which to remember and honour the dead of the First World War in many of the Allied countries (Australia, New Zealand, Canada, South Africa and the UK). It's also called Remembrance Day and Veterans' Day. In the UK, people often observe two minutes of silence in public places on 11 November.

You may also hear this day called Poppy Day. A poppy is a small red flower with a black centre. The flower symbolises the fields of northern France, covered with poppies in the spring, on which so many soldiers died. On Armistice Day the streets of many of the cities in the UK have people selling plastic poppies, which you can put in the buttonhole of your jacket or shirt.

Chapter 18

Ten Phrases That Make You Sound Fluent in English

In This Chapter

▶ Sounding like a native

▶ Avoiding common pitfalls

Sounding like a native in most languages involves having enough every-day language to be able to talk to people on different levels – sometimes it's just social, like talking about the weather and asking about friends and family, and sometimes it's work-related, like being able to talk about your job. Often it's a mix of the two.

But most countries have little stock phrases that are in constant use, and these phrases can help you fit in a little better and sound a little more like a native speaker.

We can't cover all of the phrases in this chapter, but here we present ten that can make a difference in certain situations. Of course, it's important not to use the phrases too often – listen to other speakers of English and see how often they use them, and when, and you'll soon be sounding native yourself.

Actually

People are divided in their opinions over the use of the word *actually*: some people think that British people use it too much and should think about other ways of starting sentences; others use it all the time and have no problem with the word. In the most basic form, *actually* means something along the lines of 'in actual fact' or 'really' – but you find it starting a lot of sentences in English, and almost with no real meaning any more. It's just a word to introduce thoughts, ideas or . . . well, anything, really. Here are some examples – you can try taking the word *actually* out of them to see if they still make sense:

- ✔ Actually, I need to finish this report before I go home.
- ✔ Actually, he's not working this week.
- ✔ Actually, we're staying in tonight – too much work to do!

You can safely remove the word *actually* and the sentences are unchanged. But it's a very popular word in English, so using it gives you that 'native' edge.

You may also hear people starting or finishing similar sentences with the phrase 'as it happens' – this doesn't mean much either, it simply introduces or highlights a piece of information into a discussion, and people often use this phrase instead of *actually*:

- ✔ As it happens, she's on holiday this week.
- ✔ I don't really like Italian food, as it happens.

Bless You!

Sneezing is supposed to be a very simple thing – you sneeze, you perhaps excuse yourself for making such a noise and then everybody carries on doing what they were doing. But of course it's more complicated than that, because in many countries and languages it's customary for people to react to a sneeze.

In English people generally say 'bless you' when somebody sneezes. This is a short form of the phrase 'God bless you', and people have many theories for why we say this. Most of the theories involve religion, bad luck or disease. If you want to know more about the possible origins, take a look at the Wikipedia entry here: `http://en.wikipedia.org/wiki/Bless_you`.

What you don't want to do is shout out a translation of 'bless you' in your native language. For example, if you're Spanish and visiting London, you don't want to shout out 'Jesus!' (the Spanish translation of 'bless you') when someone sneezes. In English, people often use 'Jesus!' as a sign of frustration and so this wouldn't have the same meaning as 'bless you'.

You can find out more about different linguistic reactions to sneezing around the world here: `www.mamalisa.com/blog/how-do-you-sneeze-in-your-country`.

Bon Appétit!

It's a popular myth that British food is terrible – and impossible to find among the Italian, Chinese, Greek and other restaurants usually found in most towns and cities – and critics tell you that this is why the British have no set phrase to offer diners before eating, such as 'bon appétit'. In a lot of countries when people sit down to eat they wish each other an enjoyable meal. Indeed, in some countries you even see such phrases printed on table-cloths and placemats.

Where we live, in Catalonia in Spain, it's normal to see white paper place-mats with 'buen provecho' (Spanish), 'bon profit' (Catalan) and 'bon appétit' (French) written on them around the edges. On the fourth edge you can often find 'good profit', which is considered to be the English version – but that's wrong, because the Brits don't use this phrase at all! When diners enter res-taurants in Spain and pass by your table, they often say 'buen provecho' (or similar) to wish you a happy dinner or lunch, but you won't find the same thing happening in Britain. Brits usually just get on with the eating!

Some people say 'enjoy your meal', but it always sounds a little forced and a little uncomfortable. It's normal for restaurant staff in the UK to say this when they serve your food, but what do Brits say to each other when they sit down to eat? The answer, often, is the French phrase 'bon appétit'.

Perhaps Brits use the phrase because the French have a good reputation for the quality of their cuisine (there's another French word!) or perhaps 'bon appétit' is an old-style phrase from the days when the top restaurants often had French waiting staff, or perhaps it's a little snobbishness?

Whatever the reason, listen carefully and you'll probably hear that Brits are a little reluctant to say 'bon appétit' and when they do they often say it with a slightly comical, overdone French accent. It's as if Brits know it's an odd thing to say, so they try to make it a little funny.

Come to Think of It . . .

Like 'hang on a minute', which we mention later, Brits often use 'come to think of it' when a new idea occurs to them, or they suddenly remember something. The phrase reflects a sudden thought or memory, or something that you need to consider in a certain context.

Katy:	So, I'll get the food and you organise the drinks.
Mike:	That's fine. Is there anything else we need to do?
Katy:	Come to think of it, we should get him a leaving present – we usually get something when people are leaving the company.
Mike:	Right, good idea! Shall I do that, or will you?

Katy: Not being funny, but you're terrible at buying presents!

Mike: No, you're absolutely right. I think I'll leave that up to you then.

Katy: I thought you'd say that!

Do You See What I Mean?

You can ask people if they understand what you're saying, or whether they agree with you in lots of ways. These often have different meanings – sometimes you expect people to agree with you, sometimes you allow them to disagree and sometimes you're just checking to make sure they understand you. So:

✔ **Do you agree with me?**

- Wouldn't you agree?

- Wouldn't you say?

- Don't you think?

✔ **Do you understand me?**

- (Do you) see what I mean?

- Do you get me?

- Are you with me?

Hang on a Minute

This phrase, like so many others in English, has two quite different meanings and uses. The first is probably quite obvious – it means 'please wait a moment':

Sally: We're going out for a walk. Are you coming?

Piotr: Hang on a minute, I just need to finish this email.

Sally: Okay – no rush.

The other use of 'hang on a minute' is when you've just had an idea or a thought. It means something like 'wait, I've just thought of something':

James: So we do the shopping, then go to the bank and then we can get some lunch.

Michelle:	Hang on a minute.
James:	What?
Michelle:	Won't the banks be closed by the time we finish the shopping?
James:	You're right, I hadn't thought of that. Maybe we should go to the bank first?
Michelle:	I think so, just to be on the safe side.

Lovely Day!

Ah, the British weather! Now it's certainly not going to be a lovely day every day in Britain. In fact, you'll see plenty of rain, grey skies and some even worse weather. But the British have a reputation of making the best out of something bad and of not complaining very often.

This can be a bad thing (the British often suffer terrible food in restaurants because they're not very good at complaining), but the trait is part of the British character and more often than not you find people using these optimistic phrases.

You often hear the phrases 'Lovely day!' and '(it's) turned out nice again!', even when you think it's cold and grey and miserable. The fact is, unless you are in the middle of a snowstorm then you're more likely to hear how 'nice' the weather is than to hear someone complaining about it. More British irony, certainly – but this is part of being British and keeping a positive attitude in the face of adversity, and that's part of the British stereotype!

This positive attitude also carries over into other parts of life. So, when someone asks how you are, you may reply 'Can't complain', or 'Mustn't grumble' or 'Not so bad'.

Read this conversation between Sergio from Spain and his British colleague John. Notice Sergio's mistakes!

John:	Lovely day!
Sergio:	Not really. It's cold, grey and miserable. It's much nicer in Spain.
John:	Oh, I see.
Sergio:	Yes, I really need some sun.

John:	Still, you look well!
Sergio:	Not really, I've got a terrible headache and a sore throat.
John:	Oh . . .

Here Sergio has confused poor John by 'not playing the game', but instead complaining about the weather *and* his health! If you're ill it's best to see a doctor, who at least is paid to be sympathetic and listen to your troubles! But make sure you don't complain about the weather to him – he's not paid for that . . .

Not Being Funny, But . . .

British people don't like to criticise things or seem too pessimistic about anything, but on some occasions you may want to say something negative about someone or tell someone something that you think she won't like. In many languages and cultures it's quite acceptable to come right out and say it, but in English you often want to introduce the subject slowly and carefully – or to 'sweeten the pill', to borrow a phrase from medicine.

In these circumstances the phrase '(I'm) not being funny, but . . .' is a good introduction. Basically, it tells the person you're talking to that something a little negative is coming, that it's probably personal, but that you're only trying to help and you're not being deliberately difficult. Here's an example:

Clara:	John, could I have a word, please?
John:	Sure, Clara – what's the problem?
Clara:	Well, I'm not being funny, but those clothes aren't really suitable for having meetings with clients.
John:	Really?
Clara:	I think so – a shirt and tie, or suit and shirt would be better.
John:	Sure – no problem. It's always difficult to know what 'smart casual' really means. I'll pop home and change.
Clara:	Thanks, John, I'm glad you understand.

The Thing Is . . .

This phrase is a little complicated. It often introduces an unpopular idea or something that the speaker thinks is important and should be discussed, but a lot of the time it's simply at the start of a sentence with no real meaning.

A study in 2008 found that approximately 10 per cent of all British speech is made up of these words called *fillers* – words that have no real meaning but you use them to give you time to think.

This phrase is one that's often followed by a slight pause. You might, for example, hear the phrase beginning a sentence in a discussion between a couple who are breaking up, or between an employer and an employee. Perhaps like this:

Alan:	We need to look at the sales figures for this month, Jacques.
Jacques:	Sure – what's the problem?
Alan:	The thing is, sales are down 25 per cent, and we're going to have to make some changes.
Jacques:	Changes?
Alan:	Yes, reductions . . . ummm . . . in the, umm . . . workforce.
Jacques:	You mean redundancies?
Alan:	Umm . . . yes, I suppose I do.

Here Alan uses the phrase to signal some unpopular information, and to help Jacques prepare for that information.

You Know What?

This phrase is excellent for starting a conversation or for introducing a new idea or a suggestion, or simply for making a comment. In fact, this is just a great phrase for joining in with any conversation! It generally means something like 'listen to me, because I'm about to say something interesting or useful'.

It looks like a question, of course – and it is, to some extent. But it's not a question that you expect an answer to! In fact, when you start a conversation with 'You know what?', you don't expect anyone to answer you, because you're introducing something that you know or think and are about to explain to everyone else.

After saying 'You know what?', it's customary to leave a small gap and wait for a response. Sometimes you get one – a single word, 'What?' – and sometimes you simply get silence, which indicates that you can continue and explain what's on your mind. A typical conversation might go something like this:

Alan:	I'm really not sure what to do tonight.
Sarah:	You know what?
Alan:	What?
Sarah:	I think we should stay in and save some money for a change.

Here we use the phrase to introduce a suggestion. There are some variations on this theme. In a discussion or argument you may see the phrase 'You know what I think?' to introduce an opinion, usually a strong one!

You may also see the short 'Guess what?'. Of course, you're not actually expected to guess what the other person is thinking, and you have a couple of possible answers: you can answer with a simple 'What?' or something longer, such as 'I don't know', What?' or 'You tell me!'.

Sacha:	Guess what?
Crystal:	What?
Sacha:	I've been promoted!
Crystal:	Really? Congratulations!

Note that on these occasions, the use of the word *what* is entirely appropriate, but be aware that some people find *what* quite rude in certain contexts. If you're in very polite company and someone starts talking to you with 'Excuse me?' then it's often impolite to answer 'What?'. Here you should try something like 'Yes, can I help you?'.

Part V
Appendices

In this part . . .

We have a list of super-handy appendices. Appendix A looks at phrasal verbs, which are very common in spoken English. You can sound quite fluent in English if you use phrasal verbs well! Sometimes the meaning of a phrasal verb can be difficult to understand, so we give you examples of verbs and explain carefully what they mean.

Appendix B looks at some of the most common verbs in English, such as 'have' and 'do'. Here we look at how to use these common verbs in several different ways. We also look at the most common past tense irregular verbs. Many learners find it useful to memorise these. Finally, in Appendix C, we give you a guide to the contents of the audio CD that comes with this book. We hope you enjoy it.

Appendix A

Phrasal Verbs

. . . .

*O*ne problem many people have with English is with the concept of phrasal verbs. Most English verbs are far less complex than verbs in other languages, with fewer forms for each tense – but with phrasal verbs English enters a whole new world of complexity.

In this appendix we help you understand the nature of phrasal verbs, and how and when to use them, and show you the difference between the five types of phrasal verb. We also give a list of the most common phrasal verbs in English.

For loads more detail about verbs and all things grammar-related, check out *English Grammar For Dummies* (Wiley).

Defining Phrasal Verbs

A *phrasal verb* is a verb followed by a particle (a preposition or an adverb). If all that terminology makes you nervous, simply think of a phrasal verb as a verb made up of more than one word.

Some books refer to phrasal verbs as 'two-word verbs', 'multi-word verbs' or 'prepositional verbs'.

You probably already know the following phrasal verbs:

- **Carry on:** Continue doing (your work, talking, watching TV).
    - *Carry on* with your work and I'll be back in half an hour.
- **Fill in:** Complete (an application form).
    - Could you *fill in* two copies of this form, please?
- **Hang on:** Wait.
    - *Hang on* for a few minutes – I'm nearly finished.

✔ **Look up:** Find information (a word in a dictionary).

  • Could you *look up* the train times to Birmingham, please?

✔ **Set off:** Leave (on a journey).

  • If we *set off* at ten, we'll be there in time for lunch.

Most phrasal verbs are made up of a few very common verbs (come, set, go, get, put) and a few common prepositions or adverbs (up, away, off, in). Sometimes it's quite easy to guess what they mean:

✔ **Hang up:** End a phone conversation (this comes from the old days of telephones when phones were usually on the wall and you'd literally 'hang' the receiver on the phone after a conversation).

  • Please *hang up* and try calling again in a few minutes.

Another easy-to-guess phrasal verb is *sit down*. When you sit it's usually down on a chair or a sofa. The verb tells you the principal action, and the direction of that action; for example 'Sit down and eat your dinner!'.

But many phrasal verbs often signify something quite different from what the words suggest:

✔ **Wear out:** Become very tired, or unusable.

  • He's *worn out* after all that exercise (very tired).

  • I've *worn out* these sandals with all the walking (broken, unusable).

Or how about *sit up*? This doesn't normally mean to take a seat somewhere higher. Sit up means to sit straight, and not slouch in a chair. You usually hear parents tell their kids to 'sit up and eat properly', meaning to straighten their backs, sit properly and have their dinner. The difference between *sit down* and *sit up* can cause problems for people learning English.

Phrasal verbs are very common in English, particularly in less formal and spoken English. A general rule is that phrasal verbs are informal and the Latinate equivalent is more formal, but this is only a general rule, and as with much of English you find exceptions.

Have a look at these two examples:

✔ **Informal:** I'll call in on Bob later for a quick coffee.

✔ **Formal:** Mr Jones will be visiting head office on Monday 12 August.

In the formal version you see the verb *visit*, which is the form that comes from the Latin, but in the informal version you see *call in on*, the phrasal verb that also means 'to visit'. In spoken English you often sound more formal if you use the Latinate form, but in formal contexts such as business you may sound too informal if you use common phrasal verbs. Again, observing how others speak and write is a good way to understand when to use – and when not to use – certain words or phrases.

Seeing Why Phrasal Verbs Are Special

Phrasal verbs have their own grammar and you need to understand the basics of that grammar in order to use them properly. The five types of phrasal verb are as follows (the verbs are in bold and italics; the objects are in bold):

✔ **Intransitive (an intransitive verb has no object):**

- *Get up*: to rise from bed.

- *Get up*, David! You're going to be late for work.

- You can use these phrasal verbs on their own; they don't take an object. So, you can tell people to 'get up' or 'slow down' and so on.

✔ **Transitive (a transitive verb has an object) with moveable object:**

- *Fill out*: complete a form.

- Please *fill out* **the application form** in black ink.

- Please *fill* **the application form** *out* in black ink.

- With these verbs, the object (in this case '**the application form**') can come after the phrasal verb or it can come in the middle of it. These phrasal verbs are often called *separable phrasal verbs* because you can separate the two parts – *fill* and *out* – with the object.

✔ **Transitive with fixed object in the middle of the verb:**

- *Set apart*: distinguish.

- Ron's research really *sets* **him** *apart* from the other journalists.

- With these verbs, the object **must** separate the parts of the phrasal verb.

✔ **Transitive with fixed object after the verb:**

- *Run into*: Meet by chance.

- I *ran into* **John** the other day in the Italian restaurant near work (not 'I ran John into the other day in the Italian restaurant near work').

- With these verbs the object must always come after the complete phrasal verb. These verbs are often called *inseparable* because you can't separate the parts of the phrasal verb with the object.

> ✔ **Transitive with two objects, separable:**
>
>   • *Put down to*: Attribute.
>
>   • They *put* **their exam success** *down to* **plenty of studying**.
>
>   • These phrasal verbs have two objects ('**exam success**' and '**plenty of studying**'). One of the objects separates the verb ('*put* **their exam success** *down to*') and the other comes after the verb itself ('**plenty of studying**').

Practising Phrasal Verbs

Unfortunately, there's no really easy way of learning phrasal verbs. We don't recommend looking for long lists of them and trying to memorise them – even though we do include a list of phrasal verbs in this appendix.

Try listening out for phrasal verbs and make a note when you hear one. Later, think about the context and who used it and you'll soon build up a list in your head and active vocabulary. When you note a new phrasal verb, take a look at this appendix and see what kind of verb it is – this helps you work out how to use the verb.

Try not to think of phrasal verbs as multi-word but instead to practise them as single vocabulary items. Keep notes of new phrasal verbs, perhaps with a translation or a cartoon or a couple of example sentences to help you remember. You can also add verbs that mean the opposite (if they exist) and perhaps the more 'formal' Latinate version of each verb:

Verb:	Look up
Meaning:	Research, look for
Context:	Dictionary, website, timetable, phone directory
Objects: number	A word, some information, train times, a phone
Verb type:	Type 2 – transitive, moveable object
Examples:	'Could you look up John's phone number, please?'
	'If you don't know a word, look it up in the dictionary.'
Latinate form:	Research, investigate

Try to group phrasal verbs together. We show you how you can group them grammatically earlier in this Appendix, but here are some other ways:

✔ **According to particle:** In many cases the particle gives clues to the meaning of the verb. For example, the particle *up* is often associated with movement (get up), an increase (speak up, hurry up) or the end of something (fill up, finish up).

✔ **According to verb:** For example, get, put, look. For example, for the verb *get* you might have get on, get up, get over, get off.

✔ **According to theme:** Try remembering the verbs as thematic objects connected with different things in your life: work, travel and so on. So, for travel you might have get away (for a break), check in (to a hotel), check in (for a flight), take off (plane), check out (of a hotel) and go on (an excursion).

The best way to practise phrasal verbs is simply to use them as soon as you encounter them. By using these verbs regularly you soon remember them and begin to feel comfortable with them. Use them in informal writing and speaking. But remember, too much of anything can turn out to sound a little artificial – so don't overdo it!

Meeting the Most Common Phrasal Verbs

Here are some of the most frequently used phrasal verbs in English. Listen for people using them in everyday conversations, and then use our tips in the earlier section 'Practising Phrasal Verbs' to help you incorporate them into your vocabulary.

ask [somebody] out

back [somebody] up

back [something] up

bear with [somebody]

believe in [something / somebody]

break down

break into [something]

break [something] off

break up with [somebody]

bring [something] out

bring [somebody] up

bring [something] up

buy up [something]

call [somebody] back

call [something] off

to call on [somebody]

call [somebody] up

calm down

care for [somebody]

carry on with [something]

catch up with [something / somebody]

chat [somebody] up

check up on [somebody]

cheer [somebody] up

clean up / clear up

close [something] down

come across [something / somebody]

come down with [something]

come out

come up with [something]

count on [something / somebody]

cross [something] out

cut down on [something]

deal with [something]

do away with [something]

do [something] up

do without [something]

doze off

dress up

drink up

drop in on [somebody]

drop off

drop out of [something]

eat out

end up

face up to [something]

fall down

fall for [somebody]

fall in love with [somebody]

fall off [something]

fall out with [somebody]

fall over

fall through

figure [something] out

to fill [something] in / out

fill in for [somebody]

fill [something] up

find out

get on with [somebody]

get in / out of [something]

get on / off [something]

get on with [somebody]

get over [something]

get rid of [something]

get up

get used to [something]

give [something] away

give [something] back

go on (with) [something]

go out with [somebody]

go over [something]

go through [something]

hand [something] in

hand [something] out

hang around

hang up

hear from [somebody]

hold [something / somebody] up

hurry up

join in with [something]

keep on [doing something]

keep up with [something / some-body]

kick [somebody] out

knock [something] down

leave [somebody] alone

leave [something] out

let [somebody] down

lie down

lie in

lift up

look after [something / somebody]

look for [something]

look forward to [something]

look into [something]

look out for [something / somebody]

make for [something / somebody]

make off with [something]

make sure of [something]

make [something] up

make up for [something]

mix [things] up

open up

pass [something] on

pass [something] up

pick [something] out

pick [somebody] up

point [something] out

put [something] away

put [somebody] down

put [something] off

put [something]

put [something] out

put [somebody] through

put [somebody] up

put up with [somebody]

read [something] over

refer to [something]

get rid of [something]

ring [somebody] up

rule [something] out

run into [somebody]

run out of [something]

see to [something]

set off [for]

set [something] up

slow down

sort [something] out

speak up

take after [somebody]

take [something] away

take [something] back

take care of [something / somebody]

take [something] down

take [something] in

take [something] off

talk [something]

think [something] over

throw [something] away

try [something] out

turn [something / somebody] down

turn [something] off

turn [something] on

turn up

use [something] up

wake up

walk out on [somebody]

watch out [for] [something / somebody]

wear [something / somebody] out

wind [something / somebody] up

wrap [something] up

write [something] down

Appendix B

Common and Irregular Verbs

• •

*E*nglish verbs aren't too tricky to learn. Unlike many other languages, English verbs have very few *inflections* (endings), so you don't have to learn lots of different forms for the same verb. As we explain in Chapter 2, the main inflections that you need to learn are those for the past tense (+ ed for regular past simple verbs) and those for the third person present simple (+ s or + es for all verbs).

In this appendix we look at some of the most common verbs in English and when to use them. We also look at irregular past tense verbs.

Considering Common Verbs in English

Estimates vary, but as a general guide you need approximately 2,000 words of vocabulary to communicate at a basic level in English. Many of these words are verbs. Of the most common verbs in English, here are the top 25, in order of popularity:

- ✔ Be
- ✔ Have
- ✔ Do
- ✔ Say
- ✔ Get
- ✔ Make
- ✔ Go
- ✔ Know
- ✔ Take
- ✔ See
- ✔ Come
- ✔ Think
- ✔ Look

- ✔ Want
- ✔ Give
- ✔ Use
- ✔ Find
- ✔ Tell
- ✔ Ask
- ✔ Work
- ✔ Seem
- ✔ Feel
- ✔ Try
- ✔ Leave
- ✔ Call

The most common verbs express basic concepts such as being, having, doing and looking. You may notice that all these top 25 verbs are only one syllable long – this makes pronunciation much easier.

Can / be able to

You use *can* and *be able to* to talk about things that you know how to do (general ability). Here are some examples:

- ✔ Jorge *can* speak three languages.
- ✔ Jorge *is able to* speak three languages.
- ✔ I *can't* swim very well.
- ✔ I'*m not able to* swim very well.

You can use both *can* and *be able to* in the present tense, as in these examples, or in the past tense. In the present tense, *can* is more common than *be able to*. Here are some examples using the past tense:

- ✔ Jorge *could* speak fluent Japanese when he lived in Japan, but he has forgotten a lot now.
- ✔ Jorge *was able to* speak fluent Japanese when he lived in Japan, but he has forgotten a lot now.
- ✔ I *could* play tennis very well when I was younger.
- ✔ I *was able to* play tennis very well when I was younger.

You also use *can* and *be able to* when you talk about being able to do something in the future.

> ✔ Jorge *can* practise his Japanese when he visits Tokyo next month. (Notice that you can't say 'Jorge will can practise his Japanese'.)
>
> ✔ Jorge *will be able to* practise his Japanese when he visits Tokyo next month.

However, more commonly people use *will be able to* in the future. For example:

> ✔ I *will be able to* play better tennis if I practise more.

You *don't* say 'I *can* play better tennis if I practise more'.

Do

Do is a very common verb in English. In Chapter 2 we look at how we use *do* as an auxiliary verb in questions and negatives. In this section we consider *do* as a full verb, not an auxiliary verb. *Do* is similar in meaning to *make*, which we consider later in this chapter. You use *do* in conjunction with a lot of words and short expressions. Here are a few examples.

Talking about general tasks and activities

You can use the verb *do* to talk about general activities, or when you don't name the exact activity. You often use *do* with the words *something, nothing, anything* and *everything* in this context. For example:

> ✔ What shall we *do* today?
>
> ✔ Mark will join us at the pub later; he first has to *do* something with his mother.
>
> ✔ Paula is *doing* nothing at the moment; she's on the dole.
>
> ✔ She *does* everything around the house, and he never lifts a finger!
>
> ✔ *Do* something about it!
>
> ✔ **Jorge:** Are you *doing* anything on Friday evening? We're all going down to the pub if you'd like to come?
>
> **Juana:** Sorry, I'm already *doing* something on Friday. I hope I can come next time.

Talking about work

You can use *do* to talk about work in general. For example:

- ✔ Do business
- ✔ Do some work
- ✔ Do a job

You may also hear the expression 'a job well *done*', which means that someone has carried out a piece of work to a high standard.

Talking about jobs around the house

You can use *do* (and *make*, which we explain in a moment) to talk about jobs around the house, or housework. For example:

- ✔ Do the washing (this refers to washing clothing)
- ✔ Do the washing up (this refers to washing dishes, cutlery and so on)
- ✔ Do the dishes
- ✔ Do the ironing
- ✔ Do the cooking
- ✔ Do the housework
- ✔ Do your homework

Using idiomatic expressions and phrases

You use *do* in fixed expressions and sometimes to refer to good or bad, or to qualities that you can judge to be good or bad. You even hear the phrase *a do-gooder*: a person who goes through life doing good things for others. Here are some more examples of *do*:

- ✔ Do good / do harm
- ✔ Do well / do badly
- ✔ Do someone a favour
- ✔ Do what is best
- ✔ Do one's best
- ✔ Do someone a good turn

Get

Get is another English verb that you may know; the past tense of *get* is *got*. You're much more likely to hear *get* in spoken language than to read it in written language – some people consider *get* too informal and colloquial to use in formal writing. One of the most difficult things about *get* is that people use the word in many different ways, and in a lot of different expressions. Here are the four main uses of *get*.

Obtaining or receiving

One common meaning of *get* is to obtain, to receive or to fetch. Here are some examples:

- ✔ I *got* some really nice perfume for my birthday (*got* means *received* here).
- ✔ Jan *got* a clean glass from the cupboard (*got* means *fetched* here).
- ✔ Sofia *got* a first class degree in French literature from the Sorbonne (*got* means *obtained* here).

Causing change

When *get* is followed by an adjective, infinite or participle, it often refers to a change and has a similar meaning to *become*. Here are some examples:

- ✔ Otto and Dietlinde *are getting married* next week.
- ✔ She often *gets angry* for no reason.
- ✔ The glass *got cracked* when I put it in the microwave.
- ✔ Let's *get going* – it's already very late.
- ✔ The more time you spend in the UK, the more you *get to practise* your English.

Arriving

You can use *get* to mean *arrive*. Yu can also use *get* with other words to express movement. Here are some examples:

- ✔ What time does the bus *get* to Cambridge?
- ✔ How do I *get* to the post office from here?
- ✔ Can I *get* the Underground from Piccadilly Circus direct to Heathrow Airport?

Using 'get' in common expressions

You hear several expressions with *get* used a lot. Learn these expressions yourself and try to use them in conversation. Here are some examples:

- ✔ Get married / engaged / divorced / separated
- ✔ Get dressed / undressed
- ✔ Get lost
- ✔ Get damaged
- ✔ Get up
- ✔ Get out
- ✔ Get away

You can find a list of phrasal verbs with *get* in Appendix A.

Have

Have is a common verb that you can use in a lot of different situations. In Chapter 2 we use *have* as an auxiliary verb in the present perfect tense ('I *haven't seen* Jim for ages'). Here we look at using *have* as a full verb.

Possessing something

In British English, the expression *have got* is very common. It's not used that often in American English, where *have* by itself is more common. You can use *have got* to talk about possessions, certain illnesses and relationships, and you use it mostly in the present tense. Here are some examples:

- ✔ I've *got* three brothers.
- ✔ They've *got* a fantastic flat overlooking the river!
- ✔ She's *got* an appointment for four o'clock.
- ✔ I've *got* a terrible headache today.
- ✔ Isabel is off work again today because she's *got* a stomach ache.

As you can see from the above examples, you usually contract *have got* in the spoken form, so you say 'I've got' rather than 'I have got'.

Note also that *have got* is less common in the past tense – you usually use the verb *have* in the past tense. For example, you say 'I *had* a terrible headache yesterday', not 'I *had got* a terrible headache yesterday'.

You can always use the simple verb _have_ instead of _have got_. So in all the above examples, you could replace _have got_ with _have_:

- ✔ I _have_ three brothers.

- ✔ They _have_ a fantastic flat overlooking the river!

- ✔ She _has_ an appointment for four o'clock.

- ✔ I _have_ a terrible headache today.

- ✔ Isabel is off work again today because she _has_ a stomach ache.

If you're unsure about how to use _have got_, you can simply use _have_! Remember that you form the question and negative in a different way with _have_:

- ✔ '_Do_ you _have_ the time?' instead of '_Have_ you _got_ the time?'

- ✔ 'I _don't have_ the time' instead of 'I _haven't got_ the time'

Describing actions

You can use _have_ with a direct object to describe different kinds of actions. Here are some examples:

- ✔ Have lunch / breakfast / dinner / tea / a meal / a drink / a glass of wine / a beer.

- ✔ Have a bath / a shower / a wash / a shave.

- ✔ Have a break / a holiday / the day off.

- ✔ Have a swim / a walk / a run.

- ✔ Have a chat / a talk / a conversation / an argument / a disagreement / a fight.

- ✔ Have a word with somebody.

- ✔ Have a look.

- ✔ Have a go / a try.

- ✔ Have a nice evening / a good day / a bad day / a good time.

- ✔ Have a baby.

Look

Look has two main meanings, which we explore in a moment. _Look_ is a verb that you can easily confuse with the verbs _see_ and _watch_, which have very similar meanings.

Seeming or appearing

When *look* is followed by an adjective then the meaning is similar to *seem* or *appear*. For example, if you say 'Olga looks angry', you mean that she seems or appears angry, and you deduce this from her behaviour or by her expression. Here are some more examples:

> ✔ Jaume *looks* very unhappy at the moment – is something wrong?
>
> ✔ Maria *is looking* excited about the wedding.
>
> ✔ She *looks* tired; I think she needs a holiday.

With this meaning of *look*, you can use the present simple or the present continuous / progression without changing the meaning of the sentence.

Looking, seeing and watching

Looking, seeing and watching are three verbs that people often confuse, because they mean very similar things – all are ways of seeing.

You often use *look* with adverbial phrases (for example, look at, look back, look into, look up). Some of these uses of *look* with adverbial phrases have literal meanings, but they can also other meanings. For example, *look into* literally means to look into something (for example, you can look into a room), but *look into* can also mean to investigate or research ('I'll *look into* the matter and get back to you'). You can find a list of phrasal verbs with *look* in Appendix A.

The most important thing to remember about *look* is that it suggests concentration. You usually *deliberately* look at something – and *look at* (plus object) is one of the most common uses of the verb. Here are some examples:

> ✔ Jorg *looked* carefully *at* the report, but he couldn't find any reference to the Berlin job.
>
> ✔ Please *look at* this email for me; I need some feedback.

You use *see* to suggest that a visual impression or image comes to your eyes. Unlike *look*, *see* isn't always deliberate; it can be accidental. You can also use *see* in a more general sense than *look*. Here are some examples:

> ✔ She suddenly *saw* him across the road.
>
> ✔ I *didn't see* him until he touched me on the arm.

You also use *see* in some fixed expressions:

> ✔ Seeing is believing.
>
> ✔ I'll see what I can do.
>
> ✔ We'll see about that!

Watch is a less common verb than *look* or *see*. *Watch* is very similar in meaning to *look at*, but it suggests that something is going to happen – you pay a lot of attention when you watch something. Here are some examples:

- *Watch* how he does it and you'll learn how to do it yourself.
- Dinner is on the stove – can you *watch* it for me while I quickly go down to the shop?
- *Watch out*! That car is driving really fast!

You commonly use *watch* with TV and sports, for example:

- I *watched* a really good film on TV last night (here you can also say 'I saw a really good film').
- She *watched* her first cricket match when she came to England.

Make

Make is similar in meaning to *do*, and you also use the word in certain fixed expressions or with certain words. The most common mistake that non-English speakers make is to confuse *make* and *do* – the best way to learn whether to use *make* or *do* is to memorise the expressions. But when you're not sure whether to use *do* or *make*, choose *make* because it's more likely to be right!

Doing the housework
- Make the bed
- Make breakfast / lunch / dinner
- Make food
- Make a cake
- Make a cup of tea / coffee
- Make a mess

Doing business
You also use *make* in certain expressions related to the business world. Here are some examples:

- Make a change / changes
- Make a complaint
- Make a deal
- Make a decision
- Make a demand

- Make an effort
- Make a loss
- Make money
- Make an offer
- Make a phone call
- Make a profit

Using 'make' with other expressions

Finally, you can use *make* with other expressions, as in these examples below:

- Make an attempt
- Make arrangements
- Make an exception
- Make an excuse
- Make love
- Make a mistake
- Make a noise
- Make peace
- Make a suggestion
- Make war

Investigating Irregular Verbs in English

Here's a list of useful irregular verbs.

Infinitive	Past Simple	Past Participle
Be	Was/Were	Been
Become	Became	Become
Begin	Began	Begun
Bite	Bit	Bitten
Blow	Blew	Blown
Break	Broke	Broken
Bring	Brought	Brought
Build	Built	Built

Infinitive	*Past Simple*	*Past Participle*
Buy	Bought	Bought
Catch	Caught	Caught
Choose	Chose	Chosen
Come	Came	Come
Cost	Cost	Cost
Cut	Cut	Cut
Do	Did	Done
Draw	Drew	Drawn
Drive	Drove	Driven
Drink	Drank	Drunk
Eat	Ate	Eaten
Fall	Fell	Fallen
Feel	Felt	Felt
Find	Found	Found
Fly	Flew	Flown
Forget	Forgot	Forgotten
Get	Got	Got
Give	Gave	Given
Go	Went	Gone
Grow	Grew	Grown
Have	Had	Had
Hide	Hid	Hidden
Hold	Held	Held
Keep	Kept	Kept
Know	Knew	Known
Leave	Left	Left
Let	Let	Let
Lose	Lost	Lost
Make	Made	Made
Mean	Meant	Meant
Meet	Met	Met
Put	Put	Put

Infinitive	*Past Simple*	*Past Participle*
Ride	Rode	Ridden
Ring	Rang	Rung
Say	Said	Said
See	Saw	Seen
Send	Sent	Sent
Sing	Sang	Sung
Sit	Sat	Sat
Speak	Spoke	Spoken
Swim	Swam	Swum
Take	Took	Taken
Teach	Taught	Taught
Think	Thought	Thought
Understand	Understood	Understood
Wake	Woke	Woken
Wear	Wore	Worn
Win	Won	Won
Write	Wrote	Written

Meeting Modal Verbs

One area that makes English verbs a little different from any other languages is that of auxiliary verbs. As we explain in Chapter 2, you use auxiliary verbs to create questions and negative forms. You use *do* and *does* in the present simple tense, and *did* in the past simple.

Other special verbs, like *do* and *does*, are usually followed by a full verb. These are called modal auxiliary verbs, or modal verbs. Grammar books often group modal verbs according to their function and meaning. In this section we look at two main concepts expressed by modal verbs: possibility and probability, and obligation, permission and prohibition.

Possibility and probability

You use some modal verbs when you want to express possibility, or if you're unsure of something. Here are some examples:

✔ Joe *might* go to Italy this summer.

✔ I *may* call Yvonne to see whether she can come to the cinema.

✔ I *could* have the file – I'll check for you if you like.

In the examples above, the words *might, may* and *could* all express possibility. Look at them again:

✔ Joe *might* go to Italy this summer. (This implies that Joe isn't sure whether he's going to Italy this summer.)

✔ I *may* call Yvonne to see whether she can come to the cinema. (I haven't decided yet whether I'm going to call Yvonne.)

✔ I *could* have the file – I'll check for you if you like. (I'm not sure that I have the file you need.)

When you're absolutely sure of something, you use *must* and *can't*. For example:

✔ That *must* be Mike in the photo, standing next to Yvette. (I'm sure that that is Mike.)

✔ That *can't* be John in the photo – John has blond hair, and this man's dark! (Here I'm sure that it's not John.)

Obligation, permission and prohibition

You use some modal verbs to express permission or prohibition. Here are some examples:

✔ You *can* help yourself to tea or coffee whenever you like.

✔ You *can't* go into that room; it's private.

✔ You *must* wear a seatbelt at all times when driving.

✔ You *mustn't* smoke in here.

✔ You *have to* leave the country if they don't renew your visa.

In the previous examples, *can* and *can't*, *must* and *mustn't* and *have to* express permission, obligation or prohibition. Look at the examples again:

- ✔ You *can* help yourself to tea or coffee whenever you like. (Permission – it's okay to help yourself to tea or coffee whenever you like.)

- ✔ You *can't* go into that room; it's private. (Prohibition – you aren't allowed to go into that room.)

- ✔ You *must* wear a seatbelt at all times when driving. (Obligation – it's necessary for you to wear a seatbelt.)

- ✔ You *mustn't* smoke in here. (Prohibition – you aren't allowed to smoke in here.)

- ✔ You *have to* leave the country if they don't renew your visa. (Obligation – it's necessary for you to leave the country if they don't renew your visa.)

Appendix C

On the CD

Following is a list of the tracks that appear on this book's audio CD, which you can find inside the back cover. Note that this is an audio-only CD – just pop it into your CD player like a regular music CD.

Table A-1	The Tracks on the Audio CD	
Track	*Title*	*Page*
1. Chapter 1, Track 1	Pronunciation	16
2. Chapter 1, Track 2	Intonations	18
3. Chapter 3, Track 1	Greetings	42
4. Chapter 3, Track 2	Small talk	44
5. Chapter 3, Track 3	Family ties	46
6. Chapter 3, Track 4	Telling a joke	47
7. Chapter 3, Track 5	Telling an anecdote	48
8. Chapter 4, Track 1	Shopping at the bakery	57
9. Chapter 4, Track 2	Shopping in the newsagent's	58
10. Chapter 4, Track 3	Buying clothes	60
11. Chapter 4, Track 4	Buying shoes	63
12. Chapter 4, Track 5	At the supermarket	64
13. Chapter 4, Track 6	At the market	68
14. Chapter 4, Track 7	Talking numbers on the phone	72
15. Chapter 5, Track 1	At the chip shop	78
16. Chapter 5, Track 2	Having lunch in a pub	81
17. Chapter 5, Track 3	Discussing eating out	84
18. Chapter 5, Track 4	Booking a table at a restaurant	86
19. Chapter 5, Track 5	Arriving at a restaurant	87

(continued)

Table A-1 *(continued)*

Track	Title	Page
20. Chapter 5, Track 6	Ordering food in a restaurant	88
21. Chapter 5, Track 7	Complaining about the food	90
22. Chapter 5, Track 8	Ordering dessert	91
23. Chapter 5, Track 9	Asking for the bill	93
24. Chapter 6, Track 1	Asking someone on a date	100
25. Chapter 6, Track 2	Arranging to meet	101
26. Chapter 6, Track 3	Choosing a place and time to meet	103
27. Chapter 6, Track 4	Picking a film to see	105
28. Chapter 6, Track 5	Socialising in the pub	109
29. Chapter 6, Track 6	Inviting colleagues for dinner on the phone	111
30. Chapter 7, Track 1	Sightseeing in London	119
31. Chapter 7, Track 2	Chatting about TV programmes	122
32. Chapter 7, Track 3	Inviting a colleague for a game of tennis	126
33. Chapter 7, Track 4	Discussing a football match	127
34. Chapter 8, Track 1	Inviting a friend to the cinema	134
35. Chapter 8, Track 2	Inquiring about a room for rent	137
36. Chapter 8, Track 3	Calling a rail service enquiry line	138
37. Chapter 8, Track 4	Listening to an automated phone message	139
38. Chapter 8, Track 5	Calling a colleague about a work order	140
39. Chapter 8, Track 6	Taking part in a conference call	142
40. Chapter 8, Track 7	On a crackly phone line	149
41. Chapter 9, Track 1	At the employment agency	155
42. Chapter 9, Track 2	Being introduced to colleagues	159
43. Chapter 9, Track 3	Taking out a magazine subscription	164
44. Chapter 9, Track 4	Inquiring about a host family	172
45. Chapter 10, Track 1	Chatting about the personal ads	181
46. Chapter 10, Track 2	Discussing horoscopes	183
47. Chapter 10, Track 3	Applying for a tourist visa	187
48. Chapter 11, Track 1	Cancelling a stolen credit card	202
49. Chapter 11, Track 2	Changing currency	205

Track	Title	Page
50. Chapter 11, Track 3	Sending money abroad	207
51. Chapter 12, Track 1	Finding out about accommodation at the tourist office	213
52. Chapter 12, Track 2	Booking a hotel room	217
53. Chapter 13, Track 1	Booking a flight	230
54. Chapter 13, Track 2	Checking in at the airport	233
55. Chapter 13, Track 3	Buying a train ticket	240
56. Chapter 13, Track 4	Asking for directions	247
57. Chapter 14, Track 1	Going to see the doctor	255
58. Chapter 14, Track 2	Informing the police about a stolen bag	261

Index

FOR DUMMIES®

Making Everything Easier!™

UK editions

BUSINESS

978-0-470-51806-9

978-0-470-74381-2

978-0-470-71382-2

FINANCE

978-0-470-99280-7

978-0-470-71432-4

978-0-470-69515-9

HOBBIES

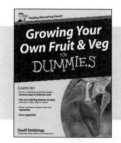

978-0-470-69960-7

978-0-470-74535-9

978-0-470-75857-1

British Sign Language
For Dummies
978-0-470-69477-0

Business NLP For Dummies
978-0-470-69757-3

Competitive Strategy For Dummies
978-0-470-77930-9

Cricket For Dummies
978-0-470-03454-5

CVs For Dummies, 2nd Edition
978-0-470-74491-8

Digital Marketing For Dummies
978-0-470-05793-3

Divorce For Dummies, 2nd Edition
978-0-470-74128-3

eBay.co.uk Business All-in-One
For Dummies
978-0-470-72125-4

Emotional Freedom Technique For
Dummies
978-0-470-75876-2

English Grammar For Dummies
978-0-470-05752-0

Flirting For Dummies
978-0-470-74259-4

Golf For Dummies
978-0-470-01811-8

Green Living For Dummies
978-0-470-06038-4

Hypnotherapy For Dummies
978-0-470-01930-6

IBS For Dummies
978-0-470-51737-6

Lean Six Sigma For Dummies
978-0-470-75626-3

8041_p1

FOR DUMMIES

A world of resources to help you grow

UK editions

SELF-HELP

Cognitive Behavioural Therapy For Dummies
978-0-470-01838-5

Neuro-linguistic Programming For Dummies
978-0-7645-7028-5

Boosting Self-Esteem For Dummies
978-0-470-74193-1

Motivation For Dummies
978-0-470-76035-2

Overcoming Depression For Dummies
978-0-470-69430-5

Personal Development All-In-One For Dummies
978-0-470-51501-3

Positive Psychology For Dummies
978-0-470-72136-0

PRINCE2 For Dummies
978-0-470-51919-6

Psychometric Tests For Dummies
978-0-470-75366-8

Raising Happy Children For Dummies
978-0-470-05978-4

Sage 50 Accounts For Dummies
978-0-470-71558-1

Succeeding at Assessment Centres For Dummies
978-0-470-72101-8

Sudoku For Dummies
978-0-470-01892-7

Teaching English as a Foreign Language For Dummies
978-0-470-74576-2

Teaching Skills For Dummies
978-0-470-74084-2

Time Management For Dummies
978-0-470-77765-7

Understanding and Paying Less Property Tax For Dummies
978-0-470-75872-4

Work-Life Balance For Dummies
978-0-470-71380-8

STUDENTS

Study Skills For Dummies
978-0-470-74047-7

Student Cookbook For Dummies
978-0-470-74711-7

Writing Essays For Dummies
978-0-470-74290-7

HISTORY

British History For Dummies
978-0-470-99468-9

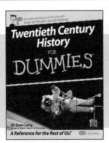
Twentieth Century History For Dummies
978-0-470-51015-5

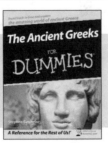
The Ancient Greeks For Dummies
978-0-470-98787-2

FOR DUMMIES®

The easy way to get more done and have more fun

FOR DUMMIES®

Helping you expand your horizons and achieve your potential

COMPUTER BASICS

978-0-470-27759-1

978-0-470-13728-4

978-0-470-49743-2

DIGITAL PHOTOGRAPHY

978-0-470-25074-7

978-0-470-46606-3

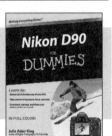

978-0-470-45772-6

MAC BASICS

978-0-470-27817-8

978-0-470-46661-2

978-0-470-43543-4

08049_p4